# STORIES OF DELIVERANCE

# STORIES OF DELIVERANCE

## SPEAKING WITH MEN AND WOMEN WHO RESCUED JEWS FROM THE HOLOCAUST

### MAREK HALTER

TRANSLATED BY MICHAEL BERNARD

Open Court
Chicago and La Salle, Illinois

Cover illustration © 1997 Larry Rivers/Licensed by VAGA, New York, NY. *Europe I*, Larry Rivers, 1956, 72 x 48 inches, oil on canvas, Minneapolis Institute of Arts.

Marek Halter made a film based on his interviews with the subjects of *La force du Bien* (*The Power of the Good*, translated as *Stories of Deliverance*). This movie, *Tzedek: Les Justes*, is referred to in the present translation as *Tzedek: The Just*. It has been released in the English-speaking world as *Tzedek: The Righteous*. The French word *juste* means both 'just' and 'righteous'.

Originally published as *La force du Bien*, © Editions Robert Laffont, S.A., Paris, 1995

Copyright © 1998 by Carus Publishing Company

First printing 1998

Printed and bound in the United States of America.

**Library of Congress Cataloging-in-Publication Data**

Halter, Marek.
    [Force du bien. English]
    Stories of deliverance : speaking with men and women who rescued Jews from the Holocaust / Marek Halter ; translated by Michael Bernard.
        p.      cm.
    Includes index.
    ISBN 0-8126-9364-7 (paper : alk. paper)
    1. Righteous Gentiles in the Holocaust—Interviews. 2. World War, 1939-1945—Jews—Rescue—Interviews. 3. Holocaust, Jewish (1939-1945) I. Title.
D804.65.H3513   1998
362.87'81'0922—dc21
                                                                97-27114
                                                                     CIP

It should have been said a long time ago, said loud and strong: in these times dominated by bullies and killers, that there are some individuals who allow us not to despair of humanity, some men and some women who did not hesitate to risk death in order to save lives.

Irena, Polish, took 2,500 children out from the Ghetto, under the nose of the Germans. Berthold, German industrialist, had the idea of employing Jews in his factory, thus saving them from the death camps. Nuns have sheltered hundreds of hunted children, in convents . . .

This is what I have discovered during my voyage to the country of the Just, without doubt: Good does exist; and this disposition for goodwill, which every man carries inside himself, cannot ever be destroyed by the worst totalitarian system.

In paying homage to these Just Men and Women, in bringing to light their evidence, long kept in silence, I have tried to create a "Memory of Good." For Good is hope. And without hope one cannot live.

M.H.

# Contents

# About the Author

Marek Halter was born in 1936 in Warsaw, a city which was then 40 percent Jewish. His mother Pearl was a Yiddish poet, his father Solomon a printer and descendant of a long line of printers, commencing in Strasbourg at the beginning of the fifteenth century with an ancestor who worked with Gutenberg.

Marek was three when the Nazis closed the Warsaw ghetto. He and his parents, along with all other Jews in the city, were trapped, but a year later, the Halters escaped to the Soviet Union. After a brief stay in Moscow, as it was being bombarded by the invading Germans, the family moved to a collective farm in Uzbekistan, where Marek's little sister died of hunger. As an Uzbekistan delegate for the Communist youth organization, Marek attended the victory celebration in Moscow in 1945, and presented a bouquet to Stalin.

The following year, the family returned to Poland, where antisemitism was resurgent. Marek was involved in Jewish self-defense groups for children and adolescents. Pneumonia with complications prevented his leaving for Palestine with many of his friends. After Marek's father had located one of his brothers in France, the family were able to obtain a French visa and moved to Paris in 1950.

At the age of 15, Halter began to study mime with Marcel Marceau, but then became more attracted by art, and assiduously frequented the Louvre. In 1953 he entered the École Nationale de Beaux Arts and a year later was awarded the

Deauville International Painting Prize. He exhibited his paintings in Buenos Aires and became closely linked with President Juan Perón.

Returning to France, Halter published articles and agitated for human rights, against racism, and for peace in the Middle East. On the eve of the Six Day War, he was received at the Elysée Palace by General de Gaulle, and when the Arab armies surrounded Israel he launched an international appeal in defense of Israel and for peace. With his wife Clara he later founded an international committee for a negotiated peace in the Middle East, with the participation of Hannah Arendt, Saul Bellow, Engène Ionesco, Primo Levi, Alberto Moravia, Iris Murdoch, Jean-François Revel, Jean-Paul Sartre, C.P. Snow, François Truffaut, and Elie Wiesel. President of this committee from 1967 to 1973, he returned to the Middle East many times, working to persuade Israelis and Arabs to enter into a dialogue.

In 1976, Halter published his first book, *The Jester and the Kings,* which became a best-seller and won the Prix Aujourd'hui, the French equivalent of the Pulitzer Prize. He also initiated international campaigns for the rights of Soviet Jews, founded a committee for the liberation of Soviet writer Edward Kuznetsov, began a campaign for the liberation of Argentinian journalist Jacobo Timmerman, launched an appeal to boycott the soccer World Cup in Buenos Aires, appealed for the boycott of the 1980 Moscow Olympics, and helped found an organization to fight hunger in Ethiopia. With cellist Mstislav Rostropovich, he organized the first international campaign for Andrei Sakharov. In 1981 he helped found Radio Free Kabul. Halter has also been involved in numerous other journalistic and persuasive endeavors, and has become a well-known and highly respected leader of French opinion and culture.

In 1983 he published his novel, *The Memory of Abraham,* covering two thousands years in the life of a Jewish family. Six years later he published its sequel, *The Sons of Abraham.* Both books were European best-sellers.

His book *La force du Bien* (translated as *Stories of Deliverance*) appeared in 1995, and remained in the French best-seller charts for 14 weeks. The following year, his novel, *The Messiah* (on the life of sixteenth-century David Reubeni, who pursued the objective of a Jewish state in Palestine and was considered by many Jews at the time to be the Messiah), spent 12 weeks in the French best-seller charts. In 1997, Halter presented on French television a series of true stories, *The Adventures of Good*, derived from his work on *Stories of Deliverance* and pursuing the theme of heroism of ordinary people.

# Translator's Note

We have all read the horror stories of the Holocaust. ***This book is NOT one of them!*** Marek Halter sets out on a journey, through fourteen countries, world-wide, to find the stories with happy endings: to find the people who made the happy endings possible.

The book is written as a series of short stories, told by these people and their friends, who range from simple peasants on the Polish border through Willy Brandt, the ex-Chancellor in Germany, to John Paul II, the present Pope.

Marek Halter has then taken an interesting point of view, using the Biblical origins of the stories of Just Men, and linked these stories together, with the aim of convincing us of two things. The first is to be able to affirm that there are always Good people in the world who will give us the hope needed to continue in whatever times of oppression we will find ourselves. The second is to remind us that it is only with memories of *good* deeds from the past that we will be able to adequately deal with Evil, today and in the future, which is specially relevant as we approach a new millennium.

When I first read this book I was fascinated by both the stories of the "Just" and the theme of Hope, allied to the constant battle we must wage against Evil; to the extent that I was determined to translate it and make the result of this painstaking research, told in such a sympathetic manner, available to the English-speaking world.

Originally published in France in 1995, this book makes us ever more aware of the need to fight oppression, wherever it may be, in Chechnya, Rwanda, Bosnia, etc., by talking about the good side of human nature, rather than the bad, . . . very different from most books that deal mainly with the ugly side of the Holocaust and its aftermath.

M.B.

# Author's Introduction

True Goodness—does it exist?

Does it appear at all times and in all places?

This book is the true story of a man who goes in search of the least glimmer, the smallest spark of Good in the abyss of Evil.

It is the tale of a journey from which I have not yet finished receiving echoes—a journey across hearts, minds, and souls.

These days people laugh at such words.

Now, at the time when, under our very eyes, civil war and injustices are spreading, these words must be at the heart of our thoughts. Sarajevo, Kigali, Algiers, Grosny, Erevan, Lima, Quito—without forgetting the Middle East, which is no nearer peace: the funereal litany of today's massacres inexorably prolongs yesterday's extermination.

"Don't laugh or cry: understand," Spinoza wrote. Understand, then, these women and these men who, in times gone by, although ruled and dominated by cowardly killers, did not, themselves, hesitate to save lives.

We are talking, it is very true, of a minority, and, for the most part, of simple spontaneous people. Not strategists, nor heroes, nor saints: The Just.

With each generation, they are there, according to the Talmud, to support the world. "The world depends on thirty-six Just men," says Rabbi Abaye. "On 18,000," says Rabbi Rabba. And Pascal estimated the incalculable at 9,000 . . .

Why have I not thought sooner about this part of our history? Why have I waited so long to trace the work of these Just People, to tell their story? Perhaps I was convinced, like all Jews, that to bear witness to Evil was enough. Perhaps I, also, considered that the whole world without exception was guilty.

I know that the deeds of these Just People doesn't diminish by one iota the shame of those who have killed or have turned a blind eye. In the end they make them even more shameful. For, if some men stretched out their hands to people in distress, why did others not do so?

It should have been said long ago, said loud and strong: these individuals were there so that we do not despair of humanity. And if I am so concerned about it, it is because they constitute the only positive examples in this period of our history. It is vital, it seems to me, to try to understand this consciousness of Good, that these people have so strongly manifested at peril of their lives. It intrigues me and forces me to respect it. It is that, in their faces and the intonation of their voices, in the lights that sparkle in the depths of the eyes of these old people, that I am going to try, even surreptitiously, to grasp hold of and make sense of.

The thoughts of the journeys that I have had to make, armed with information, sometimes enigmatic, in order to meet these Just Men and Women makes them difficult for me, today, to forget, since they bring back anew, within me, such a turmoil of reminiscences. Such journeys repeat themselves endlessly.

Generations come and go, but memory is perhaps our only, and living, eternity!

What place, in that memory, are we keeping for the Just?

Are we missing a memory of the Just?

This memory of the Just, will it not be our one hope and, who knows, our last chance?

But what is this "Just"?

# 1
# Poland 1994

*Don't cry,*
*don't cry my child,*
*because the day is sad,*
*because the day is bad,*
*because the day is ugly.*
*Know that above the clouds*
*the sky is blue,*
*always blue.*

Everything starts, everything begins again, with a Yiddish song, a lullaby written by my mother. Whenever I hear it, it leads me to thoughts of my childhood, to Warsaw, where I was born.

Warsaw, therefore, is the start of my search. I haven't been here for over forty years. A sad town. In January 1994, it is cold, it is snowing. Passers-by, still dressed in Russian style (muddy boots, plastic coats, imitation furs), cross the streets in groups, with hurried footsteps. The sky is heavy. The women make themselves look worse with knitted bonnets. The old red trams go by, their wheels squealing along the metal tracks and the metallic cry of their brakes, which I have not heard for so long, makes me shiver.

I watch the Vistula. The water is low and leaves several sandbanks uncovered. In my pocket, the list of five righteous people for whom I have come: five Poles who, I have been told, saved some Jews during the war. Without thinking, my footsteps led me first straight to my childhood street, Smozca.

Truthfully, why had I come to look, here, in this Poland where I was born and where the Jews had lived for more than a thousand years?

Jews have lived in Poland since the seventh century. The Chronicles of Master Vincent (Kadeluba) lead one to believe

1

that, around 1170–1180, the Jews, placed under the king's protection, were already numerous in Cracow—and that at a time when they were persecuted practically everywhere else in Europe.

Three and a half million Jews, that is 10 percent of the country's population, lived in Poland before the war. Only 100,000, of which the majority escaped and found refuge in the Soviet Union, survived the Nazi persecution. Today only 8,000 remain, mainly old and sick. This Jewish presence has, however, left indelible traces in classical Polish literature and in the history books.

But of my street, of my district in my city, nothing is left. Everything has been destroyed. Everything was rebuilt after the war. No matter how. On top of the unleveled rubble. This part of town, for centuries, made up the Jewish quarter. The ground is all built over. A few steps, or a sharp slope, and you are there. Following immemorial custom, houses for the living have been piled on top of houses of the dead. This slope, these few steps indicate that down below exists a buried world. A complete world, with its courtyards, its offices, its shops, its workshops, its libraries, its streets and lanes, its staircases, its washhouses, its wells, its fountains, its schools.

Of Smozca Street, all that remains is an enamelled plaque on the side of a wall. The sole tangible indications of the location of my birthplace is therefore this plaque bearing the name of the street and also this red brick church, so plain, if not ugly, which had been saved from the bombs and which I saw as a child from our balcony.

But where is this balcony? Where is the old street?

This obliterated world retains a sickness at its heart, a sonorous silence: that of a language, my mother tongue, Yiddish. Yes, I feel again this silence like an open wound, like something missing.

Yiddish! I speak of Yiddish while nobody or almost nobody speaks it in Poland today. And yet . . .

Before the war, certain villages, certain regions of Poland

were 100 percent Jewish. Warsaw, city of my birth, had nearly a million inhabitants, of which 368,000 were Jews, with their primary schools and their yeshivot, six theater companies, daily newspapers, revues, fifteen publishing houses, and as many political parties. And these women and these men thought, spoke, and wrote in the Yiddish language.

From Alsace to the Urals, Yiddish was, at that time, the language of 10 million people, a living language in which they sang, cried, laughed, and above all dreamed of saving humanity.

Indispensable link between East and West, between nations and the Universe, knowledge which crossed all scientific research and all political battles: this world, this language, and the world of this language, one ended by thinking them immortals.

However, it is enough for me to rest my eyes on the extent of the old Ghetto and to listen to this silence of my mother tongue all around to understand that here, with yesterday's streets and houses, the immortal had also been swallowed up.

I approach a front door, I knock. The door opens. A middle-aged woman whom I have never seen before looks at me. I ask if there are any Jews in this district. Her face hardens:

"Jews? Don't know."

This woman, besides her frosty appearance, confirmed reports. Jews, no trace could be found here except in some abandoned cemeteries and at concentration camp sites.

More than 3 million people assassinated in three years, and even their cemeteries are dying!

However, it is in visiting one of these ruined Jewish cemeteries, in which hardly anyone in Poland is interested today, that I am going to be put on the track of an exceptional woman, one of the Just for whom I am looking. She is not on my list, a list which I have patiently built up thanks to statements from escapees. No one up till now had spoken of this woman. The young rabbi who mentioned her to me thus calls me back to my task. It pulls me back to life.

How this woman, Irena Sendler, had pulled back to life 2,500 Jewish children, whom she brought out of the Ghetto under the nose of the Germans!

Thus, in this neglected Jewish cemetery, almost forgotten, headstones awry, overgrown with ivy and birch saplings, it is revealed to me how a human being, here, in Warsaw, did the impossible.

# 2

# The Warsaw Ghetto

A tiny chapel of the Virgin, distempered in white, backs onto the wall of a block of flats like one often sees in Poland. I am in a square dilapidated courtyard, all around which, typically Polish, stand the buildings. It is here, in the working-class district of Mokotow, that Irena Sendler lives in three little rooms each about four meters square, on the second floor of a decrepit apartment block. She is eighty-four years old. Infirm, she cannot move without her walker. But her round firm face still shows a youthfulness. She smiles, flashing her eyes with girlish mischief. Her hair is white, but styled like a teacher from the thirties: a shiny hair-slide, just above her forehead, holds up a carefully brushed lock of hair.

"To give a hand to someone who needs help?" she says. "But . . . that's only normal!"

It is during this first meeting that she tells me that, with the complicity of her friends, she has saved so many Jewish children. She worked with them before the war. She continued to do so under the eyes of the Nazis! Being a social worker she was one of those rare people whom the Germans authorized to come and go across the Ghetto. She had profited by this to organize the exit, necessarily clandestine, of the children. And this way she was able to save 2,500.

"Perhaps we could have saved more," she adds. "I torment myself with this thought. We should have saved even more. We were young, we didn't know enough to take them . . ."

I had always been told that in Poland Jews could not find anyone to lend them a hand, and yet here is a woman who, with help from her friends, succeeded in saving so many children! Irena Sendler feels my surprise, my incredulity. Because of this I start to think of the terrible comparison made by a Polish Jewess, Margaret Acher, who owes her own survival to the Sisters of a convent at Plody:

"It needs a thousand Poles to save one Jew. But it only takes one Pole to denounce a thousand Jews."

Irena Sendler averred that she had wished to write her story for a long time, but that life had passed too quickly. She had evidence, letters from those she had assisted, who, themselves now adult, continue to show affection and recognition. She would show me all that tomorrow.

When I arrived back at her house, at noon, she was waiting all smiles. She is made up; she has dressed up. She is wearing a pretty pearl necklace on top of a blouse of little blue and white checks. Her looks sparkle under the silvery circle of her hair: her documents, letters, and photos are ready, as well as about thirty pages of close writing.

She gives them to me: "I have made some notes for you. Read them."

I read. At the end of several lines, I understand that a whole story is hidden here. Her father, a doctor, cared for many destitute Jews in the district, free of charge. All her childhood, little Irena had passed her time playing with Jews of her own age. She spoke Yiddish. When the doctor died of typhus, representatives of the Jewish community extended an offer to Irena's mother to take charge of Irena's education, as a sign of gratitude for her father's good deeds and so that they could honor his memory. Her mother, too proud, declined the offer, preferring to work in a restaurant to ensure her daughters' studies, but they continued, of course, to keep contact with their many Jewish friends.

"Since that time," explained Irena Sendler, "I always felt I owed something to the Jewish nation."

*The Jewish Nation . . .* these words went straight to my

heart. For, in short, the Sendler family along with all the other health-worker friends of Irena were Catholics. In the thirties, Irena Sendler never hesitated in putting on a brave front to oppose the anti-Semitic atmosphere which, at that time, pervaded the University of Warsaw.

Students' cards featured the words *Jew* or *Polish:* outraged, she scored out *Polish* on her own. Suspended from the university, it was five years later before, thanks to some liberal teachers, she was granted her diploma in sociology. She describes all that smiling all the while, and I can sense the ardor of the young girl of long ago, who led her friends to oppose injustice.

"But the Ghetto? The children you saved? The war?"

"Yes . . . You must remember . . . it was the Warsaw Ghetto . . . to understand," she said.

Irena Sendler is right. Many could not understand—many today do not understand it yet. In September 1939, on the Day of Atonement, Yom Kippur, Poland was invaded by Hitler's army. One year later, on the 2nd of October 1940, the Nazi governor Ludwig Fisher decreed the creation of the Warsaw Ghetto. All the Jews in the city, some 368,000 people, along with those from the suburbs and the neighboring countryside, that is to say 600,000 beings in all—the equivalent of the population of a city the size of Lyon—were brought together and shut up in a space of a few streets, within a small area of about one and a half square miles, literally cut off from the world.

"Ah, the Ghetto!" continued Irena Sendler. "The Germans locked it up in the autumn of 1940. My best friend, Eva, was a Jew, and suddenly she found herself on the wrong side of the wall! Everything happened because of Eva. I had to save her, I could not leave her in there! I asked her to come and hide with me. She refused. She thought she would be needed inside the Ghetto. She only accepted my offer in the end, several days before the uprising, in April 1943."

"What did your friend Eva do for a living?"

"She was a social worker, like me. Before, we looked after

the poor, Poles and Jews, and above all children. The Germans, when they occupied Warsaw, cut off all social services from the Jews. And, when the Ghetto was closed, with exit forbidden, their situation became worse. Then I organized ways, with some friends, in which to help them. And . . ."

Here it is, the chain of a thousand Poles necessary to save one Jew . . . "Who were these friends?"

"My colleagues. As we had an official budget, we gave money to the Jews as we had in the past. We only had to invent Polish names on the forms . . ."

"You went into the Ghetto?"

"Yes."

"I thought you needed a pass."

"The Germans were frightened of epidemics and allowed disinfection vehicles and ambulances to go in. Thanks to Dr. Makowski, a doctor in charge of the sanitary department of the 'non-Jewish' part of the city, we had passes which allowed us in and out of the Ghetto in the health vehicles. We doled out the money and food. But the famine took hold, and the children were the worst affected. I decided to save them at any cost. I knew of places ready to welcome them outside the Ghetto: all it needed was to get them out. There were several possibilities, first choice the ambulances. I said that I was going to evacuate a contagious invalid. When we came out with some children hidden in the back, the Germans let us out without inspection, for fear of contamination. We were also able to bribe some guards. And, after all, the Ghetto was not totally hermetically sealed. Certain houses looked onto different streets, one into the Ghetto, another into 'normal' Warsaw. Several public buildings were like this: the Courts, for example, or the tramway depot in Kraskinski Place. Then . . . we knew of ways out through caves and underground . . ."

# 3

# Save the little children

Yes, it was possible to risk breaking the law, to get out of the Ghetto. But was it enough to take off your yellow star and, false papers in pocket, walk along as if nothing had happened? And then, where to go? You must have friends you could be sure of, or a trustworthy network that could give addresses, hideouts, and stopping-off places. A great many of the Jews in the Ghetto knew that: they could not go ten steps outside without being arrested—2,000 years of exile had had no effect on the blackness of their hair, so easily spotted among the blond heads of the Polish crowd.

"And the children, Mrs. Sendler, how did you gather them?"

"Within the framework of our social duties, my friend Eva worked with the leaders of the Jewish community, who gave us the addresses of needy families, and I went there. Imagine: I went to homes of these people who had never seen me before, and announced that I could save their child. All of them asked the same question: could I guarantee that their son or their daughter would survive? But there were no guarantees. I wasn't even sure of getting out of the Ghetto alive. Certain parents were suspicious, and refused to let their child go. I would go back the next day in the hope of convincing them, and sometimes their flat was in ruins. The Nazis had set it on fire just for the pleasure of seeing Jews burn. But more often they gave me their child. The father, the mother, and the grandparents would be crying, and I would lead the little one away. What a tragedy, each time! The children, separated from their mothers, sobbed ceaselessly all along the road, and we were crying as well. To avoid alerting the Germans with their cries, our driver had found a solution: he brought a fierce dog in the ambulance. As the guards approached we made him walk and his barking covered the children's cries . . .''

I listen to Irena Sendler. The yellow walls of her apartment disappear, and I imagine, at that time, at the age of thirty, tears filling her eyes, making a dog howl to fool the SS. Such courage, such guile to allow her charges to pass, saved by a bad dog . . . I think of all those whom other dogs have tracked, flushed out in front of machine-guns.

Irena Sendler continued:

"We weren't heroes. It was the Jewish children who were the real heroes. Before their departure, their parents explained: 'Listen well. Your name isn't Rachel, but Roma. Your name isn't Isaac, but Yacek. Repeat it. Repeat it ten times, 100 times, 1,000 times. And your sister and you, you are Polish.' To be able to survive, they learned this way to deny their name, their family, their parents. Yes, they are the heroes. After all those years, I still hear them, in my dreams, learning and crying their new identity before being separated from their parents . . .

"With some friends, I arranged for four social assistance centers, where they could stay as long as necessary—days, weeks, whole months—to overcome the shock into which this situation had plunged them. We even had to teach them to laugh again. Only then could we place them. Sometimes in welcoming families, but more often in convents, with the complicity of the Mothers Superior. No one ever refused to take a child from me. I placed them with Sister Nipolanski, at the Visiting Sisters of Christ, and at the convent at Plody. We also had a house at 96 Lesno Street where we hid some of the mothers who had escaped from the Ghetto. It took a lot of money to sustain it all. Around 1942, the Germans started to control us more strictly, and we couldn't use social aid funds any more. Happily, in the autumn of that same year, Zegota was formed, a Socialist resistance organization that also wanted to help the Jews. Zegota had access to funds supplied by the Polish government in exile in London. The leader of this resistance group is, today, the Polish Ambassador in Vienna. I went to see him. He quickly decided to help us."

"Irena," I said to her, "I don't understand. How did you find enough Polish people to welcome so many children?"

My question astonished her.

"Everyone was from Warsaw! I was born in this town. I have always lived here and I knew lots of people here. I can say that in my circle the people were good. I had whole lists of volunteers, but I sent most of the children to religious establishments. I knew I could count on the Sisters. And then it wasn't only to save the children's lives. I wanted to save them for what they were, so that they knew how to stay Jewish. I wanted their families to be able to take them back after the war, or at least for them to know their origins if they were permanently orphaned. To conserve their true identity, masked by false Polish names, I made out a list. There were so many of them! For example, I noted: *Maria Kowalska equals Rachel Grindek.* For security reasons, I was the only one to have this list. When the Germans raided my house, in October 1943, I had already taken precautions, and they didn't find it. If they had, it would have been death for everyone: the children, their families, and all my friends."

"Where did you hide this list?"

"A girlfriend was staying with me. She slipped the list inside the sleeve of the dressing gown she was wearing. It was stupid: if the Germans had made us hold our arms up in the air, the papers would have fallen out. Whenever they found a man in a house, the Germans made him hold up his hands. They didn't give this order when they dealt only with women. Happily, my husband was in a concentration camp: We didn't have to put our hands up."

Afterward, the enormity of this statement hits me: "Happily, my husband was in a concentration camp"! No doubt Mrs.

Sendler was not at all happy about the fate of her husband. But the saving of this list was of such importance in her eyes, that fifty years later, she makes this hallucinatory recall.

She continues: "When I found myself in Pawiak prison, I was able to send a coded message to the Zegota organization to reassure them: 'It's OK, the Germans don't have the list.' After the war, I was able to give the list to the organization."

"And the surviving Jews, did they get their children back?"

"Yes. And those children whose whole family disappeared were later sent to Israel . . ."

This mass rescue bothered me. I was troubled. I had so ardently wished that there should have been Poles to hold out their hands to Jews in distress, and, now that I am face to face with one such person, it makes the inaction of others even more unacceptable.

"All my friends were Catholics. You know, when one decides to be a social worker, that says that you have a feeling for the misfortune of others. It was our calling."

"You tell me how your little group has saved 2,500 children. How many more thousands could have been saved with several groups like that?"

"Yes, certainly . . . But it would have taken two things: willingness and courage. You look at me and you think you have met the only Pole who felt the misfortune of the Jews. Not at all! When traveling past the Ghetto in a tram and when you see a mother throw her child out the window of a burning building in the hope that someone would pick it up, you would have needed to be made of stone not to be moved. Many Poles cried, but did nothing. They were very frightened."

"And you, were you frightened?"

"Yes, I was. But, when you are young, you are brave and courageous. I wanted to resist the Nazis. I wanted to save my friend Eva, give a hand to victims. When the Germans arrested me, I had to walk with them across the courtyard to their car. I asked myself how to hide my fear from them. It is by overcoming my fear that I can hold on . . . Today, I know myself that I did not do all I could have done. I have regrets, and I will have till the end of my days . . ."

Irena cries.

I am, myself, greatly moved. Here is an unbelievable situation. When the worst executioners, the Nazis, responsible for thousands of murders, claimed responsibility for nothing, arguing that they did nothing but obey orders, but the Righteous, the saviors, the Good, reproach themselves, and for the rest of their lives, for not having done more . . .

When I take my leave from Irena Sendler, I recall one of her first sentences:

"To give a hand to someone who needs help? But . . . that's normal!"

With this "normal" gesture, she risked her life dozens, hundreds of times. By her "normal" gesture, 2,500 children have survived. And she reproaches herself for not having done more . . .

A mystery, profound mystery that is the power of Good!

*"Throw your bread on the water, you will harvest it in the days to come,"* Book of Ecclesiastes.

In effect, a few months later, when I was in Israel for the premier of my film, *Tzedek, Les Justes,* I met, by chance, a Polish friend, Wanda Elsner, an educationalist who had a miraculous escape from the Ghetto and whom I knew in Poland after the war.

"You have filmed Irena Sendler," she said.

"Yes."

"She told you about her friend Eva, didn't she?"

"Yes."

"Eva was my sister."

I remain speechless.

"We prepared, together," continued Wanda, "the lists of children whom Irena got out of the Ghetto . . ."

Leaning on the bar in a cafe, Wanda talks. She is an old lady today. She talks about Warsaw of long ago, of Israel, of Irena . . . Warsaw of my childhood surges up before my eyes. I even remember the smell of fresh bread and salt herring which then filled the air in the stairwells of the decrepit apartment blocks and their large square courtyards.

I listen to Wanda . . . This book is, first of all, dedicated to the Good, but also in the words of Paul Ricoeur, to those that were *spared,* to those who were saved by the *Just.* Can the evidence of some of them perhaps guide us through the labyrinth of the Good without the evidence of the others? Certainly not. Only the words of all of them together can say, completely, that goodness is more deeply rooted than Evil in the hearts of men.

# 4

# Paris to Warsaw

Poland again: after leaving Irena Sendler, I decided to go to Plody, to one of the convents to which Irena trusted her charges. I consult my notes: the convent is mentioned by Margaret Acher, that Polish Jewess who, in Paris, had told me her story. She and her sister, when very young, had been picked up by a nun, one of the Just, to whom they owed their lives: Sister Ludovica. They have stayed in touch. I hold the two links in the chain, the one who was saved, and the one who saved.

First, the escapee: Margaret Acher is petite, voluble, with a lively and passionate appearance. Born in 1930 in Paris, where her parents were studying, Margaret studied at Warsaw and Paris. She came from a Polish-Jewish family, a family of 'assimilated' Jews: at home, no one spoke Hebrew, no one spoke a word of Yiddish, they didn't observe Jewish festivals, which they scarcely even remembered. Her mother, prudently, had even had her daughters baptized, so they were really Catholics. The friends of the family were intellectual Polish Catholics. Her father, a brilliant barrister, had been an officer in the Polish army.

In 1939 all the family were staying in Paris when the grandfather, also a barrister, died in Warsaw. They had to return to Poland for the funeral. The Germans arrived . . . and the Achers were taken to the trap . . . of the Ghetto. Impossible to leave. Impossible to return to France. In giving up his soul, the happy grandfather had set his family on a terrible adventure.

Inside the Ghetto, these lapsed Jews, half-Catholic, knowing no Yiddish, Hebrew forgotten, were regarded rather badly. They did have, however, a number of influential friends, well-placed—among those, the attorney general—who there, in town, could help them. But little Margaret, only ten years old, posed a problem: it is difficult for a Polish family to shelter her temporarily, let alone to hide her permanently. It is that she has, to use the correct words, a *bad face*. What a terrible expression, to identify this curse. A bad face, that is to say a Semitic face, immediately recognizable.

"I swore at it," she said, "this face. I would have preferred to be hunch-backed, to have one leg shorter than the other—but with blond hair and blue eyes! But no, I was rather pretty, without deformities—and all over dark! To go out of the Ghetto without risk of immediately being identified as a Jew, I would have to cover up with a hat along with a huge fur collar to disguise my hair and my nose. I could hide for a time at the house of the niece of the attorney general, my parents' friend. They lived with their aunt and they were going on holiday together. They left me food and I was all alone. I could neither flush the toilet nor make any noise, as the neighbors knew that they were away on holiday. I stayed there two or three weeks. It was diabolic. Then, my sister and I were taken into a convent near Warsaw, at Plody: the Convent of the Sisters of the Family of The Virgin Mary. There are several of them across Poland. At Plody, about forty Jewish children were already hidden. They were brought by different channels, through Irena Sendler's network. But certain families came with their children. Sister Ludovica told you: parents never showed themselves as such; they preferred to say they were the child's uncle or aunt, and that they were here to give them to the convent. They gave the name of the child, then left quickly, taking cover along the walls. The Sisters had to change the names and keep absolute secrecy. Every Jewish child knew that they were Jewish but did not know which others were Jews, in this community of several hundred 'orphans,' Jews and non-Jews. Sister Ludovica told me this very funny story of a little Jewish girl saying to another: 'I wouldn't like to be friends with a Jewish girl,' in total ignorance that the other girl was also Jewish. There were some incredible moments, in the convent at Plody. Fear of the blues, for example.

"The blues were the Polish police—they were called this because of their blue uniforms—who worked hand in hand with the Nazis.

"One day, a blue came to the convent. He spoke to the Mother Superior and said to her: 'I know you are hiding Jewish children and demand that you denounce them.' The Mother Superior answered him: 'Why don't you do it yourself?' Replied the blue: 'No, I can't. I am a Catholic, I was baptized here. I don't want to go to Hell . . .' And the Mother Superior retorted: 'Why would you want *me* to go to Hell in your place?' Ah well, that policeman never dared to denounce the convent to the Germans!"

Margaret Acher clearly remembers her life at Plody. She didn't know what had happened when the uprising burst out in the Warsaw Ghetto, but, from the garden of the convent, they could see in the distance an enormous cloud of smoke above the town. She asked the gardener what was happening. He replied, "It's the Jews who are cooking."

Margaret Acher relates. Her memories give off so many vibes. Like this story of the Red Army officer. The Germans were in retreat. The Soviet officer got out of his truck and asked Margaret and her sister, in bad Polish: "You are Jews?" They were scared to admit it, one never knows . . . The man pressed: "Since Stalingrad, I keep going on in the hope of saving a Jewish child . . ." But the two little girls didn't answer and went on their way. A few days later, accompanied by their father who had also been able to escape the massacres, they met the officer. Margaret told her father what had happened.

He called the Russian and explained to him. The officer turned towards the two girls: "You have given me one of the greatest heartaches of my life . . . I am a Jew. Since Stalingrad, everywhere I go, I try to find people of my community. But there is nobody left . . . I arrive here, I see two young Jewish girls, and they are frightened to tell me who they are!"

The remark made by this officer—without doubt a man out of the ordinary—summed up the situation at the time: since Stalingrad, not one Jew! Three and a half million lived in Poland before the war. I asked Margaret Acher if they weren't too numerous to be able to hide themselves.

"They were, above all, very different," she told me, "Recognizable by their accent. They used words in Yiddish or of Hebrew origin which made them very quick to identify and denounce. And then the faces, the hair . . . In France the population is mixed: my face and my dark hair don't make me particularly noticeable."

"In France also people were denounced . . ."

"Yes, my husband was denounced by his partner. And that only thirty miles from Nice!"

"In Poland did the enormous proportion of Jews denounced and massacred come from the fact that it was difficult to hide them for the simple reason they were different?"

It is then that she made that observation that I remembered in the middle of my interview with Irena Sendler: a thousand Poles to save one Jew; one Pole to denounce a thousand Jews . . . Here it is in full:

"In order to save one Jew in Poland, it needs a thousand Poles. In effect, when the place where we were hiding was not safe any more, we had to leave and find another hiding place. A chain of helpers was indispensable. But conversely, to denounce a thousand Jews one Pole was enough."

Impossible equation! It is, however, its positive dimension that I want to keep, because it shows up the difficult permanence of Good, of this chain of solidarity that works despite the ambient barbarity. The convent at Plody forms one of the high points in this. Margaret Acher has arranged a meeting for me with Sister Ludovica. She is the last, in the convent, from now on, with the power to bring back this period. Fifty years have gone by, and all the other Sisters have disappeared.

# 5
# My own escape—
# Treblinka

When one leads an inquiry, chance is often king. I am leaving
for Plody with a young Polish cinematographer, Vojtek, who is
to be my chauffeur and my guide, and . . . we lost our way. At
the same moment when Vojtek realized his error and was
ready to turn around, I noticed a road sign pointing the way to
Malkinia. This word worked on me like a can opener. Some
words exist like this in the hidden recesses of the mind as if in
closed boxes—and then, suddenly, a lid opens . . . Malkinia
was the railway marshaling yard through which the Jews
passed when they were fleeing from Warsaw to seek sanctuary
in the USSR before the eruption, in June 1941, of German–Soviet hostilities. Through Malkinia, we could find the part of
Poland occupied by the Red Army. With this place there came
to life again in my memory a key moment from my childhood.
When we fled the Ghetto, my parents, my aunt, and two of my
father's Catholic friends, printers like himself, had the intention of crossing several frontiers before reaching England,
where my father and his two colleagues intended to enroll in
the Polish National Army to fight the Nazis. But they also took
the wrong road.

I remember it. I was five, my mother was pregnant, we
walked during the night, and, during the day, we hid ourselves
in the woods. Our Catholic friends went in the villages to find
something for us to eat. When evening came, we moved on . . .

Having arrived at Malkinia, my parents saw their navigation

error, but it wasn't possible to go back; we had to go forward. In the station we were all bunched together, as were lots of people, in a goods wagon. I remember the smell of straw and cow dung—this was a cattle truck. Today, this memory raises bitter thoughts about the destiny of the Jewish people. How not to think of those innumerable railway convoys, phantomlike yet sadly real, which, across the whole of Europe, have taken— in conditions worse than those reserved for beasts—whole herds of human beings to the extermination camps, to the human slaughterhouses?

Suddenly, the doors were opened roughly; blinding search-lights were turned on us. Barking of dogs, guttural shouts, tears, unequivocal orders: "Jews to the right! Poles to the left!" They made us get down from the train. In the general confusion, a hand gripped mine; one of our Polish friends dragged me under the wagon. All of us came out on the other side, running across fields for I don't know how long, while they fired shots at us. Not one of us was hit. Luck . . . Later we were arrested by a patrol of Russian soldiers. They took us at first for spies; one of them even wanted to shoot us. Another one, older, held them up: "Eh no, these aren't spies, look at them, they are Jews fleeing the Nazis!" Things were arranged. At last, they sent us to Moscow, in February 1941. Several months later Moscow was bombarded: this was the start of the German–Soviet war. This was how, having left for London, my parents and their friends found themselves in Red Square!

So many memories out of one roadsign . . . I say to Vojtek not to turn round, to go to Malkinia. We arrived there in the snow. The station hasn't changed. Fifty years later, the same Poles, the same railway workers, dressed just the same. The freight trains are from the same era. And Vojtek told me (I didn't know) that Treblinka is five miles away . . . Thus, in the course of our flight in 1941, we came within a hair's breadth of this place where 800,000 people would be exterminated. I say "would be," as this death camp, at the time of our misadventure, did not yet exist: it was built a year later, in 1942. In 1941 Treblinka was only an ordinary Polish village. To escape the worst, we had, then, skirted these places where worse still was to carry out its devastation!

"Since we are so near Treblinka," I say to my friend, "let's go there."

I was in the process of a sort of lucid hallucination; I had the impression of hearing once more the confused mixture of noises, of barking, of crying, the crackling of machine-gun fire. Like certain horror movies, when one goes into an empty room which, all of a sudden, fills with the noise of voices. Like Rabelais, when Gargantua enters a cave and there makes his monks light a fire to warm him: voices are raised suddenly from all sides, and the monks explain to him that these are voices which have been frozen, voices of people who lived there a thousand years ago, and who, in the heat of the fire thaw and wake up.

The route we take is parallel to the rails, crossing the snowy plain, alongside the railway line. As a child I thought the rails were black scars stretching away beyond the horizon. The rails were infinity. To my eyes the rails had no end. At Treblinka this childhood vision stops dead. Here, the rails stop. You follow them, and, suddenly, no more. Bare earth. This terminus of the ironway, their jump into nothingness is common to all the concentration camps at their entrance. One difference, all the same, with Auschwitz: there where the rails end, there is this gate with its infamous inscription: *Arbeit macht frei* ("Work frees"). But at Treblinka the Nazis destroyed everything to leave no trace of their crimes. The rails stop in the snow-covered plain. As if empty. There is nothing. Only eight huge stones cut like stalagmites, no ruins. Just a sort of platform to the left, which must have been the station. There is a railway sign, with the inscription: Treblinka. That is all that remains of a place where 800,000 beings were tortured, assassinated, burnt.

Salvador Dalí, when having one of his crises as a delirious visionary, decided, when leaving a train by mistake there, that Perpignan station was the center of the world.

He was wrong: the center of the world is here, at the center of Europe, in the phantom station of Treblinka. In this vast emptiness that has seen 800,000 martyrs pass by, and where nothing can be seen anymore.

The village itself, in contrast, is just like a Chagall village, with its wooden houses, geese running about, horse-drawn carts, herds of cows. Old peasants chatting, standing in the melting snow, leaning on one of the wooden latticed fences which surround each house. Chagall's picture, yes. Only the fiddler on the roof is missing. I want to speak to one of these Treblinka locals. To ask him if he knew what happened up there, less than a mile away, in the camp.

"You are going to find anti-Semites again," predicted Vojtek.

"We'll see!"

I approach a small old man.

"Are you from here? Were you here during the war?"

"Yes."

"Were there any Jews here?"

He didn't blink.

"Yes," he replied.

"What became of them?"

Then, he gazed at me: "You don't know?"

"No."

It is with a serious tone, but not taken in by my stratagem, that he speaks: "The Nazis exterminated them at Auschwitz, and then here, a mile away."

"Did you know these Jews?"

"Certainly, yes."

"Then why did you and the others do nothing to come to their aid."

In fact, I feel a veritable verbal aggression rising in me in the encounter with this Polish peasant. He is getting angry. I am going to have a row with him . . . In all the documentaries devoted to Poland, each time one asks peasants from around Auschwitz, Majdanek, or Treblinka what they think of Jews, they seem to rejoice at their extermination. This one surprises me. He is rough, offended by my question, but damned likable in his blue work jacket, his cap screwed on to his head.

"But we, my brother and me, we hid a little Jewish girl in the house, sir! Later, my brother took her to the Russian border so that she could save herself. Then my brother was arrested, sent to Auschwitz. He escaped on the way there, but he was recaptured by the Polish police, who tortured him to death, also my father. Both dead, sir. For having saved one young Jewish girl!"

Surprised and moved by his tale, I offer my apologies; we part good friends.

Later I confide to Vojtek: "They are going to think that I chose this man deliberately, to prove positively that there are Good people."

"It was definitely pure chance," exclaimed my guide, not without cause.

Yes. Chance. But do things really happen by chance?

We left this morning for Plody, now we were here, after that wrong turn, at five o'clock in the evening. Now Plody is only seven miles from Warsaw! Actually, it was as if, to go to Marseilles, we set off in the direction for Lille—as, fifty years earlier, my parents en route for England found themselves in Moscow. These two wild detours skirted Treblinka before and after the extermination. And my mistake had allowed me to meet an unknown peasant who was part of the anonymous network of Just people without whom no Jew would have been able to survive.

# 6
## Sister Ludovica

When we arrived at Plody, two blond children were throwing snowballs at each other in the gathering darkness of this late afternoon. Without doubt, in years gone by, there would have been dark children playing in this same place. Sister Ludovica is waiting for me. When I telephoned, several days ago, for this meeting, the Mother Superior was not very encouraging:

"Sister Ludovica is very old! She has problems with her memory. I don't think she will be able to tell you anything."

I persisted, and obtained permission to come. And Sister Ludovica said this lovely thing to me: "I am so grateful that you have come to see me today, because for three days I have prayed to God that he give me back some of my memory so that I can tell you everything! And here you are, and I feel right on form!"

We are face to face to each other across a round table, in a corner of the parlor. Just behind her hangs a huge portrait of a bluish Virgin Mary wearing a gold crown. Sister Ludovica, with her somber blue habit and white collar, is both at the same time more severe and more smiling. The oval of her face, which shows from the frame of her nun's headdress, gives out an expression of sweet solemnity. For Sister Ludovica, who speaks with simplicity, everything came, she said, *from the interior:*

"I was very happy that these children were able to survive,

that they were able to get away. It gives me satisfaction, yes . . .
But, what I did was from the heart. The adults, in principle,
could shift for themselves—children, no. So, all the children
who came here were accepted. We never knew how it would all
finish. We did all we could so that they could survive, everything it was possible to do . . . It was a heart's demand, a cry
from inside."

She explained how these things had been handled in the
convent during the war: each Sister was responsible for a small
group of children; she herself was in charge of thirty-five little
Jewish girls. She told me: "Today, some of them are in
America, others in Israel, and others still in France. Regularly,
one or another comes to see me. Besides that, I have many of
their visiting cards. Hold on, I even have a list of all their
names, with their addresses. Completely accounted for: they
were saved from death, and now they have children, and some
of them are grandmothers!"

"When the Red Army liberated the region, what happened
to these children?"

"All of them were collected by their relatives, or friends,
who knew they were here, hidden in the convent. Only one,
whom nobody reclaimed, remained. Then someone came to
take her to Palestine. That was well before the creation of the
State of Israel. But she didn't want to go with them, she
preferred to stay at the convent. I don't know where she went
in the end."

"Converted?"

"Catholic, yes. Without doubt she went to one of our other
convents, I don't remember any more."

I thought of Margaret Acher, whom Sister Ludovica spoke
of with joy. Equally, I thought of other converted Jews. For the
Nazis, in Poland, these conversions were of no account. In
their eyes, up to the fifth generation of converted Jews were
still Jewish. In the Ghetto, there was, beside the red brick
church in Novopolski Street near Smozca Street, another
church in Lesno Street, a gray building, filled every day by
Catholics. These Ghetto Catholics were converted Jews, as was

their curate. All of them perished, like the other Jews who couldn't escape from the trap . . .

I ask Sister Ludovica: "I have been told that the Nazis came three times to inspect the convent?"

"They only saw Christian children," she chuckled. "You see the little chapel in the grounds? We took the children there to pray. We put the little Jewish girls furthest from the door, right up by the crucifix, close to Jesus: like that when the Germans came, they could only see blond heads."

I visit this chapel. "It has remained," Sister Ludovica said to me, "exactly how it was at that time." At the entrance, pigeonholes for the children's little ankle-boots. A picture crossed my mind, still intact within me, overwhelming. At Auschwitz, where my father had taken me on our return from Russia, right at the end of the war, there was a mountain of children's shoes. I was ten. *Crematorium oven,* I hardly understood. There was also a mountain of spectacles and a mountain of hair: I saw them without taking it in. But that . . . , that mountain, consisting only of little shoes . . . I felt that, I really knew, at that moment, the vast emptiness which that exposed. Thousands of children like me, and then nothing: shoes, an absurd mountain of shoes. I pull myself together. I go back beside Sister Ludovica.

"Why did so many Poles do nothing, all these Catholics, to help the Jewish children?"

Sister Ludovica stays silent for a fraction of a second, then looks at me and with a clear voice, begins to laugh.

"Ask *them* why!"

"Why did you, yourself, save some Jewish children?"

She smiles. Behind her strong glasses, her eyes radiate a warm simplicity.

"For God, for sure. Because God has said that you must help your neighbor. And then . . ."

She interrupts herself, in a clear voice:

"We couldn't not save Jewish children, because . . . when you save a Jewish child, it is as if you have saved the Infant Jesus."

# 7

# Memories of Evil
# to find Good

On returning to The Victoria, the old Warsaw hotel where I was staying, I glance out of the window. A caricature of a skyscraper, pompous and huge, is just across the road: a poor copy of the Empire State Building from the Stalin era, it is the Cultural Center, a free gift, ready to use with all instructions, from the Little Father of the Polish People of yesterday. I draw the curtains. Besides, my thoughts are divided, between the camp at Treblinka and the words of Sister Ludovica, at the convent in Plody.

I turn over thoughts of the contrasts of this day. Thoughts of Evil constantly emerge. Also Good.

I can't help thinking that the extermination never took place. The extermination: it is through it that I see the story. It is the gateway through which I interpret everything, my clarification, my faith in me and mine, the blackest mark against humanity. These images raise and sustain the whole of my being. I must without doubt, following the example of Elie Wiesel, preoccupy myself with evil, search to find the sources, the roots, before being able to understand the plot. Freud postulated on that which he called the *instinct of death:* he never intended, by that, to put an end to it. But, it appears to me, he never explored this antidote: the impulsion of generosity (not love) that one could also call goodwill, justice, or solidarity—impulses that arise spontaneously, as if being able to think for themselves.

Was it not this impulse which obsessed the mystics: this *je-ne-sais-quoi* which stimulated St. John de la Croix and the Christians, and, for the Jews, Zohar's statement (I,65a): *"Everything is based on this secret. Happy is the fate of the Jews in this world and the next."*

. . . Impulse to kill, then. Why? Why does it exist against Muslims, Protestants, gypsies, homosexuals, and so many others?

Why murder these and those others, so often?

Why kill Jews, always?

Will I have to go, like so many of my predecessors, on an initiation journey to investigate Evil? To ask the same questions they have so often left without answer—in the hope, on my part, of discovering at least one? Will I not need a veritable army for such a task?

No: with the same story, with the same path as the others, I am traveling among memories of Evil to find Good.

The Earth cannot only be populated with swine. One day I realized that I was alive. And I knew that it was impossible for *everyone* to wish me dead, that *everyone* applauded the extermination of the Jews.

Yes, there is a memory of Good. To explore it, to throw light on my search for these Just people appears urgent. They are the key to the dignity of Man. They alone can ward off Evil.

One of my father's two printer friends, that blond, fervent Catholic who briskly pulled me under the railway wagon, at Malkinia station, he certainly didn't wish me dead. He wanted me to live. I have never found any trace of him. He is, however, the first Just person I ever met. I was five years old. I owe him my life.

In the next few days I have appointments here, in Warsaw, with Zofia Doboszynska, Zofia Sterner, Alicia Szczepaniak— three women: three Good women. Perhaps they will help me the better to understand this generous impulse *"forgotten"* by Freud. At this moment the hotel room is filled with perfume.

My childhood is coming back to me, with all its forgotten sensations. Is this the wardrobe? Is this the floor polish? This odor mixed with the very particular smell that one senses in Eastern European cities: a mixture of mists and badly refined petrol. Yiddish has been swallowed up but not the *salt* of the air.

# 8

# From Ghetto to cupboard

I saw them one after the other, but they coalesce in my memory, these three ladies who have saved Jewish families.

Zofia Doboszynska, Zofia Sterner, Alicia Szczepaniak: I admire these Good people who have helped Jewish mothers and their children to escape from the Ghetto. They welcomed in their own small apartments, in Warsaw itself, in the middle of the Germans, those persecuted people whom none other would shelter, because it was too dangerous: a little girl and her aunt, for example, whose accent and faces stamped them as "non-Aryans."

With these three women, who relied on their husbands, their children, and complicitous silence of their neighbors (sometimes the whole apartment block), I am once more facing resources of improvised but infallible solidarity: discrete, efficacious, as if running itself. No, *all* Poles were not anti-Semites nor indifferent to the Jewish tragedy . . .

I question Zofia Doboszynska: "Madam, you are an Evangelist, your first husband was Catholic, the second was also— and, your two husbands and you saved Jews during the Second World War. Why?"

"If we talk of my first husband, he wanted to help me. He loved me. He had lost me as a wife, but he loved me very much and he thought he just had to help me, although the danger was huge—and he did help me! He hid a Jewish woman with her child, in his house, for more than two years, just because I

31

asked him. This woman, today, is in Canada where she met up with her brother again. She has done very well. One day, I received a little present from her: of silk, that she had sent with a letter to tell me that she has never forgotten that originally it was I who saved the lives of her and her child . . .''

I listen to Zofia Doboszynska, I watch her speaking. She must have been very beautiful, at that time when two men loved her. Today, in her apartment in the early evening light, peaceful in the center of her comfortably decorated flat, she described the situation with amused detachment. But this indifference was a sham: truthfully, she still savored, today, surrounded by a sort of unconditional respect, the fact that her ex-husband continued to love her. This woman had been much loved, and those who loved her stayed faithful in spirit. This faithfulness, this solidarity with her previous husband had allowed two people to be saved.

"And your second husband? Why did he help the Jews? The first did it because he loved you—but the second?"

"My second husband believed that he *had* to do it, that he had to oppose all Hitler's orders. We hated that man. All the time, both of us prayed to God for someone to kill Hitler, that a bomb would drop on Hitler. This man, Hitler, would die in such a terrible way . . . Don't ask any more."

Zofia Doboszynska shines. However, the look does not last. Only a clear determination. While speaking, she shook her head several times to emphasize what she was saying. The wavy mass of her hair shook, then, straight faced and calm again, Zofia is ready: "I must tell you that I have no one in the world more dear to me, or closer, than this little Jewish girl whom I saved from the Ghetto when she was five years old . . . We remain, today, very much in contact, her, her family, and me. When they have a party, Easter or New Year's Day, I am always invited."

She gives me a photo where I see her flanked by two little girls.

"That dates from 1990," she explains. "That's me, with the granddaughters of my little Ghetto-girl!"

"How did you snatch this child from the Ghetto?"

"I brought her out, on foot, holding her hand—and her aunt with her! My husband also brought a woman out of the Ghetto, whom I wanted to save at any price; this little girl's mother. Then the father, the mother, and the girl had to be sheltered. My husband, a fervent Catholic (I'm an Evangelist), knew where to find a convent that would welcome the little one. There remained the aunt, with her Semitic head and her weird accent, who jabbered in Polish more than spoke it . . . Actually, her accent was Lithuanian, but for the people here, that sounded like an even more 'Jewish' accent. Nobody wanted to take the risk of looking after her. OK. We took charge of her, in Praga district, Radzyminska Street. We lived in a block where only workers lived. We made her talk to all the neighbors, in her language. Everyone soon became fluent. So, she stayed there during the whole Occupation, protected by all the people in the block!"

"All the same, you were taking a great risk!"

"In Poland, at that time, hiding a Jew was punishable by torture and death."

"Fifty years later, Zofia, if the same situation arose, how would you react?"

"Oh, fifty years after, that question needs to take into consideration all that has passed since in my head, my heart, and my feelings. Could you imagine that today, at my age, I would be just as courageous? That I would again bring death so close? Because, then, death threatened me ceaselessly . . ."

"Nobody ever denounced you?"

"Ah, there was one man . . . We were suspicious of him. My husband made enquiries about him, and we learnt that he was trying to become a *Volksdeutsch* ('Honorary German'). One day he threatened my husband about our ward with the Lithuanian accent. But my husband sharply replied that the Organization would punish him if he denounced us. All Warsaw knew that the army of the interior charged itself with executing this kind of traitor. The fellow was scared, and he was killed just at the end of the war. Our Jew had been able to be saved. She stayed two and a half years with us! She was quite old even then. She has been dead, now, about twenty years. She liked me better than her family . . . When she began to be very ill, they asked me to go to her. I held her hand right at the very end."

This link, right to the end, of savior and saved, between saved and savior, this is a force which I feel I am going to find more than once in this search for the Just. More than recognition, there is such a confidence there, such a gift, such abandon to Good! I am greatly struck by it, when Zofia Sterner tells me how she led her charges out of the Ghetto. She appears to answer a question which I neglected to ask Zofia Doboszynska.

For Zofia Sterner, only one way: out through the municipal buildings. And this was not without danger.

"To get them out of the Ghetto," she explained, "you passed the finance office, and the court. There was one entrance to the 'Aryan' part of Warsaw and another to the Ghetto. I had a friend on the inside, a finance officer. It is there that it began. My husband and I had some very good friends, a mixed couple; him Polish, and she a Jewess. From one day to the next, there they were separated, and the wife obliged to live in the Ghetto! It was untenable, and, my husband and I, we took them out of there, along with two other Jewish women. As for these other two, I don't know how they fared afterwards. There were escape routes in town. As for our couple of friends, we sheltered them, for enough time to obtain false papers for the wife. After that, we also hid plenty of others, for enough time to let them find false papers. My husband worked for many clandestine organizations, he knew how such things were done . . ."

And this is how, during all of the Occupation, the Sterners devoted heart and soul to the cause which they had voluntarily chosen: to save Jews, give them comfort, and to help them leave for more secure places, with passes in their pockets.

"Your husband and you, were taking great risks! Were you frightened?"

"On reflection, I don't think so. I wasn't scared. I thought it was something quite natural. We knew we must help these people. It is not even pity, it's normal, that's all."

"Madam Sterner, fifty years later, if such horrific events were to happen again, with such a tragic situation, would you do the same things, would you, once more, help these people?"

"Yes, of course. But now I am old, I am eighty-five. I don't know if I would be strong enough . . . but I am sure that my daughter would do everything that I did!"

I look at this old lady, fragile and yet determined, and I remember that Hegel called this type of person: *noteworthy individual*. Those *"who wished for and achieved not something considered imaginary, but something just and necessary. [And] who did it because they received internal revelation"* . . .

It is possible that the tendency towards Good, that the feelings of those who are righteous are among the rare gifts of the soul which never lose their edge. But, for women like Zofia Sterner who become examples, because they become *noteworthy,* they need a "transmitter"—the word is a translation from Paul Ricoeur—an individual who can transmit their story into History. The idea set my mind in turmoil and frightened me: would I be up to this task?

With Alicia Szczepaniak, I was doing business with someone of another generation. Younger than the two Just women that I had met recently (she was thirteen in 1943), she will bear witness more for the courage of her mother, now dead, than for her own, which, however was nonetheless real. Since her father's death, in 1939, she lived with her mother in the Praga district. They lived in a single room, on the first floor, without any facilities nor the least comfort, in very hard conditions. There also, a discrete group, a litany of desperate souls, found refuge and protection, at a cost of unbelievable cunning to be able, simply, to eat. But how could one not help these people that one knew and loved?

Alicia Szczepaniak recalled: "I agreed with their being hidden. I sympathized with them, I sympathized with their fate, I knew how difficult it was. After my father died, it was so hard for my mother and I to find enough food, to survive. But they . . . they were a lot worse off than us! I thought I understood bad luck—their bad luck compared to ours. I passed months, years, shaking with fear. You couldn't make any noise in our 'apartment,' what with Tatania and Nina whom we hid in the wardrobe when a neighbor visited. Because we had to be suspicious of the neighbors. They were never able to know how many Jews stayed with us! We had practically nothing to eat— only soup which my mother made with thick potato peelings which she brought home from the workers' canteen where she worked. But no one knew . . . There was once a terrible alert with the Germans who searched every flat in the block. I was alone. I didn't open the door. A neighbor came out and told them that there was no man in the apartment. They didn't persist . . . Another time, a group of Germans started shooting just under our windows: they wounded a boy who had stolen, as many others did, coal and tires. I was very frightened both those times. I seemed to live in a state of permanent fear. This anguish was horrible because I imagined the end could come at any moment: the end of these Jews, the end for my mother, for the neighbors, for me . . . But not one of our Jewish friends was taken."

I posed the same question as I had to the others: "Madam Szczepaniak, fifty years later, if the situation repeated itself just as terrifying as before, would you again help Jews in trouble?"

"Yes, yes. I would even try to do more. I couldn't wish that on anyone, no one! But you know, after the end of the war my mother had regrets—yes, regrets! She would say that she had only done very little for these people, very little . . . What perhaps she could have done, what she ought to have done, if she had organized herself better . . . There will never again be such a situation! Hopefully! Hope for it with all your might, for our children, for our grandchildren . . ."

"We will wish for that, yes. But how do you explain that so few people took the risk of saving Jews, as your mother and you did?"

"There were reasons for that . . . But, first of all, there was fear, sir. I know there were houses, families with men, women, children, and the people feared for their children, for their wives, for themselves, feared for everything. I admired my mother so much more because of this. Our house had no man, no father, no husband. Fear or not, she made up her mind, and stuck to her decision!''

# 9

# Three types

''Open unto me the gates of the Just!'' exclaim the Psalms (CXVIII, 19). This verse is translated elsewhere as: "Open unto me the gates of Justice!" The nuance is very fine, for I who have just crossed the threshold, the thresholds, of these modest people who more often than not scarcely understand what I want to do with my stories of the Just. The word astounds them. In their simplicity, it scares them. However, it comes from a long way back, from our common religious origins. "The Just will flourish like the palm and will multiply like the Cedar of Lebanon," muse the Psalms, once more (XCII, 13)— a verse on which Rabbi Isaac, in the Kabbala, comments thus: "The world only continues to exist because of the merit of one single Just person, as it is written: And the Just are the foundation of the earth." (Proverbs, X, 1).

I did not inflict them with a lecture on the Bible nor the Kabbala, but I begin to interview like this: Through the diversity of their experiences and what they have witnessed, these people, unknown to them, have given evidence of what they have in common: an immediate sense of justice. I don't know whether Rabbi Isaac was correct to affirm that one Just man was enough to sustain the world, but I am sure that one justice, that one sense of Good, prevailed in all those I came to meet in Poland.

Here, as in Germany, to help a Jew was to risk death. These Poles, these Poles whom I call the Just deliberately put their life on the line. Little by little I can distinguish three categories among them, three families of Good people, whose motivation can be analyzed for clarity. And each one touches me and moves me.

There are those who have acted out of pride, to preserve that which they considered their dignity when faced with the Nazis. They detested Hitler and decided to resist him. To save the Jews constituted one of these acts of opposition. They would have done the same for any category of people or peoples persecuted by Hitlerian barbarity. From this type, I will meet many representatives in France, for example.

There are those who have saved Jews because they were believers: convinced Christians, fervent practitioners, applying to the letter the precepts of help and love. Among them, certain of them are distinguished by a clear leaning towards the Jewish people, seen as *"older brothers in God."* In this regard, Sister Ludovica's feelings are extraordinary: *"To save a Jewish child, it's the same as saving The Infant Jesus."*

There is in that a dimension of deep complicity, in the way of a shared secret. In the course of conversations with Cardinal Lustiger, which I will have later, he will confirm this senti-ment. For him, the rapport between Christians and Jews is a revelation. A revelation of the true faith. He thinks that anyone he would call a "true believer" cannot *not* feel a positive love for Israel: Israel, that is The Old Testament, which is our common source. You can't spit in your own spring. You cannot pollute it. You cannot block it. If you kill your source, then you dehydrate and die.

These Poles, and these Polish Catholics, these Good people, renew confidence. This then, when it is *justly* lived, is what a fervent religious life can offer: a welcome, a dignified recogni-tion of the human family of man, with, the first reaction, life saved for thousands of unfortunate people.

There is, to finish, among these Good people, people of *because.* Perhaps these interest me more than the others. I have a weakness for their silence, for their reticence. They must be pressed with questions before they will explain their actions.

In the end, when pressed, they admit: they cannot support injustice. If they see the weak mistreated by the strong, they can't stand it, that's all. From the outset they feel on the side of the persecuted. And not with intellectual speculation, weighing the pros and cons, the moral and the expedient, no: in deeds. Their solidarity carries them on, left to risk their lives: *This is the way it is. Because.* These are the most touching. You feel as if they are lifted up in spite of themselves, animated by a power which pushes them in front of those in distress.

They make me think about this *capacity for Good* which Pascal talks about, which manifests itself in spite of everything, in spite of the flagrant presence of Evil that is there watching and working away. No, I am not forgetting that these Good people were in the minority and that, although 400,000 to 500,000 Jews were saved thanks to them, 6 million were massacred in the almost general indifference.

But, I believe also with Pascal, the most Jewish of Christian philosophers, that *it is dangerous to try too hard to see how Man is similar to animals, without showing him his greatness,* and that *it is dangerous, also, to show him too much of his greatness without his baseness.* Finally, *it is still more dangerous to leave him ignorant of either one or the other.* Now, if I knew Evil in his many guises, hate and its diverse manifestations, death and his millions of victims without graves, then, there is this new thing that I will have discovered during this return to the country of my birth that this journey to Poland has been for me: the sense of Good is not a moral classification, or not only. It is a spontaneous act. It is, like Evil, part of our true nature.

Even if all, far from the truth as that may be, do not reflect this disposition, there are people, everywhere there are ordinary people, very simple sometimes, who even in spite of the horror, display this solidarity of heart with their actions.

So tenuous, so fragile, and so derisory that it hardly shows, it is there, thanks to the Good, a justice, that is to say an active goodwill, that watches, that circles—and that saves.

# 10
## Strange odors in the barn

I leave Alicia Szczepaniak with regret. I am expected at a meeting twenty miles from Warsaw, in open country, or almost.

Set in the depth of the nearby forest with, in front of it, the immensity of the plain, Szczesny farm is situated on the edge of the village, about 1,200 yards away as the crow flies.

Leszek, Maria, and Kazimierz Szczesny are imposing: tall, heavy, feet well planted in the black earth, bleached and hardened by the frost. They speak simply, without rambling, without giving themselves airs, airs of the Good, airs of the Just. During the war there were five of them: their parents were still alive.

The Jew was a tailor. He was called Abraham and his wife was called Rachel. The Szczesny's hardly knew them: Abraham's business was in the neighboring village. One day in the Spring of 1943, Abraham arrived in the farmyard, terrified, shouting, crying . . . Father Szczesny was unloading a handcart of potatoes with a shovel.

"My wife is in the woods . . . hidden . . . She is about to die of exhaustion . . . and hunger!" cried Abraham. "—What do you want of me?" replied father Szczesny. "Take my shovel and bury her there!"

"Abraham began to cry and shout louder," says Kazimierz Szczesny. "Then, my mother heard the noise and calmed everyone down . . . She took a casserole full of soup and

41

followed him . . . Rachel took three days to eat that soup. Little by little, her health improved. But she remained very weak for the rest of the war. Back home, the blues arrived and threatened my father: they were looking for two Jews . . ."

Leszek Szczesny interrupted: "Actually, they were hidden in the barn. They stayed there till the end of the war . . . Early on, our father called us together and warned us: it would be at pain of death for us to be denounced. Then we voted . . ."

"The result?"

"Everyone was for . . . Father changed his mind also, when it came to the bit."

We went to visit the famous barn. Maria Szczesny, Leszek and Kazimierz's sister, explained: "We put them in the recess where we stored the firewood. Every day, to take them their food, I took a basket and pretended to go for some wood for us. Abraham came out from time to time, being very careful not to show himself, to stretch his legs. Poor Rachel was too weak to walk. She had to be carried. They also came to the house, with us, when there was a celebration. When that happened, someone stayed outside to watch round about, in case a neighbor from the village came without warning."

"You thought of the danger?"

My question made them laugh. "Of the danger? Yes, there was some."

"That is . . . the Germans came here, a full truckload, in September 1943!" exclaimed Leszek. "And they wanted to spend the night in the barn! Impossible to say no to them . . . Without realizing it, they slept right above Abraham and Rachel's shelter . . . One of them gave us a terrible fright. He thought he could smell strange odors. He started complaining that there were other people in the barn apart from him and his friends! Insisting on searching and looking into everywhere, he finally discovered . . . the WCs which are just beside the building; that calmed him down, and he went to sleep like the others. The next day, they left and we never saw them again."

Maria Szczesny was overcome with nostalgia. She wanted to

leave the barn. She was remembering parties passed together, at home: "With all these ordeals, as days, weeks, months went by, Rachel and Abraham became our friends, and even a lot more than friends. In fact, they became part of the family. Our father, himself, who, at first, was a bit wary, said to them: 'If we ourselves survive this war, then you will survive it with us!' Much later, in the eighties, I went to see them in Israel. Abraham greeted me by throwing his arms round my neck saying: 'Maricha!' And Rachel spoke once more of my mother's soup which had saved her when she was dying of exhaustion, out there in the forest." Leszek and Kazimierz have visited Rachel and Abraham in Israel. They too, like Maria, had the feeling of finding lost close friends or relations. The ties which bind them are indestructible. Useless to ask them if, events recurring, would they do it again: Abraham and Rachel, *aren't they family?*

# 11

# You will choose life

*"Love thy neighbor as thyself."* This biblical precept, revived in the New Testament, is often cited by the Just. As if this ancient injunction is enough to explain their action.

Freud did not believe much in this ideal requirement. "Not only," he said, "does our neighbor rarely deserve our love," but on the contrary, more often he "deserves our hostility, if not our hatred."

Why should it be otherwise, Freud asked himself, when this neighbor "does not appear to have the least affection for us?" And even, "when it suits him, he has no hesitation in putting us down [ . . . ] and he appears to find pleasure in doing that."

For Freud, Man is always tempted to satisfy his need for aggression at the expense of others. Then, the psychoanalyst asks himself, what relief is Man able to find in saving his neighbor?

Recent history appears to support him, even if the men and women that I have met did not ask themselves the question. In fact, we must warn him, they have replied, ". . . the instinct of life, which is buried so deep within us, but which brings us equally pleasure and satisfaction."

I have always been fascinated by the implacable logic of Freud's analyses. But, in the case of these Just people, they do not satisfy me at all. There are those *others*, of course, that we love through desire; and there are those *others* that we love because we have to: this compulsion we learned at school, at home, or yet again in church. It constitutes the Freudian superego. But what is this sentiment which drives us to go to the aid of someone in distress without expecting one benefit in return? What is this mechanism which releases in us this supreme gesture of solidarity: to save a life, many lives—to take an interest in others who appear to be strangers to us, indeed, who are strangers to us?

"I give you the choice of life or death, blessing or curse . . . You will choose life." This choice which Deuteronomy offers us, is it anchored in every mind?

Perhaps the Bible, in its day, already answered this question. It teaches us that Adam and Eve were the first human couple on Earth. These, then, were our ancestors. This somewhat unlikely couple had two sons. One goes to kill the other. This is how our history began . . .

However, an important fact seems to have escaped us: Cain, who killed his brother Abel, was innocent. Innocent as children are. Innocent because of *lack of knowledge*.

Cain does not know what death is.

How could he know it?

He has never seen it.

It belongs to the second generation of Man. His parents, Adam and Eve, are still alive. In killing his brother, Cain cannot know that he has committed the irreparable. The concepts of Good and Evil do not yet exist. The law, morals, and the "Thou shalt not kill" of Moses are not yet the order of the day.

In these conditions, Cain ought not to be able to celebrate nor to experience shame at what he had done. To the question from the Eternal: "What have you done with your brother?" he should have to reply truthfully: "I hit him and he does not move anymore."

Now Cain dodged the question: "Am I my brother's keeper?" he replied—as if he wanted to conceal his deed, as if he *knew* that this act was reprehensible.

But who told him? Where did he learn that to kill was Evil?

From the experience of the forbidden tree, from the tree of

Knowledge, from which his parents ate the fruit in the Garden of Eden.

Thus, from generation to generation, Man inherits a consciousness of Good and Evil, even before such notions are inculcated in him by being taught the laws.

Are the Just simply the incarnation of this consciousness from *before the Law?*

Only the pursuit of my enquiries will let me give an answer.

This is why the second stage of my journey looking for Good must take place in the most unexpected, and the most revelatory area: in Germany.

# 12
# Germany—the culture

Chancellor Helmut Schmidt said to me one day: "If the Poles were anti-Semites, the Nazis, they were Germans." This sentence, coming from a German, profoundly surprised me.

I saw Germans for the first time in Warsaw. I was three years old. It was in 1939. When the noise of the bombs and the crashing of the buildings falling down had, at last, stopped, the Jews were able to hear the announcement of their destiny: *Judenrein* (a country "purified" of Jews).

Ever since, when a Jew is killed at Antwerp or in Rome, in Vienna or in Paris, it is these words from my childhood that I hear.

I met Germans for the second time in sixty years. In Germany, this time. A Pole who had fled his country and set up in Cologne had invited me to exhibit in his gallery. It was Carnival time. Germany was sad then, drunk with beer and shame. Men of forty to fifty years old told you imagined tales from memories which, each time, swept away five years of their lives, at least all those who had not been sent to the Eastern Front did. Their children cried at the stories of Warsaw, of the Ghetto, of the flight into Soviet Russia. Germany of the economic boom bent under the weight of its wretched conscience.

Here I am now back in this country, looking for Just men and women. From Strasbourg to Heidelberg, you can hardly see a border: there is even friendliness among people, countries, and towns.

"That's normal," Baron Putliz, president of the famous university, said to me, teasingly. "We are the Southerners of Germany, the Latins of Northern Europe."

I speak fluently in French or in English when I am in intellectual company, but my friends insist that, when I am in public, I address Germans in Yiddish. *"Why yes, we understand you"* they say. And, truth to tell, on condition that one avoids Hebraic elements and composes the syntax on German lines, Yiddish can pass as one of the many dialects that are common in this ultra-decentralized country.

At the university, I announce to journalists from radio and television that this language, thanks to which we are able to communicate, is called Yiddish, and that it was born here, on German soil, more than a thousand years ago; Kant and Goethe used it to produce the glory of their linguistic and literary research, and that, out of the need to resist pressure from a hostile world and preserve it, this language, based on German, enriched itself in the course of the centuries, developed and expanded across the world to the point where it created a sparkling culture in which, in 1939, ten million people participated. Annihilated with those who used it, this language does not exist anymore today, except for a few thousand old people, some a bit younger, and strangely, but unknowingly, by the Germans themselves.

The city of Berlin, capital of the old Reich, afterwards cut in half and perhaps even because of that, has unwillingly maintained an atmosphere of atonement. They walk there with muted footsteps, they speak with quiet voices.

Today, with the disappearance of The Wall, everything seems as new as possible. The latest leftists of the century, the majority in Berlin, coexist, before confronting them, with the oldest conservatives from the neighboring regions. Memory here seems indefinitely devoted to the consideration of Evil, to an impossible yet necessary meditation on horror.

The declaration of the presence in Berlin itself of several

dozen men and women who, in the Nazi era, saved Jews, raises suspicion, if not incredulity. However, their names figure on a list which I keep with me, folded in the bottom of my pocket.

Walking along the old Wall, here and there, are brightly colored panels, in the style of a Chinese hoarding, but, for illuminated graffiti, I began to doubt it myself. This wall takes me back unceasingly to another wall. This other one was raised in general indifference. One scarcely accepts it except to put a face on death. It is the wall round the Warsaw Ghetto.

In effect, for the Jew from Warsaw that I am to go in pursuit of "good Germans," here in Berlin, is a gamble, an enterprise full of traps which make constant claims upon me. In a large cafe in the town, filled with men and women of a certain age, a German journalist born after the war put me on the defensive, not unpleasantly, by asking me to distinguish between the customers those who have participated, more or less, in the massacre of the Jews. I scrutinized them carefully, I had to admit to being puzzled: in fact suspects, every one! How difficult it is to read Good and Evil from faces!

Now there exist few countries where the cultural integration of Jews was as perfect, as complete, as in Germany. The Jewish community, before Hitler, was strong there, 500,000 people, of whom a third lived in Berlin. Their presence in letters and science was legend. The German language was the language in which Freud, Einstein, Kafka, Schnitzler, Kraus, Werfel, Schönberg, Mahler wrote and thought . . . In Germany, today, there remain less than 30,000 Jews, mostly recently arrived from Russia.

The pushing aside of German Jews by the Nazi power, their banishment, first cultural then physical, surprised them, bowled them over. The abandonment of humanity in the country of humanism, its violent negation: the shock is so brutal, the deception so intense, that a remarkable series of suicides took place very quickly.

Kurt Tucholsky, critic, dramatist, suicide.

Ernst Toller, poet, suicide.

Ludwig Fulda, dramatist, suicide.

The following also committed suicide, the philosopher Walter Benjamin, the novelist Ernst Weiss, the dramatist Walter Haserchever, the composer Gustave Brecher, the novelist Stefan Zweig . . .

I bring my thoughts back to this Berlin square, rather than elsewhere, to a wall on which a commemorative plaque indicates who, in days gone by, led the people in this place.

*This was the oldest Jewish Cemetery in Berlin (1672–1943), destroyed in 1943 on orders from the Gestapo.*

As in Poland, it was not enough for the Nazis to exterminate the Jews; they needed more: to attempt to annihilate all traces of their passage on earth. To kill a cemetery. To assassinate the memory.

Despite the information I have already received, I find it hard to imagine that here, at the very center of Hitlerian power, some Jews have nevertheless been able to hide themselves, to find aid and refuge, and some of them survived. How was Good, then, able to manifest itself in the middle of a population submitted to intense propaganda, with incessant surveillance, and frantic badgering to denounce?

# 13
## The Pastor's daughter

Some way along the autobahn linking Stuttgart to Munich, a signboard indicates Nuremberg to the left, and Dachau to the right. My traveling companion, a young German, makes conversation. I don't listen to him. I am overcome. Arriving at Stuttgart, where I am to visit the first of my Just in Germany, Kaethe Schwartz, I tell her how I feel.

During the war, Kaethe Schwartz helped a Jewish woman and her daughter, Inge Deutschkron, who is a writer today and lives in Berlin. I was astonished to see this German woman, who welcomes me, share the same indignant reaction at the word *Dachau*. Is it not here that, on the 22nd of March 1933, the camp that bears this name started its existence? My questions on the reasons which led her to save Jews, on the other hand, seem to embarrass her.

"I think I reacted spontaneously, because I am like that," she said. "I would not have been able not to help Inge Deutschkron. Such terrible injustice prevailed: the Jews scurried along the walls with their yellow star on their chest, they were made to do the most degrading work . . . All that revolted me. I have never made the Nazi salute nor shouted 'Heil Hitler.' Neither did my husband. The brutality and the cowardly politicians always horrified me. Add to that, I detested Hitler. Everything he said was repugnant to me. You know, I have a very sharp keen ear: I couldn't stand the sound of his voice."

Thin, almost aesthetic, lined face, pale hazy blue eyes, but with a precise manner, Kaethe Schwartz received me in the minuscule garden of a smart little two-storied house. On the first floor the rooms seemed more elegant, but she preferred the ground floor opening out onto a terrace and some trees of which she is very proud. She sits down cautiously. I noticed that she had a slight squint.

"I am a pastor's daughter," she said with her voice clear, yet worn as if by time.

There came to my mind some sentences from a letter that Konrad Adenauer, the first Chancellor of the Federal Republic of Germany, sent at the end of 1946 to Bernard Custodis, the Pastor at Bonn who was deposed by the Nazis.

"I believe that if the bishops had taken official positions against Nazism, all together, on the same day, from their thrones, they would have been able to avoid things. They did not do it and they have no excuse. If that had meant the bishops going to prison, or to the concentration camps, we would not have regretted it, on the contrary. It didn't happen that way, so it is better to keep silent."

Silent? Kaethe Schwartz did not wish to keep it so. She believes that one must speak, to denounce injustice, and today louder than ever. On the other hand she minimizes her role in the saving of Jews: "Isn't that normal?"

The simplicity of this woman touched me. Her compassion for her neighbor made me marvel, but one thing about her caught me by surprise once more: her modesty, her deep humility. I ask myself if this is not the quality which transforms saviors into the Just.

I have often noticed that heroes love to tell of their feats of arms. All around them. In films. In books. Now, to my knowledge, there is not one story written by a Just person. *"Look for justice—and aspire to humility,"* said the prophet Sophonie.

A clarifying commentary on this subject is that of the German Jewish philosopher Hermann Cohen: *"All human heroism is vanity, all knowledge remains unfounded if it is not submitted to the ultimate test of humility."*

However, the adventures of Kaethe Schwartz, who helped Jews to survive in the city of Berlin during the Nazi period, would be able to fill a large book.

Inge Deutschkron, who owes her her life, tells: "At the end of the war, there remained in Berlin between 8,000 and 10,000 Jews. Most of them were children of mixed marriages; some of them had come back from the camps. One can estimate between 1,500 and 2,000, the number of people who were able, like me, to survive clandestinely . . ."

Inge Deutschkron is lively, serious yet smiling. Under a cap of brown hair cut like a boy's, her mobile and expressive face never ceases to captivate attention: her look tells more than her lips. The high windows of the apartment open onto leaves that I don't recognize; the evidence given by Inge Deutschkron is, for me, original and impressive. She took part in these escapes, in these *'savings,'* which took place, without her ever being caught by the Nazis, in Berlin during the twelve terrifying years that they ruled. She is very moved when she thinks of Kaethe Schwartz or Klara Munzer, two of her benefactors at that time.

I want to know more: "To survive, you say . . . But how could a Jew even *live* in the capital of The Reich? Hidden all the time in a cellar?"

"No. We lived, as I told you, in a kind of clandestine way. We did not wear the yellow star, we went about town dressed normally: we were, in the words of the times, the 'submariners.' Most of the time we didn't even have false papers; in a big town it is easier to melt into the crowd. Some days, we didn't know where we were going to be able to sleep that night. But there was always someone to help. In total, twenty Berlin families helped us, my mother and me. We often had to move from place to place. I don't know if Berliners are particularly curious, but neighbors of those people to whom we were going always finished up by asking questions, piles of questions: 'Are there many of you at home? . . . Your family, friends? . . .' etc. It was best not to offer food for suspicion, to move on, and stay with other friends for a while. We didn't have a fixed address, we had twenty . . ."

"And among these families, was Kaethe Schwartz . . ."

"Yes," went on Inge Deutschkron, "At that time, I was a salesgirl at a newsstand owned by one of our friends. I said *'Heil Hitler'* like everyone else, and no one suspected that I was a clandestine Jew until the big day when I was . . . As for other things, to survive, we also needed ration cards, for food . . ."

It was necessary then, once again, for networks of friendship, active complicity, for sure. It is at this point, between other good information, that Kaethe Schwartz intervened.

"The bookshop where Inge worked in some ways became her refuge. On one of my visits, she closed and locked the shop door and asked me to stay. Then she confided in me. Before asking me for help, she admitted that she had to change her refuge and that she knew that I was already hiding a young Jewish girl in my home. I didn't hesitate for an instant. I obtained some food for her and a few small things she needed. She often stayed with me."

"Kaethe Schwartz," added Inge, "gave us ration cards and introduced me to the Jewish girl she was hiding. This is how Kaethe entered our lives."

To listen to these two women, the one who had saved as well as the one who was saved, warmed the cockles of the heart, brought to life a breath of confidence that contrasted vividly with the noxious atmosphere in Germany up till then—which equally contrasts with certain no less disquieting contemporary situations. I remember that smoky Berlin bar where I went the evening before my visit to my two interviewees. Going through the turnstile of the revolving door, there were only shaved heads, or practically only: I had just entered a den of skinheads.

I asked them what they thought of the liquidation of millions of Jews by the Nazis. An appalling and impossible discussion followed:

"Liquidation of Jews by the Nazis? That's propaganda, a con!"

"Whose propaganda?"

"Jews themselves, of course!"

"You don't believe, then, that millions of Jews were massacred by the Nazis?"

In guise of reply, laughter.

"What do you think of Germans who helped the Jews during the war?"

"Helped . . . Jews?"

"Yes. Who hid and saved Jews, here, in Berlin and in other towns in Germany."

"That's their business . . ."

"And what do you think of those who kill Turks and other strangers in this country today?"

"But . . . that's nothing to worry about!"

Huge bursts of laughter.

I come back to Kaethe Schwartz.

"The Germans disappointed me. Profoundly disappointed. I had ration cards for one person, and I had to feed five. And none of my neighbors wanted to help me, not one. I would have . . . I would have to lie, yes, lie! That so few among us were able to help the Jews does not really surprise me. Egoism, fear . . . You know. But, all the same, the Germans disappointed me."

"How was it able to start?"

"Perhaps . . . Here or there . . . You know, *the people were not nice.*"

Some, in Germany, like Martin Walzer, don't want us to call the young racists *neo-Nazis,* for fear that they will take the word for their own purposes. "The skinheads are lacking any positive ideology," they say. Perhaps they are not wrong to refuse to apply the word *Nazi* to the skinheads. Perhaps these latter only dress in the insignia and copy the behavior of a hated era, to provoke, to show their refusal to accept these values of a society from which they feel rejected: they want them to be irretrievable.

But in the twenties, did not the youth which, in comparison, became Hitlerian have the same motivations, if not the same models?

In any case, here we are, forewarned.

For my part, I share the somber but lucid idea of Richard von Weizsacker, the President of The German Republic. According to him, *"the Weimar Republic foundered not because there were too many Nazis, but because there were too few democrats."* Too few people refused to hate. Too few—but they were there, and, by their actions, they proved that they could resist persecution by aiding, protecting, and saving lives.

Oh, gracious me, it was not easy! As to attacking the regime or its chief, we have seen that it is practically illusory to even think of it: Admiral Canaris and his friends Bonhoeffer and Hans von Dohnanyi, who plotted against Hitler in the autumn of 1942 and sent forty Jews to Switzerland, under protection of the Abwehr, were arrested and executed.

People like Kaethe Schwartz, were they conscious of the danger they were in? Yes, certainly, and the significance of their actions did not escape them.

"Without doubt I dare say I had courage," she murmured, then in a very low voice: "It was possible, since I was not bothered nor arrested. Luck! But I had to foil Hitler . . . to hinder him, so little as I could, to reduce his power to kill, always to kill . . ."

# 14

# The baker's wife

One could do Good, then, even in Hitler's Germany. One could carry out the simple gesture of giving some bread. As did Klara Munzer, who also came to the aid of Inge Deutschkron as well as other Jews that she and her husband received into their bakery, who together hid them in their home.

Slight, white curly hair with rebellious locks, Klara Munzer receives me sitting in an armchair next to a large bookcase. The presence of books in houses of the Just that I have met cannot only be by chance: it is perhaps indicative of the natural disposition of these Good people that this reinforces, educated—cultivated, even. This old lady who is in front of me, who speaks with her hands folded, whose little white blouse collar lies on a dark blue waistcoat, uses simple words. It is of experience she speaks, and this experience comes from a base of generosity itself, the most spontaneous, the least "taught." The deep furrows which time had printed on her face could not wipe out the expressions.

Gradually, as she spoke, I read in her voice a determination without emphasis, a sound of kindness which she was able to hide, to not be afraid: everything was dangerous, true, but from her point of view, *obvious*.

And then Klara Munzer laughed. She laughed like a child who has played a good trick on anti-Semites, when she explained how she had transformed Inge Deutschkron into a "veritable Aryan": "I said to her: 'Inge, I am going to turn you into a veritable Aryan! I am going to tell the police that I have a friend in distress because she has lost her papers. I will guarantee, me, a real German, that this friend and her family are called Richter, that they were the family Richter . . .'And it worked: I obtained identity papers for them. They became the Richters: a banal name, German, Aryan. And they were able thereafter to stay without danger in a hotel. The owner of the hotel, when they checked in, said to them: 'I can see that you are not Jews!'"

At this punch line in her story, Klara Munzer burst out laughing. Recovering her seriousness, she explained: "In our bakery, which was in Charlottenburg, in an area where many Jews lived, I had a ringside seat to see what was happening. They came to arrest them, and I saw that some managed to save themselves. They hid. Sometimes they came to my place, wearing a swastika or a mourning hat so that no one recognized them! They came because they knew my opinions. I took them in. I gave them food: some bread, cakes, flour."

"And the danger?"

"Sure, it was very risky. One has less fear when one is young. Today, at eighty-two, I am not so alert! But . . . you understand, it was . . . how can I say? It was love of thy neighbor. I can't stand to see someone suffering. And then I had a Catholic education; I still hear my mother saying: 'The slightest thing which you do to my brothers, you do to me; you give it to me.'"

"Did you have Nazi surveillance on your baker's shop?"

"No. But I was denounced once, accused of having sold some flour to a Jew. This was forbidden. The police were thorough. I told them that I had sold this flour to someone who had presented a ration card, and therefore how was I supposed to guess that he was a Jew. The case was dropped . . ."

I then posed a general question, which, to my mind, asked a judgment from her on the collective attitude of Germans to Jews. As we shall see, her response skips the collective dimension of my question: Klara Munzer takes it personally as being the sole responsibility that matters. And she then puts herself through a personal retrospective critique, like Irena Sendler did in Poland. Half a century later, that which most upsets these Just people, is the feeling of not having helped enough, is the pain of not knowing how to do better . . .

"Fifty years later, how do you view all that? Do you think it would have been possible to do more to help the Jews?"

"I should have given much more. Inge, for example: I didn't know that she experienced so many difficulties in feeding herself. She was very discreet, too much so. She said nothing, and I did not even imagine how serious it was at that point. When one eats one's fill, you understand, one doesn't think enough about it. I ought to have given her more, more flour, more cakes . . ."

"But at that time or, more so, before the war, the Jews were Germans like any others, weren't they?"

"Yes, and perfectly integrated: workers, intellectuals, and then suddenly, from one day to the next, rejected, general persecution! What shame for us! What tragedy for them! . . ."

Can we compare a Klara Munzer to our humanitarian activists? Would she leave to care for the wounded at Sarajevo with Medecins du Monde, or carry sacks of rice to the hungry Somalians in the trucks run by Equilibre?

"I cannot stand seeing anyone suffer," she confides to me.

If she was thirty today, Klara Munzer would, it appears to me, participate in convoys for Rwanda or Gaza.

It is not the degree of danger that a man must face which makes him a Just person, but the urgency of the demand pressed on him and the immediate instinctive and objective reply that he gives.

The spokesmen of our great humanitarian acts, those who speak of them, who write about them, could they be part of the Just?

To the kings and to the churches, the opposition spokespeople of the civil society, in the Bible, were the Prophets. They it was who questioned the powers, who criticized them and made them subjects for discussion. Also, they were the people who have always reminded the population of their choices: *"I put before you life and death, blessing and curse. You will choose life . . . "* But the Prophet—in Hebrew the *navi*, that is to say "the man who speaks"—is not one of the Just. To save the world, thirty-six Prophets are not enough. They are there to proclaim the essential: *"You will choose life."* The Prophets are there to proclaim Justice. The Just are there to practice it.

Besides, the Prophet defends Justice without referring to the example of the Just. But no one would have known about the Just without Prophets to talk about them and denounce Evil. This Evil that the Bible does not try to hide: Was Adam not spineless? Cain irresponsible? Noah weak? Did Abraham not allow his wife to be raped because he was a coward? Did Jacob not partake of a fraudulent act against his brother Esau? Was Joseph not an ambitious schemer? And the greatest of all, David himself, whose line is supposed to bring the Jewish Messiah like that of the Christians, did he not commit unpardonable acts?

*"All human beings have merits and vices,"* said Maimonides. *"He in which the merits surpass the vices is a Just Man. He in which the vices exceed the merits is a Wicked Man."*

But how does one become a Just Man?

Education?

Klara Munzer repeats: "My mother said to me: 'The slightest thing which you do to my brothers, you do to me; you give it to me.'"

And yet others like Klara Munzer, having received the same education, find themselves on the side of Evil.

I am aware that the road towards knowing the Good will be long, and that it is still keeping a few surprises for me.

Nevertheless, I leave Klara Munzer with one certitude: that whatever terror is brought down on the world, there will always be some Just Men to attempt to bring the remedy, to try to lessen the devastating effects, and take us through.

# 15
## Protestant Germany

I do not remember who recommended that I go and see Cornelia Schroeder.

But the fact that she is a Protestant and that she lives in the area of Grunenwald, which is so often mentioned in classical German literature, encouraged me to meet her. As opposed to the French Protestants, who have long been persecuted themselves, always having a fellow-feeling for their brother Jews, German Protestants, at least the majority, and because of a traditional strong nationalism, were very receptive, at first, to the policies developed by national socialism. Although the Catholic Church signed an agreement with Hitler (the *Reichskonkordat*), the Protestant Church became the official Church of the Reich, the *Reichskirche*. It is true that certain theses written by Martin Luther himself, author of a treatise titled *Jews and Their Lies*, already foreshadow some elements of Nazi ideology: the Church at the service of the State, anti-Semitism, nationalism, Germanness. All that, according to Luther, to reflect "the order of Creation as wanted by God."

From 1933 Hitler organized the Movement of German Christians, to which also belonged one-fifth of all Protestant pastors. I remember, on my first journey to Germany, having met Pastor Martin Niemoller, who during the Nazi era, had, himself, organized the emergency Association of Pastors wishing to oppose an ideology contrary to the faith that proclaimed *love thy neighbor*. Martin Niemoller and some of his friends were flung into a concentration camp in 1937. He is the sole survivor.

Why was he opposed to the Nazis? At this question, the pastor answered me with a smile: "I keep asking myself why I was taken so late. When the Nazis persecuted the Jews, I didn't react as I was not Jewish. When the Nazis arrested the communists, I kept quiet as I wasn't a communist. When they silenced the socialists, I said nothing as I wasn't a socialist. When they sought out the Catholics, I did not protest because I was not Catholic. When they came for me, there was no one else to protest . . ."

Cornelia Schroeder is a small neat woman with short white hair, a look sparkling with mischief, who lives in a house surrounded by trees. She is very much more proud of her late husband's musical compositions than of her own actions in saving Jews. At first, she cannot understand why I have come to interview her on this latter subject.

"Yes, it was in 1944," she said to me as if to brush off my question.

"One day, I received a call from an old school friend asking if I could take in a man who was married to a Jewess. He had need of work; he offered to do odd jobs, do housework—it didn't matter what inside work, in exchange for a room and board. There you are, that's how my husband and I met this couple. Soon afterwards, his Jewish wife and he could not go home because of the persecution. Then, we decided to welcome them to stay with us. It was very risky since we were on file as political suspects. In spite of that, we gave them shelter. They only had false papers and were without ration cards, but we managed . . . They lived with us until the end of the war. There, nothing exceptional in all that!"

"Why did you do it?"

"Because we had to help them!"

I admire this reply, the simplicity of the understatement, its definitive *because,* . . . end of conversation. Good does not explain itself, does not justify itself. It acts, it offers itself, it gives of itself.

Cornelia does not want to talk about the others, those who did nothing, or those who have killed. She and her husband have not saved two lives to be thanked nor because of what others may think. I had to negotiate with her for more than two hours to allow me to tell her story—and then only in this book, not in my film!

It is by Cornelia Schroeder that I am soon put on the track of an escapee, Baron Loewenstein de Witt, whom I had never heard of till now.

To the Nazis, the Baron was a *Mischling,* a "half-blood," a particular and embarrassing type: he was a child of mixed marriage, half-Aryan/half-Jew. The Hitlerian bureaucrats gave up days, weeks, months, years even! in discussing and sending from Ministry to Ministry, the question of the *Mischling.* A quasi-insoluble question in their racist problem: a Jew, you kill; an Aryan, you protect—but a "Judo-Aryan" child, what do you do with it?

At first, they decide to sterilize the *Mischling,* to put an end to the penetration of "impure" blood into Aryan blood. Then they envisaged forced divorce. But what was to be done with a *Mischling* child which an Aryan father wanted to keep? At last on the 20th of January 1942, in the spirit of the first *Final Solution,* a decision was made: deportation of the children. However, less than two months later, in March 1942, the second conference on the *Solution* finally put everything back in question.

One year later, in March 1943, the Gestapo became impatient: they rounded up a handful of these Jews who were benefiting under the category of *Mischling* and shut them in a Jewish old people's home in Berlin. Among them was Baron Loewenstein de Witt.

Inge Deutschkron gave me his address, and I am leaving to look for him. His situation like his career was not ordinary, and both of them have witnessed, with war at its height, a retreat by the Nazis in the face of public opinion. The case merits further investigation.

# 16

# The *Mischling*

When I meet him at his house, on the top floor of a modest apartment block, Baron Loewenstein de Witt moves aside to show me in. The apartment has nothing princely about it. There are many photographs on his lounge and office walls; diverse curios and elegant fine china pieces bear witness to an aristocratic patrimony in decline, if not already lost. Ancient splendor of a long line, reduced to the level of souvenirs: it seems very far away from the sumptuous luxury with which his seventeenth-century ancestor, Johann de Witt, surrounded himself, throned in wig, gown, and magnificent doublet and hose as he is portrayed in an engraving done at that time . . .

The man of the moment, the present Baron Loewenstein de Witt, answers my questions directly. He talks a lot, all the time manifesting a penchant for accuracy. His graying hair, his high bald forehead, and his glasses with certain quick funny expressions on his face: he sometimes reminds me of Woody Allen, but more serious. It is with a grave but impassioned tone that he tells me of his existence as a *Mischling* all those years ago:

"How was I able to *hold on* in the middle of Berlin? Not easily. Survival was not easy, nothing was easy when you consider the number of things that were forbidden to Jews. It was insane. Hundreds of prohibitions, for everything: we couldn't have flowers, records, cameras, a telephone . . . No right to own a car, gold, money, pictures, valuable furniture; no typewriter, no gas heaters or stoves, no oven. It was

# OPEN COURT PUBLISHING COMPANY, CHICAGO IL 60604

☐ Please send me a **FREE** Open Court catalog.

Thank you for your interest in this book. We would like to know what our readers think.
Please take a moment to complete and return this card.

Book Purchased: Title/Author _____

Purchased at _____

Did you receive this book as a gift? ☐ Yes ☐ No    Did you buy this book as a gift? ☐ Yes ☐ No

Comments

*I am interested in the following subject areas:*

☐ Biography
☐ History/Philosophy of Science
☐ Eastern Thought
☐ Social Issues
☐ Sociology
☐ Other _____

☐ Philosophy
☐ History
☐ Spirituality
☐ Occult
☐ Music

☐ Psychology
☐ Classic Texts of Western Thought
☐ Pop Culture
☐ Cosmology
☐ Lifestyle

My Name _____
My Job Title _____
Address _____
City _____ State _____ Zip _____
Telephone _____ Fax Number _____

This is my ☐ Home Address ☐ Business Address

forbidden to have an animal—no cat, no dog, parrot, or goldfish. It was equally forbidden to use lifts, or to go out on balconies overlooking the street. Outside, whole streets were forbidden to us, also public transport—except if the forced labor to which you were assigned was more than four miles from your house: then, a special pass would be given to you, but only for this exact journey and only by Metro. Buses were absolutely forbidden. In the Metro you were forbidden to sit down. Forbidden also to go to the hairdresser. And a thousand other daily victimizations! I could go on . . . To come back to the roundup in 1943, all the Jews in the capital of the Reich were brutally deported to the east, to Auschwitz. Those who had a Christian parent—as I had, my mother—were shut up in that old-age home in Berlin."

On that date, Goebbels noted in his private diary: "Unfortunately, some very annoying scenes took place outside a Jewish old-age home, around which a huge crowd gathered, which to a certain extent, was taking sides with the Jews."

Baron de Witt elaborated: "Then an extraordinary event occurred: Christian families, some of them even wearing Nazi insignia, gathered in front of the building to protest against our internment. This gathering turned itself into a demonstration which lasted several days. The Gestapo did not intervene. At the end of a week, Goebbels gave the order to free us. The end result was that we stayed in Berlin as members of that bizarre and almost untouchable sect of *Mischlings*—'half-Jews.' Of course, we had to follow to the letter each of the innumerable orders and edicts issued by the Nazis. I don't know which one we missed, but we ended up having to go into hiding. It wasn't pleasant. In a town of 4 million inhabitants like Berlin, there were perhaps, in total, a few hundred people to help us—but it is thanks to them that we did survive.

"Thus, public opinion, even in Germany, even in Berlin, could extract concessions from the Nazis! It was possible, as a *'submariner'* or as a *Mischling*, to pass through the narrow mesh of the net of informers and police. There had to be the indispensable support of a minority, but this minority existed, and was active. Goebbels, again from his private diary, paid them a backhanded compliment in complaining of the 'myopia' of certain Germans who sometimes warned the Jews, 'to such an extent that 4,000 of them have now escaped us' . . . And Goebbels continued to grumble: 'They are now in Berlin without shelter or warmth and naturally constitute a grave public danger.' He quickly reassured himself in the usual way by: 'I have ordered the police, the Wehrmacht, and the Party to do the utmost to lay their hands on them.'"

It is comforting, even fifty years later, to know that this evil man never achieved his ends. Some Just Men can sometimes loosen the vice of the repressive arsenal of the worst tyrants. Better still: Inge Deutschkron, when I met her after my visit to the Baron de Witt, revealed the existence of a 'network of the blind' who, during the war, knew how to deceive the Gestapo.

Several people have spoken to me about Otto Wayett, a blind man who saved blind Jews thanks to a protection he received from the Wehrmacht. He ran a company that made sweeping brushes. I made an arrangement to meet him way back, but he died shortly before I arrived in Berlin . . . Time wipes out everything, even the memory of a Just Man.

One day, Otto Wayett was raided by the Gestapo while his men were at work. According to witnesses, he negotiated for a long time for their release. "I must deliver my sweeping brushes to the Wehrmacht and I can't do it if you take away all my workers," he argued. And he won his case! The Gestapo gave him back his blind people and this is how you could see them, thereafter, ambling across the Grossehamburger-strasse—where the Gestapo headquarters were—a procession of blind men, yellow star on their chests, holding the ends of their white canes, like one of Brueghel's paintings, crossing the town unscathed and free, guided by their employer and savior, who was also blind . . .

# 17

# Berlin—a furniture shop

Berlin. This time it isn't snowing, it's raining. I go out of my hotel in East Berlin. Berlin is reunified, but for the Berliners' separation lives on. For me too. The rhythms of life have stayed different, like the architectural styles in the town: modern buildings in the West, avenues of facades studded with tiles "like giant bathrooms"—in the grand style loved by Stalin—in the East. Sometimes I see monuments from before the Nazi era, houses from the thirties. Reminders of a sad past, traces of bullet holes on the buildings are still there. Two steps from the Brandenburg Gate, you are in Potsdamerplatz, surrounded by the Philharmonia, the National Gallery, and the National Library. Only yesterday, this old cultural center of the town was divided across the middle by the East/West axis, and to establish this divide the DDR named their half *Leipzigerplatz*. Today Potsdamerplatz has again become the center of Berlin.

Berlin, according to Madam de Staël, is "the city at the center of Europe which can be considered the home of its leading lights." Scarcely fifty years ago, it was the home of darkness. These dark shadows which I am crossing today in search of the light. Erika Bungener lives five minutes' walking distance from Potsdamerplatz. I see her as the flickering flame of a candle. A candle in daylight lights very little. On the other hand, at night it can illuminate a vast space.

Erika Bungener is a woman with brown frizzy hair piled on

top of her head: a young woman, and her seventy-four years don't change that. She appears so much younger! The gold necklace, the white collar on the garnet-colored jacket, the natural look which is really her own, everything about her gives off a feeling of well-preserved vitality. In fact, she does not give the impression of bowing to the pressure of age at all. I divine in this person an energy as understated as it is unstoppable.

Erika Bungener was twenty-five when she was married in 1941. Her two sons were born at the height of the war, in 1941 and 1943. She and her husband owned a big furniture shop. Widowed since then, she calmly reminisces about those wartime years. Her face radiates an impression of equilibrium with strength. Large forehead, direct approach, in listening to and answering my questions, she gives me the image of one who pays *attention to others*. Yes, I sense that it must have been good, and comforting, for the oppressed, to come across a person cast in this mold.

In January 1943 she and her husband went to collect and give shelter to two Jewish families, the Mandels and the Kantoroviches, whom the Gestapo were looking for. Their furniture warehouse was a perfect hiding place, until it was bombed, on the 1st of May 1945. But the Bungeners, like the Jews they protected, came out safe and sound. During more than two years, Erika Bungener and her husband looked after all their needs, including their food: they had the benefit of supplementary ration cards because of their two underage children, and Erika's sister, sent by their parents, could also bring them a few country products in the guise of presents.

Implacable opponents of Hitler, the Bungeners did not hesitate to save hunted Jews, knowing full well that they were taking mortal risks for themselves and their two babies. Much later, Erika Bungener went to visit Israel. She also kept contact with the Mandel family, who, shortly after the war, went to Brazil, to São Paulo. To her eyes also, most of the Germans of the time carried on like cowards, "paralyzed by fear." As for herself, to have saved four human lives appears to her to be what she should have done: "How could my husband and me have done otherwise?"

"But, tell me," I say to her, "Why did you do it? Why take so many risks for these Jews? For antifascism?"

"Yes, it's true: we were antifascists—convinced antifascists!"

A flash of light appears to shine out of Erika Bungener's eyes, an ironic look, a half-smile, as if making excuses for the intensity of her convictions . . . It is very clear that she is still antifascist, and with the same vigilance, the same clarity of thought, the same resolution as fifty years ago.

This unfailing determination I am going to find in another of these Good people, Edith Berlow, a much older lady.

Slim, fair, wearing a black waistcoat over a white blouse, Edith Berlow, with large wild looks, appeared outraged each time we mentioned Hitler. She carried, towards Hitlerism, a solid hatred, persistent and inalterable. If it were not for the quiet decor of the apartment and its obvious air of tranquillity, one would have believed, from the ever-changing expressions on her face, that she was a warrior getting ready for battle. At eighty-two years old, Edith Berlow is very young at heart. Her passion animates her. And her lucidity.

Married in 1929 to a German, she is living, around 1936, with another man in her house. He is a Jew, a militant social democrat, named Hirschfeld but living under a borrowed name in Berlin, thanks to the passport of a communist friend. This latter had declared his identity card 'lost,' and this is how Edith Berlow lived with a Mr. Hirschfeld whom everyone called "Doctor Gunslav" . . . The neighbors of the villa never suspected for an instant that "Doctor Gunslav" was in fact a *Jewish submariner* who, to cap it all, each day organized antifascist demonstrations as he was the leader of a resistance group.

When I teased her by asking why she had lived with a Jew in this, ever-so-dangerous era, she answered me, eyes wide open with astonishment, half-angry, half-amused: "But . . . I loved him!"

I concede that actually it sounds quite a good reason! . . . At that time, also, her ex-husband, who continued to hold her in great esteem, was as willing to help with Edith's needs for food as much as her new companion. Very quickly, Edith Berlow's apartment became an even more dangerous place, as, on the initiative of "Doctor Gunslav," political meetings were held there.

"I don't know how it came about," she says, "but there were only Jews in the house . . ."

Not one of these Jews was caught by the Gestapo. After the war, married to "Doctor Gunslav," openly practicing surgery as Mr. Hirschfeld, she emigrated to the United States because of the anti-Semitic atmosphere which once again prevailed within the Berlin medical profession where her new husband worked. She only came back to Germany in 1974 after he died. She does not feel at ease there, and her judgments on her fellow-citizens remain unrelenting: "In that era, almost all of them were nothing but chicken-livered so and so's!—cowards who adored Hitler or pretended to do so . . . I couldn't stand it, neither to see nor to hear it!"

Edith Berlow neither compromised nor hesitated. To help him was to state the obvious, for love of her "Doctor G." and because nothing could appear more natural to her. Her convictions and her heart beat to the one tune. In her own words she has acted almost *in all innocence*.

She regards the years 1945–1974, lived with her Jewish husband in the United States, as the happiest of her life. As for her sentiments towards her fellow-countrymen, I find it on many occasions with rescuers, especially the Dutch: the post-war period is difficult for those who, having saved Jews from the middle of indifferent, hostile, fellow-citizens, represent for these latter a sort of living reproach, although silent, to their own cowardice. On their side, the saviors have to live the hurt again, as if nothing had happened, in the middle of a community that they have seen little inclined to justice or even simple care about human dignity. In the Netherlands I will find several of these saviors who stayed in their country, but I will learn that most of them preferred to emigrate far away, as far as Australia in some cases, forming in a strange way a "Diaspora of the Just" . . .

However, I have not yet finished with my German quest for these beings without whom one could legitimately doubt the presence of Good in this black period which Hitlerism inflicted on the human race.

In fact, I know that I will never be finished with it in Germany. I will never finish with Nazism! I cannot forget that the first victory was electoral: with the citizens voting for the swastika.

Neither will I finish with these Just people, who, Germans themselves, were able to show, at the peak of Nazi insanity, a little *humanity*.

Others, after me, will pursue the research. Since I have started this enquiry, I have had pointed out to me, here and there, some other Just people, men and women, too few, it is true—who are known, here, in the center where the cyclone overtook this country, to have resisted the murdering folly of Hitler. How to visit them, how to question them all? Time, by definition, is always short; it is this element that people can sometimes vanquish by erecting the only monument that will last: Memory.

Memory of the Just. Memory of the Good.

# 18

# Karpathian Oil

Oh yes, there were some Germans like me, for whom the 8th of May 1945, the day the Third Reich capitulated, was the best day in their life," the past Chancellor Willy Brandt told me.

When he received the news, he was still in Norway where, wearing that country's uniform, he had fought the Nazis as a soldier—such an unusual position for a German and yet he still dared to reproach himself . . .

That was also the happiest day in my life. But Willy Brandt also gave me some advice: "You must try to meet some of the men who were in the Nazi organization, who, from the inside, tried to save lives."

Could I leave Germany without trying to profit by this suggestion?

This is how I came to make an appointment with Berthold Beitz, the present vice-president of the Krupp establishment.

The little castle, which is the head office of the Krupp organization, on the outskirts of Essen, surmounts the top of a well-maintained hill of grass and looks like a very pleasant and vast house. Berthold Beitz receives me with courtesy and without the least ostentation. It is a very strong eighty-year-old, with a good-looking calm face, who answers my questions. A blue suit of impeccable cut, a haughty manner, the distinguished air of his person did not hinder him one little bit from being affable and spontaneous.

For Berthold Beitz, everything begins as it does in *The Damned* by Visconti.

At the beginning of the war, he was twenty-seven. With his university degree, specializing in energy, he worked in Hamburg at Royal Dutch Shell.

One evening, his grandfather, a high Nazi dignitary, invited him to dine in the Krupp headquarters. Among the guests, one of Hitler's aides, Heydrich, announced that after the attack on Russia on the 22nd of June 1941, the German army, which already had control of Rumanian petrol, had taken the powerful refineries at Boryslaw and at Drochobycz, which would be most useful to industry and the war effort by making the balance of strategic reserves and energy resources tilt in Germany's favor.

It was necessary to send petroleum production specialists there. Berthold Beitz raised his hand: he would go, accompanied by his young wife. Thanks to support from his influential grandfather, he was appointed director of the new company, Karpathian Oil, which would retain its head office at Boryslaw.

Berthold Beitz thought he was going there to find petrol: he discovered there . . . Jews.

Boryslaw: 40,000 inhabitants, of which 18,000 were Jews.

Drochobycz: 35,000 inhabitants, of which 17,500 were Jews.

When Beitz arrived in the area, the Jews were grouped together in work camps. He had scarcely taken over his new duties when he attended the first massive deportations: "One day, in 1942, at Boryslaw station, I saw several hundred Jews who had been waiting in the cold loaded on to the train for Belzec. Among them were many children in a lamentable state. One woman was clutching a little girl to her. The child was coughing in a disquieting way. I said to the SS officer who was guarding the group that he ought to find a doctor as quickly as possible. 'Where they are all going, they won't need a doctor!' he replied, guffawing."

The vision of whole trainloads of Jewish children going to their death overwhelmed the young director of Karpathian Oil and his wife. Shocked and upset, they decided to do something about the situation.

"I went to Gestapo headquarters. I said to them that I had urgent need of supplementary manpower, that it was of essential strategic importance to the Reich. That was how I was able to obtain authorization to employ as many Jews as it took. Armed with this exceptional power, I went every day to the station to grasp several young men from death.

"I could have selected a better-qualified workforce. Instead of that, I recruited tailors, hairdressers, students from talmudic colleges, etc., . . . to give them ID cards as petroleum technicians . . . I even employed one man as a simple clerk, his name was Erich Rosenberg, Professor of Economics!"

"How many did you employ like this?"

"Around 800 in the company. Most of them survived. After the war they all went away. To America, Israel, Australia, everywhere. I don't think anyone was left."

"Why did you do it? Wasn't it dangerous for you and your wife?"

"Yes, but . . . what would you have done in my place? You see a child, you see how, . . . in the street, in the station, everything is refused, everything except death—and in the early morning light this child looks at you with his big eyes, with enormous eyes: what do you do? I did it, that's all. With these children, with their mothers that I employed as secretaries by making them get off trains, thanks to my official pass, from trains ready to depart for the camps, for torture and extermination. I remember . . . Once, in Boryslaw station, I made a young woman come down from a wagon, to explain to the Nazis that she was one of my indispensable secretaries. 'Sir, Mr. Director,' she said to me, 'can I bring my mother with me?' I answered yes. At this moment, an SS arrived: 'What's this?'—My secretary.—'And the other one?'—She works for me.—'No, No! Impossible,' said the SS. 'She is too old . . . Up you go, on your way!' There was nothing I could do. Already the old lady was back with the crowd in the wagon. The secretary, aghast, begged me: 'Sir, Mr. Director, I don't want to leave my mother. Can I go back on the train?' That was a poignant situation. Mother and daughter went to their death. That day there, because of an over zealous SS, I had slipped up. I watched that train move away in the distance with rage in my heart, crying . . . But that's me: I have an innate need to help people. And I would do it again today with the same passion. If I see a child, or even an adult, mistreated in the street, I still feel this need to help them. It is a question of humanity. At home my wife hid a little Jewish boy, whom she raised, during all those years, along with our own daughter. In Israel, where we went much later, he found us, Leenhardt, now a police officer; we fell in each other's arms with such happiness. And we cried real tears of joy."

At this moment, I can see that Berthold Beitz is trembling with emotion, his voice falters, and his eyes moisten. He quickly recovers his dignity, his sense of bearing, and he smoothes his hand over his silvery hair before inviting me to ask another question.

"Did the Nazis try to arrest 'your' Jews, in town, just to annoy them?"

"No. My Jewish employees had a special armband and an identity card, a pass signed by me, which guaranteed their free movement. I organized the ghetto so that the police couldn't go there. The Jews could not be arrested."

I don't know what evil spirit makes me think it, but, as a young man, this man would have constituted a perfect image of fashion for the Nazi propaganda, if only dressed in an officer's uniform. Facing him, I put away this provocative thought. I do, however, ask the question: "Mr. Beitz, at the time, and in carrying out your work, did you ever wear uniform?"

He is absolutely astonished: "No. Why would I wear uniform? What uniform? I didn't belong to the Party, nor the SS, nor the SA. I did not belong to any party nor the armed forces. No, I remember that I traveled the streets in a horse-drawn carriage. I was a civilian, in a suit, a coat, and a hat, which, of all things, came from London!"

Elegance, again . . . I look at him. He is speaking with his elbows supported by the arms of his chair, hands together, fingers entwined. Sometimes he lifts them to the height of his eyes as if better to search among his memories. Sometimes he underlines a sentence by raising one of his hands, which then goes to rejoin the other one in a natural gesture which renews his train of thought. He emanates an air of nobility, of serenity: this man of taste never wore a uniform! All his personality goes against any sign of barbarity. However, did he not come from the very innermost part of the system? We are going to see that despite the strong and paradoxical position he adopted, he did, however, cross the boundaries of behavior acceptable to certain people.

Berthold Beitz benefited, with his grandfather being a very powerful influence, highly placed in the Nazi hierarchy, it is true, but his way of working made it difficult not to raise the suspicions of certain members of the SS. In 1943, denounced, accused by the Germans of the old guard, the "true" Germans, he is called to Breslau to explain himself in front of the Gestapo chief of the district. A dossier is open on his appearing, in which he is accused of carrying out a protection scheme for Jews. Enough, if proved, to condemn his wife and daughter to death, with him. At first, blinded by the office light, he did not recognize the Nazi officer who was interrogating him. Then the man showed himself: he was an old student friend! He had been a Divinity student then; failing his exams, he joined the SA, and rose through the ranks . . . Without pressing any further, the chief of the district smiled, tore across the file and flung the debris in the fire. The luck of Berthold Beitz . . .

"Luck?" he said. "Yes. You know, if you give the impression of not being sure of yourself, that can cost you your luck . . . But I think that if you know what you want, if you want it with all of your heart, then . . . you will make it, or someone will give you a chance!"

Give luck a chance, is this not one of the elementary gestures of every act of goodwill, of every desire for justice?

A little later, Beitz comments for me on the abominable

cliché, initiated by Hitler during a national photographic competition in 1941, that shows a German soldier in a snow-covered plain, at point-blank range, shooting a woman holding her child to her breast—and assassinating with the one shot the child with the mother.

"Is it this photo which sensitized you to the fate of the Jews?" I asked him.

"I know the photo, but until I arrived at Boryslaw I had never been at such a scene."

Berthold Beitz stayed silent for a long moment, then: "When you are present at the execution of a woman with her child in her arms and when you have a child of your own, you cannot remain indifferent."

There it is, . . . there is that disposition to immediate compassion that the worst totalitarian systems and their exterminators can never kill in man. And this compassion, one can see it in a being of the temper of Berthold Beitz, who is likely to rush at every individual if he thinks them to be one of those whom fate has placed in a master's camp, in a camp of executioners. Coming from inside the monster, this Just man has saved hundreds of Jews from what would have been their final journey.

*"Of everything which it is possible to conceive in the world,"* wrote Kant, Beitz's countryman, *"and even in general out with the world, there is nothing which can be taken as goodness, without reservation, if it is not a willing goodness."*

It is, perhaps, thanks to this *willing,* but dangerous, *goodness* in the Nazi era, both for them and their nearest and dearest, that Good people such as Berthold Beitz have proved that one can certainly do what one must—but not counter to Justice. Kant, for his part, warned: *"If Justice disappears, things without value which take its place will be what men will have on earth" (Doctrine of Rights, II, 1).*

Before I take my leave from him, Berthold Beitz confides in me: "I am now over eighty. And I am glad to be able to say that I have done something, which to tell the truth, has not had any economic effects, no . . . , but it certainly has had effects on humanity—and that, to me, is very much more important. My children, my grandchildren, and my great-grandchildren will know it. That's as it should be. From the bottom of my heart, I am proud to have helped all these Jews escape the death trains. But, truthfully, how could I have lived if I had not done it? With such an insupportable bad conscience? No, there was no other solution, no other possible choice! . . ."

# 19
# Schindler's List

The story of Berthold Beitz made me think of that other story which inspired Steven Spielberg's film, *Schindler's List*. Now, even if Oskar Schindler were still alive, I would not have included his story in this book. Because it tells of the life of someone who belongs to another category from those of the Just, to a category of *Baal Techova*—in Hebrew, the "repentants," those who came back to the right road.

Faced with his friends the executioners, Oskar Schindler at first felt admiration for them, then, much later, disgust which turned him away from them.

Faced with the same executioners, Berthold Beitz, on the contrary, is filled with revulsion.

Oskar Schindler was the hero of a classic tragedy edited and presented from the angle of a 'western.' That is probably the reason he attracted Spielberg. As in the westerns, the story starts in an innocent world which, all of a sudden, is confronted with violence and death. It always happens in a village in some vague countryside. One day the scared locals witness the arrival of a bunch of outlaws. After having cleaned out the village bank safe, stolen the farmers' cattle, and burnt their harvests, the gangsters decide to hang some of the villagers. For pleasure. Faced with this collective manifestation of the "compulsion to kill," one or more of the gangsters has pangs of conscience. One of them, who cannot accept this supreme injustice, is often the most intelligent of the band, and can draw and shoot faster than his companions. So he will succeed in saving the lives of the condemned and regain the confidence of the villagers. After having participated in the Devil's ride, this man finds himself defending the line for the Good . . .

Now a Just man, even if he is weak and oppressed, would never, even for a moment, find himself on the side of the executioner. On the contrary, when barbarity manifests itself, he himself attempts to save lives.

Oskar Schindler's career poses another problem: that of the relationship between the savior and the saved. To save somebody, must the savior love him? Must he love the persecuted person? And, is this love a prerequisite for the saving to take place?

Recapitulation: Oskar Schindler is a Nazi. At Cracow, very close to Auschwitz, he uses the free manual labor of the Jewish slaves to make himself wealthy. He knows, as well as his companions, that the Jews who are working for him are going to die. However, this does not upset him: he amasses a fortune, lives and loves well. But after a time the unforeseen happens: the man becomes used to these Jews whom he calls the *Schindlerjuden,* "Schindler's Jews." Frequently in their company, being with them every day, he even finishes by liking them. Finally, through this new feeling, the idea of their annihilation in the nearby crematorium furnaces overwhelms him, and he decides to help them, even at the risk of his own life.

If Oskar Schindler had not finished up loving these Jews, what would have happened? I tremble at the question as at the answer, which one can only too well guess. For the love of Schindler for these Jews was an exception. Did Freud not teach us that it is difficult to love thy neighbor, unless, as Dostoevsky said with his habitual cruelty, "this neighbor was faceless"?

Berthold Beitz was not twisted by such thoughts. Instinctively, he chose life. People were threatened: he helped them. He neither loved nor hated them. I have met Just people who have saved men for whom they had not the slightest sympathy. "When one dives in a river to save a man in danger," said one of these Just people to me, "one does not have time to check up on the good and bad qualities of the one who is drowning: one only tries to bring him back to the bank." The relationship the Just have with Justice is not motivated by sympathy for the person to be saved.

*It is not Justice that makes the Just, but the Just who make Justice.*

But what is this humility?

It is, in Man, the conscious knowledge of not being God. That comes before actions which risk placing man on an equal footing with God, the saving of a life for instance. Above all, if one follows the affirmation of the Talmud on this point "*. . . he who saves a life, it is as if he would save the whole of humanity . . .*"

Now, the Just, when taking action, do not think about our ultimate appreciation of their attitude. They do not act because of written reports, or theories, or out of moral rectitude. They keep to the course of *real* action: on the side of *acts which save* more than the idea of being a theoretical savior.

Berthold Beitz knows that his action was exceptional; it is therefore natural that he lays claim to it. But he knows also, with Montaigne, that ". . . however clever he would like to think he is, he is only a man—and is he not therefore the more mortal, the more miserable of men?"

There are Just people who are humble out of lack of knowledge, and others because of that very knowledge. To which category belongs Richard Abel, whom I am going to meet next in Birschtein-Allfeld, near Frankfurt?

# 20

# Tunisia

I know that the use of Yiddish, in Germany, often produces an unease that pleases me—or moves me. Thus, in the eighties, at Tübingen, in the very heart of the university that continues to venerate the memory of Kepler, Hölderlin, and Hegel, this young student approached me, at the end of a conference I had just held in Yiddish, to say to me, "I believe, by listening to you, that I have discovered in me the Jewish part of the German soul." I often think that when the world will have forgotten all about Auschwitz, there will be two races who will remember it: the Germans and the Jews. And, without doubt, it is in Yiddish that they will be able to murmur: "I remember."

In which language will they say: "I understand"?

To understand. I have always wanted to understand. And, in the case of the Just, to understand the mechanism, the motivation of the Good. This is why I have chosen to leave Germany, to find out about the deeds of Richard Abel. Although I am meeting him near Frankfurt, his story will carry our thoughts to Tunisia, the only North African country to have known "Occupation."

It was Dr. Louis Beretvas who was the first to speak to me about Richard Abel, this German who, over there, saved life half a century ago. Once more death has tried to fuzzy the memory, to cut the path, by taking Dr. Louis Beretvas. However this latter had left me a note, a lightning conductor. Thanks to this ultimate act, and with the help of Mme. Nelly Beretvas, his widow, I have been able to reconstruct the events.

In Tunisia, in 1942, the Jews were living in expectation and insecurity. Like many of them, Louis Beretvas, then twenty-two, only knew that their whole fate was in play thousands of miles away from there, at El-Alamein and Stalingrad. His personal situation was scarcely brilliant. Excluded from the University of Algiers by numerous regulations, he was tutoring in Latin and English. When the Americans disembarked in Algeria and Morocco on the 8th of November 1942, the Germans, who at that moment were retreating through Libya, decided as a consequence, in order to protect their rear, to occupy Tunisia.

With four of his friends, Louis Beretvas secretly escapes from Tunis in the hope of joining the Free French forces in Algeria. En route, the five friends stop for the night at Depienne (today Smiega), with parents of one of them, Yvan Enriquez. Alas, a neighboring Italian farmer denounces them to the Germans. A commando group arrives, led by feldwebel Richard Abel, and they are arrested. Louis Beretvas, who speaks German, understands their jailers' conversation. He and his four pals are in the soup: they are suspected, not only of being Jews, but also of being spies—they are going to be shot as quickly as possible, that is to say, at dawn.

In the absence of Louis Beretvas, I have to use the evidence of Yvan Enriquez, who remembers that strange and terrible night with great emotion: "You can image our feelings at that moment! Fear, anguish . . . when suddenly the German officer, feldwebel Richard Abel, calls Louis over. We stay there, in the tent waiting. A long, long time . . . When Louis returns, he is nervous. He confirms what we already know: in effect, the officer announces that they will come for us at dawn to shoot us . . . And then the extraordinary events begin. As Louis appeared dumb, or paralyzed by the situation, the German said to him, 'You're not going to wait quietly till someone comes to shoot you, are you?! You've only to flee from the camp, and without delay! I'll help you . . .'"

Nelly Beretvas explained that as a measure to show his good faith Richard Abel gave his revolver to Louis, as well as a plan to escape to Algeria. In exchange, Louis had given the German officer his parents' address in Tunis, scribbled in haste on a scrap of paper.

The five young men managed to escape and reached Algeria.

Later, when the Allies arrived in Tunis, a German officer presented himself at the Beretvas' home: It was Richard Abel.

He explains that he refuses to follow Hitler's armies any more, but he definitely does not wish to be taken prisoner. The only address he knows in Tunis is that of Louis Beretvas' parents. He places his fate in their hands.

Nelly Beretvas tells me the end of the story: "Louis's parents gave him civilian clothes and sheltered him by hiding him in their house. With the complicity of all the family, they helped him to leave Tunisia at the end of the war. Think of it . . . a German saved by the Jews!"

This exceptional link was to be maintained and prolonged long after the war: "Since these events took place, not a month goes by without us speaking to Richard on the telephone, and not a year goes by without us meeting him! And as Richard has never started a family; he considers our family as his own, our children as his own: he came to their weddings . . . He even came to the bar mitzvah of one of my grandchildren!"

For this adventure concerning the savior saved, I am at last going, not far from Frankfurt, to meet the key person. A side road off the impeccable German autobahn leads to Birschtein-Allfeld. The car stops in front of an inn. The entrance is through a large rustic hallway, and there, sitting near the fire, waits a white-haired man: Richard Abel. He starts without beating about the bush:

"My reasons for acting as I did? It's simple: I never was a Nazi. When I was called up, they sent me first to Poland, then to the Russian front. There, in 1942, we were decimated; the survivors were parachuted into Tunisia. Hitler's Reich, which was going to last a thousand years, had stolen my youth . . .

After the arrest of the five young Jews from Tunis, I decided to help them, as I had other men, that's all. I must say that knowledge of the education my parents gave me is essential to understand my attitude with regard to the Jews."

Richard Abel was born in 1916, in the middle of a world war, in a suburb of Frankfurt. His father was wounded at Douaumont and at Verdun. His grandmother, an ardent Catholic believer, raised her relations in the Catholic faith. She is the one being to whom he has always felt very close. On his grandfather's death, the family moved into his house. Two villas, on the corner of the street, belonged to Jews. Their children were young Richard's companions at play, and they often visited each other's houses . . . The Abel family obviously belonged to those Germans who only discovered the *Jewish problem* with the arrival of Hitler to power. But, even more rare phenomena, they are some of those who took action and spoke up for the persecuted Jews.

"I have always considered the Jews as brother human beings," went on Richard Abel. "I think that every man has the right of respect and to life, whatever the color of his skin, his opinions, or his nationality. What more can I say? I did not wish to be taken prisoner, and the Beretvas family helped me to leave Tunis. I love these people like my own family, it's true. I was, however, captured by the Allies after my escape from Tunisia . . . In every story, what counts, is to have brothers . . ."

When I leave him, I again go through Frankfurt. I remember my last visit to this town. It was in 1985. I had a meeting there with Jews, Rabbis—survivors from here and there, of those who had been lucky enough, at least once, to be considered as *human brothers*. It is with them in heart and mind, that I am going to conclude this German voyage of discovery.

# 21

# Frankfurt

The Great Synagogue at Frankfurt survived Hitler. Built at the end of the nineteenth century, it is right in the middle of the bourgeois houses of the district, and this configuration protected it. Not being able to knock it down without destroying the whole district, the Nazis therefore preserved it, contenting themselves, if one can say that, by desecrating the interior.

"But, today it is all refurbished, in a modern style," as I was assured without thinking anything of it, by the warden.

Yes, and with no style! I remember the group that I met in the hall: mostly young but some older adults. They were unwinding after the Sabbath service. Addressing myself to them in Yiddish, I asked them why they lived in Germany . . . Embarrassed smiles from the adults, who, without answering me, questioned me in their turn, wanting to know where I came from, and what I was doing in Frankfurt, etc.

Who were these Jews? A study by Nathan Lewison, the great Rabbi of Baden and Hamburg, himself of German origin and returned from exile in American uniform, is better able to answer that question.

The almost 28,000 Jews in Germany today can be divided into five main categories: the *illegal survivors,* that is to say in Nazi terminology those who managed to stay hidden in the heart of the population; privileged Jews, otherwise "mixed-blood," or *Mischling,* children of mixed marriages, often taken in and protected by Catholic or Protestant institutions; Jews liberated when the *camps* were opened, mostly from Eastern countries, but who, too hard hit, stayed where they were; and at last the *Germans:* Jews from Germany who were able to go into exile at the time and who came back after the war; to which we must add a heterogeneous group of some hundreds of *Russian* émigrés established in Berlin. I must explain that these observations and figures are derived from official West German sources concerning the situation before the Berlin Wall came down and reunification took place. One day I must try and investigate the situation of those Jews who were in the old East Germany.

Here, at Frankfurt, a young man, Georg Horny, assumed to be a future leader of the community, replies to the question that my interlocutors at the synagogue had avoided: why do Jews still live in Germany?

"You need to understand them," he says to me. "They are all ill . . . sick in their heads. They live here, but they are ashamed of it. So much so that for most of them, it is not even the land of their fathers, but the land of their executioners."

Nathan Lewison, much later, in welcoming me at a late hour into his lounge, in Heidelberg, will confirm Georg's diagnosis:

"It is true, they are sick people. But I hope they stay here."

"Why?"

"To deprive Hitler of something that would be his most important and ultimate victory: a German *Judenrein,* Germany *purified* of Jews."

From the despair which he implies, to his sad willingness to witness an *effective presence,* over and above everything else, of Jews in the country which programmed their elimination, the paradoxical nature of this statement by Nathan Lewison has the merit of not covering up a truth: there are some in Germany, there are some survivors, there are Jews who have stayed to witness the failure in extremis of the sinister *Final Solution.*

It is true: Hitler did not succeed in exterminating *all* the Jews, there still are some in his so-called "Reich." This fact does not in any way allow us to believe we are sheltered from Evil. That one world, one Germany without Jews is inconceivable, that is one obvious lesson from history, but also a second lesson: the first of these lessons rests on the fact that this world from which the Jews would have been radically eliminated was, however, thought about, conceived, *programmed*—but, in Poland as in Germany, this horrible program has been practically totally realized.

This systematic horror, is it enough to denounce it to avoid repetition?

I often ask myself if the perpetual transmission of the story of the Holocaust will protect us forever against another such return. Knowing about an illness, does that stop us from falling ill?

We know, only too well, that it does not. The proof is furnished by present-day Yugoslavia, where the "principle" and the practice of "ethnic cleansing" triumphs before our eyes.

Perhaps we have made a mistake in our assessment: we have believed it to be enough to expose suffering and injustice to incite humanity to be tolerant and to show distaste for violence. To sum up, we have assumed that man was naturally good, but ignorant. And we discover, with consternation, incredulity, horror, that the executioner fascinates the victim, we are attracted to Evil as much as, if not more than, to Good; "Every conscious being seeks the death of the others," wrote Hegel, thoughtfully. "In every man there is a potential war criminal," who can be controlled, thinks Rudolph Augstein, Director of *Der Spiegel*. These damning thoughts ought to alert us: they tend to trivialize Evil, and that is the opposite of what those who have encountered it know, for their part, as it manifested itself to the saviors, the Just.

*Good subjugates Evil as water puts out fire. Because one splash of water is insufficient to extinguish a spark, is it necessary to conclude that water is powerless against fire?*

# 22

# The Chief of Police

"Her Majesty 'Chance' does three quarters of the work, " wrote Frederick II, on the 2nd of November 1759, to Voltaire. He was not wrong. It is in Berlin, the native town of this enlightened king, in a house of one of the Just people that I have come to interview, that I discover an old issue of *Der Zeit* dating from the 4th of November 1988. The page which I hold in my hand is torn in half. It starts with a sentence which catches my attention:

> On the night of the 10th December 1938, Wichard von Bredow, Assistant Chief of Police in the Schlossberg area of East Prussia, received a telex from the headquarters of the region telling him that all the synagogues in Germany were in flames.

I carry on reading:

> 'The police and the fire brigade must not intervene.' Bredow put on his uniform and took leave of his wife, mother of five children, with these words: 'I am going to the synagogue at Schierwindt; as much Christian as German, I want to foil one of the greatest crimes in this sector with everything in my power.'

He knew that he risked his life or that he could be sent to a concentration camp by the Gestapo. "I could not act in any other way!" said he. When the SA, the SS, and the men from the Nazi Party charged in to set the fire, the Assistant Chief of Police was already there, in front of the house of God. Faced with the incendiaries, he fired his pistol: he warned them that they would have to cross over his dead body to get near to the synagogue. No one dared take on the Assistant Chief of Police. The Nazis dispersed . . . This was the only synagogue to escape the destruction in that round.

That synagogue had been saved, but, 267 in total, were destroyed on that night of the 10th of November 1938, which Goebbels called *"Crystallnacht"*—Night of Glass.

Concentrating on the synagogue at Schierwindt, may we not forget all the others which were burned down? The Just people who figure in this book and all those I have been unable to question, do they risk, by their entry into the history of the Nazi era, obscuring the memory of other men who took away life, hundreds of thousands of executioners, and millions of cowards?

Or better still, in completing the information gathering on this period of our history, will the evidence of these Just people not, in the end, permit us to learn some real lessons from it?

In fact, if you do not know the upper levels of a water course, how can you prevent floods? Where will I learn that better than in Holland? That country has more Just men than anywhere else: a third of the 9,295 listed in Europe—but, paradoxically, one also finds there the largest proportion of Jewish deportations in Western Europe. Out of 143,000 deported Jews, only 20,000 have survived.

Is this information going to change my attitude and my feelings towards Anne Frank's country? One of the sentences in her *Diary* could easily be a quotation from my book: "I continue to believe that man is fundamentally good and generous."

Truth to tell, my interest in Holland owes less to tulips or windmills than to the individual Menasse ben Israel. He was a rabbi. He founded the first large Jewish firm of printers in Amsterdam at the beginning of the seventeenth century. It was there in that print shop that one of my ancestors, Herschel, worked, and he that the persecution in Poland once more set on the road to exile.

This Jewish community in Amsterdam, with its contradictions, its passions, its violence, its learning, its creative genius, has always aroused my curiosity. More: It pulls me towards it. It gives me a mirror—through the presence of my forefather Herschel and the figures of Menasse ben Israel, Rembrandt, Spinoza, and Uriel da Costa. This northern town with its Portuguese synagogue filled with memories—a constellation of familiar signs, a sympathy, outside of time itself, which doubtless explains why I always feel "at home" in Amsterdam.

I knew that, during the war, Just people had saved some Jews there. I also knew that in Anne Frank's country 80 percent of the Dutch Jews were deported with the active cooperation of the general population, the administration, the police, and the Dutch Nazi Party, who only had about 80,000 militant members—zealous agent-informers for the Gestapo. They furnished them with addresses, maps and detailed plans, places and inns where some Good people were hiding Jews.

However, on the 25th of February 1941, one year after the invasion of Holland, shortly after the roundup of Jews on the 9th of February 1941, the towns of Amsterdam, Haarlem, Weesp, Utrecht, and Hilversum went on strike. This was the one and only visible collective manifestation of the Dutch in favor of their Jewish compatriots. Following that, the resistance movements had given a little help, but this assistance really arose from individuals' initiative, from saviors moved by generosity.

It was essential, there again, that the Dutch, free-thinking, defenders of the right of respect for others, that the Just, at least, acted to avoid the annihilation of a people, and to preserve that which the Jewish philosopher Uriel da Costa, who lived in Amsterdam in the seventeenth century, named *the dignity of Man*.

# 23

# Amsterdam

Amsterdam: I love this merchant city, prosperous, huge yet somehow compact, sectioned off by its canals and small streets under the soft light of a gray sky. I am walking along Vilenburgstraat on the Oude Schaus and I am once more thinking of that sentence of Margaret Acher's about Poland. They tell me in Holland that you can, alas, transpose it and that, if it took one thousand Dutchmen to save a Jew, it only took one Dutchman to denounce a thousand Jews.

Victor Halberstadt, professor of economics, great academic, saved, in the war, by one of these chains of Just men, said it directly: "Without the active participation of the Dutch fascists and the administration, the Germans would never have been able to deport so many Jews! Look at this document: it is a plan of Amsterdam; very detailed. Look at these red dots, sometimes several in the same street, and even for one apartment block: these are Jewish houses, their apartments, their rooms, their number of occupants. This map was produced by the Dutch fascists. The central file was also held by a Dutchman, Tom Cate. These administrative documents were prepared for the Germans and were given to them. This collaboration with the Nazis was, from the point of view of these latter, 'exemplary.'"

At this point, I question Ed Van Thijn, mayor of Amsterdam, who also escaped: "You are the mayor of a large city, with an imposing administration under your command. Do you think

92

that, if the Nazi terror returned, the present administration would collaborate, as did that of yesteryear, in delivering the Jews to their executioners?"

Round-faced, large round glasses, pointed nose, frizzy hair with a dense tuft on the top of his head, Ed Van Thijn searched inside himself, in deep reflection, to find the true answer. He wanted his comments to be optimistic. They left me with a certain bitterness, an unease, and a doubt.

"Oh, I know that the only hope depends on this: the young people who work nowadays in the Town Hall or in the various town administrative offices are so rebellious and undisciplined that perhaps they would refuse to obey collaborationist orders which they would be given . . ."

For my part, I would not like to put my hand in the fire. I say so to my interviewee. He laughs. I have the impression that neither would he like to put this salutary indiscipline to the test! Besides, he added that the disciplined functionaries themselves were just like their predecessors: from the way they organized denunciation to please the overlords . . . He himself, after a thousand dodges to avoid the roundups, finished up by being denounced and arrested in the final moments of the war, just before the arrival of the Americans, the Canadians, and the Jewish Brigade. He was only twelve, but it was already good to kill: at that time the Germans had decided to empty the last of the Jews out of the Dutch camps in order to send them to Auschwitz. Ed Van Thijn was with them. This was when the Dutch railway workers, for the first time, delivered a decisive resistant action in sabotaging the railway lines so that the trains could not leave. Magnificent gesture, to which, among many others, Ed Van Thijn still owes his life.

All the same, I could not hold myself back from asking a rather embarrassing question: "But why could the sabotage intended to prevent movement of the death trains not have been organized sooner?"

Question without answer. It forms part of those which one shouts out as an insult, at election time . . . Over fifty years, this debate resurfaces every time: how could they turn a blind eye to so much apathy and compliance with crime in a country with such a long history of tolerance and humanity, in a country where the French Huguenots found refuge, in a country which welcomed Diderot's Encyclopedists and the Lumières (French pre-Revolutionary thinkers and philosophers).

Ed Van Thijn shakes his head. Such an interview is painful, and none of it is likely to bring clarifying explanations nor produce any decisive analyses.

In default of tackling the origin of the turpitude, the mayor of Amsterdam, whose face expresses, in turn, sadness and doubt, comes back to emphasizing the positive of those times past. For the present he insists on the chain of solidarity, on "the thousand to save one."

You know, I have had eighteen mothers and eighteen fathers! . . .

"I have hidden in eighteen different places, with all kinds of people, Protestants, laity, Catholics, thanks to an organization founded by a group of young people."

"What was this organization called?"

"Ah! . . . 'The enterprise with no name,' that which defines it as a truly anonymous society, because those young people did not want to claim any glory for their action. This network hid 200 Jewish children. Each child needed at least four, or five, hiding places—which in total indicates between 800 and 1,000 hideouts, and the 'Enterprise without name,' with a strength of twenty, devoted itself to finding them, and they found them! Every Jewish child rescued has been through twenty, thirty, or even forty families . . . Imagine deploying this working network across the whole of Holland: as invisible as anonymous, but all the same efficacious in respect of the means at its disposal."

Ed Van Thijn's face, smiling at the memory of successful rescues, loses its color. He can hardly swallow. He is depressed. Reminiscences jostle each other, and those of rescues which failed wring his heart: "All the same," said he in a voice altered by sadness, "many of these young men were denounced to the Germans, arrested, tortured, killed. Some of the survivors didn't want to stay in Holland, after the war . . ."

Here we are again in front of this paradox: the shame of the Just!

They are ashamed of the attitude of the majority of their fellow citizens, so quick to collaborate with the Nazis, to denounce the Jews during the whole of the war, and who, when peace came, regarded these saviors, who had risked their own lives to help persecuted people, with a troubled eye full of guilty conscience and veiled hostility. Good numbers of these saviors, then, have left. Many went to South Africa to rejoin the Boers—among them the woman who saved Ed Van Thijn. They prefer to join the descendants of their Dutch forefathers who left four centuries before them, rather than continue to live as if nothing had happened in the middle of contemporaries whose comportment during the war, appeared loathsome, and afterwards hypocritical. Others also emigrated, but farther away: to Canada and Australia, as if they wanted to put the maximum distance between themselves and the Dutch.

This troubles me. Everything unfolds here as if something of the Jewish destiny has passed into the very life itself of these saviors who helped these Jews: as a kind of "Diaspora of the Just from Holland," but freely chosen by those exiled beings.

# 24
## Mother and sons

If the Dutch saviors had a tendency to disperse to the four corners of the earth (not all of them, for sure), the rescued Jews do go back to meet each other from time to time. The first meeting of this kind in Amsterdam was organized by Victor Halberstadt. I was there. And it was a strange and paradoxical evening: these people who had known each other for thirty, forty, or sometimes more years, since childhood, since school, who were one another's friends, even brothers and sisters, were brought together on that evening to *get to know each other*, to talk as if they have never done so before, to tell about events they have never told each other, in particular certain episodes of their wild escapes and how they were saved! Afterwards, they even tried to make sense of and analyze the reasons which had made it so difficult for them to access the memory of this period in their lives. Difficult, yes, . . . as if they make themselves martyrs by speaking about it. On the other hand, they do want to highlight the part played by their saviors: they talk about them as "family," saying to their children: "Oh, that was the time we didn't visit your aunt in Maastricht, or your uncle in Haarlem, or your cousin in Utrecht." I was astonished: "There are Jews in Utrecht?" And they laughed: these "aunts," these "uncles" were the people who hid them, saved their lives, educated and cared for them when their real relations perished in Auschwitz. Their relationship with their saviors is of a particular nature, filial—and this filial aspect percolates through to the children who speak of them in an 'accepted' way: "Yes, Dad lived there, we don't know any more quite how 'he is family' with them, but they are well and truly family, and we are happy to speak about him and happy to go and see them."

Up till today, I have only come across one case illustrating this strange family connection between children of escapees and children of their saviors. That was in France. René Frydman, well-known doctor, was born in the middle of the war, in 1943, at Soumoulou, a little village in the Pau region where his parents were hidden. Now his parents are no longer of this world, and neither are the couple who saved them. But, fifty years on, the son of the escapee, René Frydman, and the son of their saviors, André Cazenave, are still friends.

Thinking of them I make my way to Willie Wiechmann's house, where Victor Halberstadt awaits me.

In the small apartment, seated in an armchair beside his old savior, Victor smiles. In this gentle setting, where the shelves are full of books, he is at ease, he is at home, or almost so. The first time he entered this house, in February 1942, his sister was with him; she was five then and he himself was two. That house, where he had been hidden, fed, cared for, raised: it was his home. The intensity of Willie Wiechmann's warm and maternal look was the same for him as for her own son who was also present. More surprising still: Victor acted as if he was always here, whilst Willie Wiechmann's son looked like a guest. They had grown up together, but one had no risk of being taken in a roundup, and the other had to remain in hiding; one could almost think that Mrs. Wiechmann, by force of events, had had to take better care of this child under threat of death, and that it had to be looked after with even more vigilance than she gave to her own.

She reviewed the period of the war by thinking of the small—and dangerous—daily tasks: "After the arrest of my husband, I moved to this house. One day a man asked me to hide his wife and child. Later, this woman begged me to hide a Jewish boy. My house also served as a refuge and transitory hiding place for employees of the Jewish hospital. When Victor and his sister arrived, I was already sheltering two people, one of whom belonged to the Resistance, and I had to feed all of them. Our Jewish Resistance man took on that job, with all the attendant risks: he had to go out, to find official papers and ration coupons. Those coupons were numbered and checked. At distribution time it was indispensable to know a lot about the controlling officer. He was always a Dutchman. If he was pro-German, the risk of seeing him confiscate a Jew's ration card was great. Condition number one so that everything went well was to apply to a neutral officer. All this strategy of research into the identity of the serving officer was fundamental: in case of being stopped, no food coupons, then no more hiding place . . .''

"One day," Victor Halberstadt remembered, "the Germans and the Dutch SS encircled our district. My mother, my sister, and I had to climb on the rooftops, then we were given refuge by some neighbors. My mother shuttled back and forth between her parents and ourselves to fetch us clothes and papers. One day, she had been arrested . . . I was then placed here with my second mother, Willie . . . The role of the Jewish clandestine organizations must not be forgotten. It was through their intervention that the saviors could find ration cards, medicines . . . In those days, a ration card was as important as an identity card—whether in Holland, Belgium, France, Italy, or elsewhere."

Once more this ambivalence, once more this balancing act, once more daily life intensified, suspended between Good and Evil, between loyalty of some and the cowardliness—absorbing the taste of death—of others.

On leaving this discussion with an escapee and his rescuer, I see for a moment a little girl playing Hopscotch near the new Amsterdam Opera house. Right beside her, on the ground, there was another design from that on which this youngster was amusing herself. It is oblong and the writing is in white stones which read as follows: *Site of the old Jewish Orphanage, founded in 1759, and used until 1943, when the residents were led away by the Nazis. None of these children came back from the deportation.*

One other sentence, written in German was superimposed: *In every man there is a potential war criminal.*

Today, reviewing these sentences, I discover another one: *"Now God watched over the persecuted,"* says Ecclesiastes (III, 10). *"I look everywhere under the sun: in the place of goodness, there is crime; in the place of the Just, there is the criminal. And I say to myself: The Just and the criminal, God will judge them, for there is a time for all things and for all actions here."*

"God will judge them," "there is a time for everything"— God, yes, . . . perhaps. But us, can we at least understand? Perhaps not: if we understood, would we still be able to judge? Then can we, with so little that we can do, avoid the return of persecution? And if we cannot do even that, will we be able to find enough Just people in the whole world to prevent the worst ones from being totally victorious?

# 25

# Reflections

Amsterdam, now. It is cold. A current of air, which, since morning, has swirled around the old streets, suddenly gusts out on the canal. It catches me by surprise on a bridge, among dozens of cyclists, and freezes me to the bone.

I am en route to meet a Just person. Another Just. To ask him some questions: why did he act in that way? What were his motivations? Why him and why not others?

At this point in my enquiry, am I going to find something, as I did at the beginning, an answer which gives me a quiver? Perhaps. We must, however, and quickly, find an answer in this world, which in spite of its victory over Nazism, has inherited from the Hitler adventure this incredible faculty of accepting the unacceptable.

Perhaps should I call a halt—to recover my breath, to rethink my project? . . . I was thinking along these lines, wandering at random through the small streets, when suddenly I was brought up short as abruptly in front of me there appeared a slightly dilapidated building: called Anne Frank's School. The facade, covered in brightly colored texts written by the deported young girl, is less unusual than the way in which I have found myself here, without knowing the place, without having premeditated my route. I am surprised to decipher on the wall this sentence which I know by heart: *I continue to believe that Man is fundamentally generous and good.*

I feel as if I am inside Jonah's body, on his way to Niniveh, when he wished to escape from his mission. Now, the Talmud warns us, *". . . you don't have to finish the job, but you have no right at all to hide from it."*

Now . . . perhaps it would be more sensible, faced with the massacres which since the Holocaust have tormented my mind—Biafra, Cambodia, Bosnia, Rwanda, Chechny—to take some precautions, even if only verbal, before facing the next step in my strange wanderings.

Before looking for the Just people in Sodom and Gomorrah, Abraham himself tried to justify his approach before the Eternal: *". . . Here am I, I who have dared to talk to Thee, I who am nothing but cinders and dust. But He who sees all the Earth and Who exercises Justice, is He going to condemn for the crimes of a few, pell-mell, the Just and the criminals?"*

A friend remarked to me that to talk of Good, here, in Holland, in a country where so many Jews have been exterminated, could appear as a willingness to wipe out the crimes, the sins, the mistakes, and could be interpreted as the end of these "times of the coffin" of which Freud speaks, as the beginning of the reconciliation of everything with the past. Stupidity! The past is irrevocable and all truth is eternal. God himself cannot in any way make that which has taken place as if it never had. From the past, we can only try to extract lessons in the hope of preventing repetition of the massacres. To reduce the return of crimes, we have to remind ourselves of those of long ago as well as yesterday. Baruch Spinoza, in Amsterdam, in the seventeenth century, had foreseen it when writing in his notebook this vigilant motto: *"Caute*, that is to say 'beware.' "* It is told that, one day having been stabbed by a fanatic, he kept his pierced body armor for the rest of his life so as not to forget this aggression, neither, without doubt, this lesson. We do not know if the philosopher had pardoned his aggressor, but we do know that he wanted neither to efface nor forget it.

There are few towns in Europe where, as in Amsterdam, on looking around our gaze alights on so many memorial plaques, monuments, and reminders of all sorts of the deportation of the Jews. Also it was there that there lived a zealous official who invented an identity card which could not be falsified, which he hastened to offer, with the blessing of his superiors, to the Gestapo in Berlin. "From 1940 to 1945, observed a Dutch historian, there was no worse plague than this awful identity card, which inflicted the Jewish people with the most singular wounds."

To pardon then? But "*. . . why should we pardon those who regret so little and so rarely their monstrous acts?*" Vladimir Jankelevitch asked himself, and added: "*Because if the crimes which are not atoned for are precisely those which need pardoning, the unrepentant criminals are exactly those who do not need pardoning.*"

For my part, I have always thought that it is the memory of Evil which has so often stirred me, much more than I have been, and at that very modestly, by that of Good. Now, in spite of the doubts which assail me, and the questions still unanswered, this is what stimulates me, what encourages me, on these Amsterdam quays with their icy wind whistling, to continue my search for the Just.

The person I am going to meet is unknown to me. I made the acquaintance of her granddaughter, Irit, at my friend's, Victor Halberstadt's house. Bravado of a young girl or truth? She fired at me: "You are looking for the Just? Then you must go and see my grandmother, Henriette Kroon! . . ."

# 26

# Henriette and Annie

A door bangs. Another opens onto a narrow caged staircase. The wooden steps are very steep and smell of polish. Bicycles are hanging on the right-hand wall. Farther up, a beautiful old lady is waiting for me as she releases the door entry control with a press button. The door locks itself. The old lady ushers me in, smiles, and goes to sit beside Irit, who has arranged our interview. Irit's grandmother sits in front of me: Henriette Kroon, a Dutch woman who had saved Jews during the war.

White hair in an oval sweep around her face, large earrings, smart spectacles, a bright jacket like a pack of cards (it is covered in the four colored symbols: clubs, diamonds, hearts, and spades!), this appeared to be a young grandmother. She is an alert petite woman, full of life: she looks about seventy but in good shape—really she is not far off ninety . . . She is one of those people who appear fragile and strong both at the same time. When she raises her eyebrows or frowns when speaking, it is like children do, in a fresh and spontaneous manner. But what she says is perfectly lucid, and very determined, no less collected nor categoric for being simple. She has forgotten nothing of that time when she sheltered unhappy and persecuted people from the Nazi barbarity.

"Yes," says Henriette Kroon, "the things that went on in this very house . . . And up there on the fourth floor, where my granddaughter stays today, there was one of our friends. It was all together very risky, but no one knew. The Jews we hid never left the house. They didn't go out. It was difficult for the men. But they must not go out."

"And the Germans?"

"The Germans? No, they didn't come into my house. They never put foot inside."

"Good luck! And the Dutch police?"

"When the Dutch SS knocked on the door, I didn't open it. One time, they came. They hammered violently on the door, and one of our Jews was hiding in the house. Horrible moment for him and for us . . . I didn't open. Then they left without forcing the issue. I never knew what they wanted to ask us that day . . . The other Jew, who lived on the top floor, had been warned. We had a bell, and our code was to ring three times. He knew what that meant."

"They had constructed a double wall," explains Irit, Henriette Kroon's granddaughter, "so that he could cross the corridor . . . And he hid. He stayed hidden in a cupboard . . . That day when the Nazis were far away we again sounded the bell: so that he knew that the alert was over, and that he was safe. After events like this we were always in shock for a while."

"I can see that you were well organized: the little bell, the codes, a double wall . . ."

"Very true. It was indispensable."

"And fear?"

"It was there, sometimes, yes . . . But really we were not too frightened. We had to do something. And then we received help, food and medical care. There was also the Organization: we were very few, but we were not completely alone . . . that helped us to cope!"

"The first time that your neighbors asked you to take in their nephew, why did you agree?"

"Out of human kindness. And it was my way of showing opposition to Hitler, if you see what I mean . . ."

Henriette Kroon was part of a network. Her opposition to Hitler was categoric, and her determination, absolute. Cost what it may, she had to resist Nazism, and, if Hitler had decided to deport redheads, no doubt she would have saved redheads!

After the war, a strange thing happened; one of her daughters met a soldier in the Jewish Brigade, fell in love, and went to live with him in Israel. And this is how Henriette Kroon's grand-daughter, Irit, is an Israeli who speaks Hebrew and Dutch! At present, she is studying in Amsterdam, and living with her grandmother. It is she who often persuades her grandmother to tell and explain about the savagery which the Jews sustained during the war. And her grandmother, from the height of her eighty-eight years, smiles and remembers. She accompanies her granddaughter, from time to time, on visits to Israel to see her own daughter, and the family. She hid these Jews in her house, and here they are now part of the family . . .

Henriette Kroon laughs: "Destiny! . . ."

"Why did you do it all?"

She raises her head, an astonished look on her face, then, defiantly: "Why not?"

"Are you a Believer?"

Henriette Kroon smiles at my question.

"Yes, most certainly," she says to me.

She crosses herself. Her smile grows and radiates. All her face glows.

"I am a Protestant. But, you know, what I did, it was humane, that's all: it was never dictated by belief . . ."

"Fifty years after, if it was to reoccur? . . ."

"I hope I would do it all again!"

At the bottom of her heart, she did not doubt for a single instant! Yes, she would do it again—I am sure of that. She plays with her rings while speaking to me, turning them with the tips of her fingers, one hand at a time, and I feel so indignant at the idea that so much misery and desolation could possibly return to shatter the world.

Uplifted by this meeting, I decide to leave today for Wester-borg where, in an old farm, another Dutch woman, Annie Baetsen, and her husband hid Jews during the war. On the way, traversing a region dotted with windmills, I suddenly think of this sentence from *Don Quixote: "A good experience is more marvelous than a bad possession . . ."* I smile quietly to myself and ask myself if by chance, in the course of this research on the mechanics of Good, I would not discover more easily the workings of hope.

I was accompanied by Sira Sodentrop, wife of the great Rabbi of Haarlem, who was saved, long ago, by Annie Baetsen. This latter called Sira her "older daughter," and very long ago Sira had called her rescuer "mama." We will come back to this filial link later.

Annie Baetsen, in spite of her seventy-three years, still looks young. Here, half a century ago, when she was saving Jews, she was scarcely twenty. One must not forget this passing of the decades, this distance in time which reappears unceasingly in this research for the Just: I am speaking to people as they were aged at the time of their life, long ago, of the life they led then when they were very young, in an era when the choice was to follow death or save a life.

But, contrary to that, because of this distance in time, the intensity of these memories which remain tied to those events has not faded. Annie Baetsen, like other Justs whom I have already met, retains a very live consciousness of the period.

"We were in the Resistance with my brother," she said to me. "At home, we hid antifascists and members of the Resistance. One evening, in February 1944, we had to hide some Jews: Sira's father and mother. They were on the run, they were in danger everywhere. One month later, Sira joined us in her turn. She was one year old! And then there were other Jews, many other Jews and sick people, and wounded, all here. We had to be very careful. Here in the country there were members of the NSP, Dutch Nazis, who watched everything.

"Did you know any Jews before the war?"

"No. The ones we sheltered came from Amsterdam, the towns."

"Yes, but in a general way, what did 'a Jew' mean to you?"

"It didn't make any difference whether they were Jews or otherwise. However, when we had Jews in the house, we never accepted any others. From prudence. There could be anti-Semites anywhere, and even perhaps among some of our friends. We could also be betrayed. I always told everyone that Sira was one of the family. I invented plenty of things on that subject . . .''

"Here, it was a farm. What did you do on it?"

"I worked in the house: housework, preparing food."

"We had to make our own bread and cultivate our vegetables. Sometimes we went to the village looking for things we lacked, but that took hours and hours. By good luck, all the same, we had ration cards, because my brother, at that time, was a lawyers clerk, and had been placed in the distribution office. But, nevertheless, the hours waiting for everything . . . Ration coupons, don't talk to me about them! There were so many of us at home, and my sister as well, she was going to have a baby. I too was pregnant, and all alone to organize everything, to run the house, and feed the world! Over and above, you must understand that the front line was just here. The Germans were all over the place, and all that huge field, in front of you, was mined. To go to the village, you had to go around the house and out through the back!

"Were you frightened?"

"No, no. Not at the time. Until, one fine day, a neighbor said to me: 'My . . . you're hiding a little Jewish girl here! Are you a fool? There are plenty of traitors in this area, many NSP— nothing but fascists! You should move!' We moved immediately, we went to live in Drenthe. Even there we heard the people gossiping, about Sira, in the sort of way: 'That's never a child of that family, perhaps she's a little Jewess,' and then I became afraid of denunciation. One day, I called a doctor whom I didn't know—of course, I took a chance—but Sira was very ill. This doctor guessed immediately. He said to me, 'You are lucky; I could have been a pro-German doctor. Me, I won't say anything. I have never seen any little Jewish girl here . . .' But, there also, in Drenthe we were surrounded by NSP People. My brother passed them every day, he said 'good morning' to them as if nothing was amiss. In that district there was a Jewish child whose father had been arrested. There I was really scared. I passed whole nights without being able to sleep. And then, in September, I had a little girl, 'my second,' since 'the first' was Sira . . . She is one year and four months younger than you, eh, Sira?"

Sira smiled and acquiesced.

"You now see," she said to me, "what I told you about my two mothers. Because my natural mother, herself, stayed safe, during the war years. And I called Aunt Annie 'Mum.' I couldn't bring myself to call her 'Aunt Annie' until much later . . . And when I do show affection to one, I have a guilty conscience: as if I have at one stroke stolen a little bit of love from the other. But, what could I do. All my childhood was marked by that. When my Aunt 'Annie' said to people: 'How pretty my little girl is,' I felt proud and happy, and then I would think of my real Mum and ask myself: 'If she heard that, how would she take it? . . .' However, the family integration was total, I was family, with Aunt Annie who was my Mum . . . Besides, when I was married, I said to my husband, Rabbi Sodentrop: 'Come on, I must introduce you to my other mother: Annie Baetsen.' I phoned here to warn Aunt Annie that we were coming . . . We arrived in a car, my husband and me, with presents, an enormous bouquet of flowers, etc., I knew that we were expected, and that there would be a copious feast. A party, to sum it up! I went up to the main door . . . I rang—nothing. I rang again—still not a sign of life. Somewhat disquieted, I went round to the back of the house, and arrived at the back door, the one to the kitchen. They were all there, waiting. The bell? They hadn't heard it . . . And then Aunt Annie said, smiling: 'What my girl, aren't you family? It is only acquaintances, or strangers, who ring the front doorbell. Why can't you come in by the kitchen door as usual?'"

The two ladies burst out laughing.

I revert to the war years. I want to know why Annie Baetsen, despite all the risks, saved Jews.

"You know, you must understand . . . You must imagine what would have happened if no one had done anything against the Nazis: that would have been chaos. It was hellish, yes, but that would have been chaos. We well knew it was dangerous, but here, on the farm, I was never frightened. It was later that I was very frightened, there, in Drenthe. Here there was always somewhere to hide. Look, for example, you see that thicket, those big bushes, there, in front of the house? Well, when we had visitors, I sent the Jews there so that they would be hidden from idle curiosity. But I never spent my time asking why I did all that. I did it, that's all. One wants to help others, one wants to help one's neighbor—one cannot do otherwise!

"Fifty years later, how do you see all that? Have you any regrets?"

"Regrets? Oh, no, none at all! And if there was another war, I would do the same things again! Why should I regret having helped other people? If I had to, I would take them home right now! And then, for Sira, such a sweet child, so adorable, I was so happy to have her close to me: how could I feel regret? You can be sure I would hide her again!"

Annie Baetsen laughs heartily. She squeezes Sira's hand in her own. How could a Hitler, or anyone like him, whatever his strength or ferocity, be able to efface all trace of the goodness of the human heart? It did not succeed with Annie Baetsen nor her "little girl." It did not succeed with hundreds of others, with thousands of others of these Just people and their protégés. In certain extreme moments of history, Evil can appear to deck itself out with the vain symbols of tyranny and deal out the worst means of extermination: it presents itself at such times as *absolute* Evil. But the word is in error, inexact, and out of place. This absolute Evil is only transitory. During the same period when it appears to triumph shamelessly, the spirit of Goodness is already sapping its foundations. Even supposing Hitler had succeeded in winning this war, his so-called Reich would not have lasted a thousand years, as his delirium would have had him think: I would like to think that Justice cannot be suffocated for so long, and these Just people that I am meeting make me feel that this hope is not ill-founded—that I am not fishing out of optimism in supposing that the Good, badly battered as they may be, remain invincible.

I am looking for the Good and speaking again about hope. But, is one not the dream of the other? The historian Yosef Hayim Yerushalami hoped one day to write a *History of hope*. To relieve our solitude. To "*. . . understand that we are not the first to whom despair is no stranger, nor hope a gracious gift.*" He believed that this route, that this research would, without doubt, make us understand that we would not be the last. And this thoughtful prize would be, according to him, "*. . . a little step towards hope itself.*"

# 27

# The Jew from Shanghai

All enquiries often take unforeseen paths. Some individuals were pointed out to me that I had never heard of before. Somehow in the course of my journeys around Holland, word went before me. In the Jewish community of Amsterdam, they gossiped about my interest in the history of the last war, and not just in the Nazis, Auschwitz, and Treblinka, but also in the survivors and those who saved them. And they organized some meetings of consequence . . . Where was it written that I must meet this astonishing man, who looks like a very typical Englishman, but speaks with a Yiddish accent: *The Jew from Shanghai?*

Nathan Gutwirth, for that is his name, presented himself to me, not without humor, under this title. Actually, he is a native of Antwerp but with Dutch nationality, and his destiny had been to travel the world across places and people. With him, I am soon going to bring back memories of great journeys: Lithuania first, from where he had to flee, not without difficulties; then the USSR, Japan, China, Indonesia . . .

"What were you doing in Lithuania, Mr. Nathan Gutwirth?"

"The Talmud! I went there, in 1936, to study the Talmud at Vilnius Yeshiva. I had left Holland, where my family lived, after I finished school. Vilnius had 154,000 inhabitants of which a third were Jews. Don't forget that they called Vilnius the 'Jerusalem of the North,' because it had the largest Yeshiva in the world at that time: a sort of international university, with students coming from all over, the United States and even Australia. When war broke out, I was still there; I was twenty-two.

"But . . . these talmudic studies, did you intend becoming a rabbi?"

"No. With us, as you know, people study for studying's sake, just to know the Talmud."

"For pleasure, . . . what sort?"

"Yes, if you like! . . . Because you must work hard, exactly like students at any university. We, simply, studied the Talmud and the Law."

"What was the situation in 1939 in Lithuania?"

"The Jews didn't fare too badly. The Lithuanian Jews originally came from Russia since, until the First World War, Lithuania was part of Russia. They had their culture, their schools, their newspapers . . . At Kaunus, a little town of 15,000 inhabitants, where all the Lithuanian rabbis studied, they even had a theatre. It was a good life, a pleasant life even."

"And, when war broke out? . . ."

"In September 1939 we saw the arrival of tens of thousands of Polish Jews, from recently invaded Poland. The Lithuanian Jews welcomed them with open arms. Most of them were men, come alone, because they thought the Germans wouldn't do anything to women and children. And then, in June '40, the Soviets occupied Lithuania and Estonia, which they then declared to be an integral part of the Soviet Union. Everything was nationalized. Shops belonging to the Jews, the Yeshiva, and the ordinary schools were closed. A wind of panic rushed through the Jewish community. By then the war was at its height, Holland was occupied, and the Germans were advancing on Lithuania: we were cornered between Stalin, already in situ, and Hitler who perhaps would soon be here. We were frightened. We had to leave. There were 253,000 Jews in this country, caught in a terrible mousetrap! . . . At first a few hundred managed to escape through Stockholm to Palestine, others through Turkey—then these routes dried up: the German army advanced and blocked the way. I wanted to leave, but, unable to return to Holland, I had to choose between the Dutch colonies or Curaçao. I opted for Curaçao because it was close to America. To do it, I would have to cross territory belonging to the USSR, with whom Holland did not maintain diplomatic relations, and I would need valid papers. The Dutch Embassy attested that a visa was not required for Curaçao. That is how we ended up at the Japanese Embassy, Zorah Wehrhaftig and me, to find a sympathetic hearing. Zorah Wehrhaftig was one of the leaders of the Jewish community (he became, much later, the Minister of Culture in the State of Israel). He made contact with the Japanese Consul at Kaunus to obtain Japanese visas to permit Dutch Jews to go to Curaçao, via Japan. Having the correct official documents— the famous visas—the Russians would allow us to cross their territory . . . There were only five Dutch people in Lithuania, and the Consul, Mr. Sugihara, agreed to furnish the visas and transit cards. But the news traveled fast through the Jewish community, and especially among the Polish refugees. Thousands gathered in front of the Japanese Consulate: everyone wanted a visa!''

"The war between Germany and the Soviets hadn't yet started, then?"

"No."

I will now learn about the troubles of Tempo Sugihara, the Japanese Consul. For his part, he had telegraphed his government three times to request authorization to issue visas to all the thousands of Jews waiting in front of his Consulate. Three times the same response came back: No.

His widow, Yukoko Sugihara, who I will meet later, will explain to me that they hadn't had a wink of sleep all night, when, at six o'clock in the morning, having put some decent clothes on, they decided together, without a word, what they must do: they were going to ignore their government's instructions and issue as many visas as they could manage.

"There were hundreds and hundreds of applicants, and we knew that others would follow," she explained to me. "The answer from the Foreign Ministry in Japan was negative, but we knew—and it was insupportable—that they were killing the Jews, and the massacres were going on and on! So we gave out the visas on our own authority. All of August, my husband never stopped giving out visas. Right up to the time the Russians ordered us to close the consulate. When we had to go, I remember, there were still twelve people standing in the street: they had a lost look, completely bewildered, and we could do nothing more for them. It was heartrending."

About 6,000 visas were prepared and issued in this hasty manner. Time was pressing. The Russians advancing from one side and the Germans from the other. At the last minute, these Jews boarded full trains to take them to the Far East, across the Soviet Union, armed with valid papers. They crossed over the whole of Russia, through Vladivostok and descended in Japan: a collective escape by the Trans-Siberian Railway!

Nathan Gutwirth describes this diversion: "Imagine when we arrived in Japan, after a journey lasting three weeks on the Trans-Siberian, just after Pearl Harbor, on the 7th of December 1941: the place was crawling with Wehrmacht military missions, there to plan projects with their allies, the Japanese army. And then, they saw disembarking, from bulk food carriers arriving from Vladivostok, thousands of Jews coming from the extreme end of Lithuania! They must have thought they were having nightmares . . ."

As for the Japanese, they were caught off guard. For sure, they had delegated their function to their Consul, Tempo Sugihara, in Lithuania. To deal with the problem, they quickly shunted all the Jews to China, to Shanghai, which they controlled. This is how a Jewish quarter was created in Shanghai, and how Nathan Gutwirth was to become "The Jew from Shanghai." But apparently, there was another episode to this story, another savage twist: "While in Japan," explains Nathan Gutwirth, "we were well treated during the period while the Japanese Government made up its mind what to do with us. Thousands of us were able to land in Japan with no problems—and—suddenly, the latest Jews who arrived were turned back. Seventy-two of them would have to reembark on the first ship which was to leave for Vladivostock in three days time: in fact, they would have to do the whole journey in reverse, back to Lithuania. What a tragedy for them, what despair! . . . I went to see the Dutch Consul in Japan, and told him about the situation. He gave me a hundred official forms— on Consulate headed paper—which he still had, and he managed to find the official and indispensable seal to authenticate them. We filled out the forms, and I took them to him. He stamped and signed them. All the Jews on the boat for Vladivostok were able to be saved, as well as a few others.

"After that, what happened to you? You didn't stay in Shanghai long, did you? Did you ever reach Curaçao?"

"No, never! . . . I left for Indonesia because I had a cousin who already lived there. I worked there, in my cousin's office. Then the Americans entered the war against the Japanese. I found myself in the army, and I was taken prisoner. That was hard. I was sent to many different camps: in Java, Flores, and other islands. In the end, when the island was being liberated, all we prisoners thought we were going to be wiped out in the course of the battles which were taking place between the Allies and the Japanese. But we were liberated without that being the case."

"Tell me, Mr. Nathan Gutwirth, are you conscious of the paradoxical nature of your adventure? You were saved by a Japanese Consul, and you had to call on the Dutch Consul in Japan to intervene on your behalf!"

"It is paradoxical, yes. And all that, thanks to documents which were more or less legitimate, more or less false—but above all thanks to the decision of Tempo Sugihara, who from the start, took the courageous initiative of disobeying his own government! The Jews that he saved are the only ones who were in Lithuania and survived: 90 percent of the Jewish population of that country was massacred by the Nazis between 1941 and 1944. Yes, it was better to have left . . ."

The odyssey of Nathan Gutwirth will not remain without a follow-up in my enquiry. In Amsterdam I learnt that there were still a few Jews in Lithuania. I have decided, therefore, to go there. I do not know that a surprise awaits me and that, after having met the "Jew from Shanghai," I am going to make contact with the "Japanese from Vilnius," when they honor his memory. I am also definitely going to Belgium, thereafter, to meet a diamond dealer, the son of one of the Just—who himself, in a strange way, is the "Japanese from Jerusalem."

# 28

# The Japanese from Jerusalem

A few years ago, who in my family would have thought that I would one day go to Vilnius? The Jews, chased out of Western Europe, settled there in the twelfth century. In 1658 Vilnius had 12,000 inhabitants, of which 3,000 were Jews. As a child, how many times did I hear the story of Vilnius and its genius, Rabbi Elie ben Salomon Zalmann? And how many anecdotes of the many writers and Yiddish poets from whose works my mother recited to me?

Arriving in the capital of Lithuania, I discovered an airport smaller than Perpignan station, a small Polish-looking town with squares built around fountains, streets paved with big round stones, houses of one or two stories with huge court-yards. Only one large hotel, a 'skyscraper' of eight floors, built by the Soviets, and already dilapidated, overlooked the town. I stayed there. I learn that during the war the Nazis had experimented, very close to here, with the first mobile gas-chamber in a lorry. I start my enquiries with the President of Lithuania, Vitas Landsbergis.

I tell him about my search for the Just, and ask him if he knows about the Japanese Consul, Tempo Sugihara, who saved between 5,000 and 6,000 Jews here during the war . . . He smiles and, mysteriously: "If you come on such and such a day to such and such a place, you will see . . . I predict a surprise . . . No: *two* surprises!"

On the appointed day, a presidential limousine comes for

me and takes me to a place in town where, very unusual in such a place, there is a large crowd of Japanese walking around. Particular attention is being paid to an enormous mass draped with material. I ask what all the fuss is about. The mass is unveiled: a monument to, and of, Tempo Sugihara is revealed. The competition organized to design and create this work of art had been won by some Japanese sculptors. Vitas Landsbergis gives a speech. A moving ceremony. It is the great posthumous rehabilitation of this Just man who was Tempo Sugihara: apart from the honors rendered by Lithuania, the Consul of old is no longer disrespected in his own country. The Japanese Government, on the demands of the Lithuanian and Israeli governments, has actually come to accept, half a century after the deed, the cleansing of the "error" which he committed in disobeying his own Ministry when it forbade him to save the Jews . . .

President Landsbergis, in giving me this surprise, has spoilt me. I know that a second surprise awaits me, but I must stay here a moment with Tempo Sugihara's son, the son of this Good man from so far away, from the country of the Rising Sun, to remember the death of thousands of people.

Nobuki Sugihara, Tempo's son, is a diamond merchant, aged forty-four, who works in the capital city of the precious stone. Antwerp. He is conscious of the importance of his father's action, and is concentrating, looking very serious, remembering the period that he only knows from stories others have told him. I look at him: he speaks calmly, often accompanying his words with measured gestures with hands, normally together on the table in front of him, that he moves to underline this or that point. His eyebrows are very black. Nobuki Sugihara is a child of this generation that was completely horrified by the 1939–1945 war. He explains to me, in English, how his father, after having been disciplined for his initiative in Vilnius, was sent to a lower post in the Japanese Embassy in Romania. When the Soviets arrived there, they sent all the Japanese diplomats to the camps in Siberia. He was there six months. When peace came, he was relieved of all his positions in Japan.

Nobuki Sugihara clarified: "Only now they are rehabilitating him . . . posthumously."

"Such a long time afterwards!"

"Yes . . . When Lithuania became independent again: it was done as a gesture of the Japanese Government to the new Lithuania. Only about a year before the Lithuanian Government erected this statue which you saw."

Silence. And, after a moment: "Now, he who 'disobeyed' has become a hero, and his story is studied by children at school . . ."

"Tell me about your father. What did he say about what he had done?"

"I wasn't born then, and, when I was very small he never told us much about that period. Later he started to explain, but modestly, by allusions. I didn't really know about it until, in 1968, some Israeli diplomats came to Tokyo. The Israeli Commercial Attaché was one of the thousands of Lithuanian Jews saved by my father, and he came to thank him. That is how I was able to gather all the facts of the story."

"Why did he make this decision to grant visas to the Lithuanian Jews when the Japanese Government had forbidden him to do so? What did 'Jew' signify for him, for your family?"

Nobuki Sugihara kept silent for a long time, then: "You know, there were these thousands of people camped around the consulate begging someone to give them visas . . . Whatever they were, Jews or non-Jews, he had to help them in some way. I am sure that would have been his answer. Jews, in our eyes, what are they? Just strangers. That is to say: people who aren't Japanese. Jews, Christians, for us it is all the same thing . . ."

Nobuki Sugihara didn't tell me, but I guessed that it must have been very difficult, in Japan after the war, to be the son of an ex-diplomat banned from the administration, suspect, fingers pointed, and more or less without means. It was out with society's norms and that would be all over the school and the university. It was the visit of the Israeli Commercial Attaché, who had come to pay homage to Tempo Sugihara, which was going to change everything: the son was going to find out, at last, the enormity of his father's deeds, he was going to be able to realize a wish that he had been cherishing in secret. He wanted to go and study abroad. The atmosphere in Japan weighed him down. He opened up to the Israeli visitor. "Don't worry about that!" the latter exclaimed. "Your father, among others, saved Zorah Wehrhaftig: today, he is a Minister in the Israeli Government. I will ask him to give you a scholarship to go and study at the University in Jerusalem . . ." Once in Israel, he felt so good there that he stayed ten years!

"But," I said to him (still in English), "you had to speak . . . to learn Hebrew?"

Then, unsuspected situation, totally unexpected, and to me bizarre in the extreme: Nobuki Sugihara smiles, and answers me . . . in Hebrew!

I have before me the "Japanese from Jerusalem"!

The conversation from now on would continue in Hebrew, even if, truth be told, he masters it better than me . . .

"Yes," he says, "I speak Hebrew, perhaps better than Japanese! I even speak a little Yiddish . . . I am forty-four years old. I left Japan at the age of nineteen, I lived ten years in Israel, and now I am the only Japanese diamond dealer in Belgium!"

This son of that Japanese Just man is a true 'wandering Jew' . . . As if he had wanted to travel the world in the opposite direction to those his father had saved. With, above all, the same point of anchorage: Israel.

"Each time I return," he sighed, *"I feel at home."*

Some time from now, and in Jerusalem, I will meet Zorah Wehrhaftig, the only one, out of 6,000 Lithuanian Jews saved by Tempo Sugihara, to have become a Government Minister. In the days of the Reich, Zorah Wehrhaftig belonged to the directorate of the Jewish Agency for Palestine and to the Party for Religious Workers, in the Mizrahi. Yarmulke perched on the back of his almost bald head where the white hair has nearly all gone, he reminisces, with great emotion, about the period. High forehead, appearing larger by contrast with his gray goatee beard, Zorah Wehrhaftig speaks quickly, his flow of words no less active than his hands, which are always ready to fly, with positives and negatives emphasized by his spirited gesture.

"When I learnt of the entry of the Nazis into Poland," he said, "I rushed to Warsaw to join the Polish army. I had hoped that the Poles would repel the Nazi troops. I was mistaken. And as it was impossible to face their advance, I had, in company with many other Jews, to go to Vilnius in Lithuania. I did not know yet that I would also have to flee from there. In fact, we were going to find ourselves cornered, as if in a trap. When the news of the possibility of escape, thanks to the Japanese Consulate, spread through the crowds, thousands of Jews rushed to the Consulate in Kaunus. You had to reason, negotiate, plead with the Consul, find the money necessary for the journey. I was busy with all that . . ."

"This famous journey, how did it go?"

"The first three weeks on the Trans-Siberian to get to Vladivostok, then a week waiting, and finally a day on a boat to take us to Kobe, in Japan. In the meantime Pearl Harbor. Japan, now at war with America, dispatched us off to Shanghai. At the end of the war, many of us left to go to America, and, later, Israel."

"Did you ever see Tempo Sugihara and his wife Yukoko again?"

"Certainly I did. And, since the death of Tempo, I have seen even more of Yukoko. I know Nobuki, their son, for whom I organized a scholarship so that he could come and study in Israel . . ."

I will suspend this "Judeo-Japanese" evocation here, this rescue of 6,000 Jews: Vitas Landsbergis, in his family home at Kotcherguine, near Kaunus, is keeping another surprise for me.

# 29

# The President of Lithuania

After the unveiling of the monument dedicated to Tempo Sugihara, in Vilnius, President Landsbergis took me to his house, near Kaunus, for a chat.

Affable, alert sixty-year-old with clear eyes, sporting a neat beard trimmed to a point, Vitas Landsbergis, from behind his spectacles, every so often throws out a smiling glance to soften the serious expression—a presidential necessity—that he wore. Here, at Kotcherguine, in the family dacha constructed with whole trees, he has no rows of pens lined up in front of the dozen telephones as he does in his office in Vilnius. There is no saber decorated with dried flowers, nor the Lithuanian flag hanging out. The official ceremonial stays in town. And it is with a friendlier voice, in softer tones, that Vitas Landsbergis speaks to me.

"At the time of the war," says he, "I was a child. I did know that there was a ghetto in Kaunus, but I didn't exactly know what went on there. I saw people who hid in my parents' house as well as at my aunt's, where we sometimes went with my mother. That's how I remember clearly a little girl with black eyes and black hair. I didn't know she was Jewish, and they made me swear not to tell anyone about her, under any pretext. She was called Bella. I remember that my mother had told her to wear a scarf, as her hair was so dark it was sure to attract attention. Everyone here is so fair . . . I also knew that my aunt's husband was in hiding, because he too was Jewish. All the family was mobilized to hide him, to save him."

"That's normal, isn't it?"

"Normal? How do you mean? I tell you, the many Lithuanians who had Jews in their families were not inclined to denounce them quickly, compared to the Germans! . . . Our uncle depended on us not to. We kept him two years in a cupboard. We took him food in there, he had a chamber pot, etc. In case of danger we knocked on the door: he wouldn't move anymore, he held his breath and stayed immobile. When he came out of there he was half blind and could hardly stand up straight. It took him six months to learn to walk again . . . But, as I said: I was very young, and it wasn't until after the war that I learnt and understood that he had passed two years in our house, hidden in a cupboard."

"If your parents were able to hide a little Jewish girl, as well as your uncle, what of the others, of those who did nothing? Have they the least excuse?"

"I agree with you. All the same, I hesitate to speak badly of our neighbors who, for their part, although they did not hide Jewish families, equally *did not denounce us*. Perhaps, in their case, the situation did not present itself, and they did not have the opportunity to show what they could do. It is difficult to judge. If you are walking along a riverbank and you see someone drowning, not far from your side, you go to his aid— but, if you are on the far side of the river, it is not so simple . . ."

The mousetrap that Lithuania in those times was for the Jews was remarkably effective. Occupied by the USSR on the 15th of June 1940, then on the 21st of the following July declared a Soviet Republic, Lithuania first suffered, from the Soviets, a repression directed against the priests of the Catholic Church, before being invaded from 1941 to 1944 by the Germans. The latter practiced a true policy of extermination against the Jews. On the 27th of July 1941, Himmler gave orders to form local auxiliaries: the Lithuanian commandos were formed and organized to reinforce the anti-Jewish measures taken by the Germans.

On the 31st of July, these commandos, with the aid of the local authority, created the Kaunus Ghetto.

Two hundred and fifty-three thousand Jews lived in this country before the war. Close to 230,000 are dead, deported, or assassinated here with the ignominious cooperation of the local fascists.

We were talking about these historic events, just at the moment when Vitas Landsbergis shows me a book with a red-and-black cover.

"You are thinking that we didn't have any Just people here, aren't you? OK, here they are! And there was even a photo of my mother . . . And then . . . ," he added, screwing up his eyes with obvious pleasure behind his spectacles, "I promised you another surprise, yes . . . ?"

"You did," I said to him.

"OK, I now present my father to you! He too is one of the Just. He it was who took care of Bella, the little Jewess whom I was talking about, a while back. It was he who saved her."

I see an old man whom the years have not deprived of humor nor smiles, coming, supported on crutches. Light jacket, well brushed white hair, slightly disheveled on top, big wide open and welcoming blue eyes; he is affable, happy to meet everybody, to take part in the conversation. He seems in good form, and his relative plumpness speaks to a happy character, with the soul of a bon viveur. When the introductions are over and Mr. Landsbergis senior is seated, I cannot resist asking his age.

"A hundred!" he replies laughing. "A hundred! I was born in 1893 . . ."

"Mr. Vytautas Landsbergis, do you remember anything about the young Jewish girl you hid here?"

"Indeed I do. She was called Bella. The curate of the Parish of Zapiche, quite close to here, gave us the papers of a little girl who died. The age and description corresponded quite closely to Bella who was thirteen or fourteen then. Later we pretended she was our children's nurse. She stayed here, with us at Kotcherguine, with these false papers. Later still, we had to take her to friends of ours in the country: one of my sons was arrested by the Nazis, the situation became very dangerous— we had to find a safe place for Bella."

"You began to be afraid?"

"Sure I did. If we were discovered, all our family could be shot for hiding Jews."

"Why did you do it?"

Mr. Vytautas Landsbergis needs the question translated and repeated several times. When you speak to him, he has to put his ear closer: he is a little deaf, but only a little—just enough that he sometimes has to ask people to repeat what has been said. With a twinkling eye, he leans, with delight and curiosity, close to the interpreter as she repeats . . . But this question obviously disconcerts him. He is astounded. He shakes his head and says: "What kind of a question is that? Funny question. How can I answer? Why did I continue to hide this imp? . . . I am a man, sir. I have a heart. It is my heart which says to do this. How could one not act in this way? I cannot answer your question. I did what my heart told me to do."

"Others did differently. And as they were men, they also had a heart . . ."

"Ah! if we start to talk of others, we'll never finish! I don't want to talk about the others . . ."

Mr. Landsbergis, senior, begins to laugh. He promises me to live long enough to read this book. He exclaims, as we are leaving, "Is it not 'incredible!,' you are the second writer who has come to see me in fifty years! The first was Milosz . . . ?"

Magnificent vitality of this centenarian, of this Just man. He would, however, be betrayed by life: he died two months after this interview.

# 30

# The Danish Nation

Today, after the collapse of Communism, there is no problem going from Lithuania to Denmark. The airplane flight takes less than one and a quarter hours—and then we are to discover Copenhagen, Hans Christian Andersen's town, home of his *Tales*, his famous "The Emperor with no Clothes," which, as a child, so often set me dreaming.

The King of Denmark and his people, a population of Just men, made me dream later on, when, after the war, I discovered the amplitude of the disaster.

For my part, I have begun to ask myself this terrible and penetrating question: Why?

Denmark, in the Europe of the Second World War, was an exception. Hitler, after having invaded the country without firing a single shot, on the 9th of April 1940, showed them strange favors for a long time. It is true that his troops are there to "protect the Kingdom" . . . The government, with its Social Democrat Prime Minister, stayed in place with its policy said to be one of "cooperation" with the occupying power. Until 1943, the Jews were not worried. Better, they weren't even forced to wear the yellow star . . .

But, on the 28th of September 1943, the Danish government, all of a sudden, ceased to "cooperate" and resigned en bloc. The Nazis had to take over running the country themselves. And, on the 28th of September 1943, a German officer warned his Danish friends that a general roundup of the Jews was planned for the nights of the 1st and 2nd of October.

The news went through the population like wildfire. Immediately, the churches, the intellectuals, about forty charity organizations and other groups, political and denominational, united their efforts. Niels Bohr, Nobel Prize winner for Physics, arranged with the Swedish King for the Danish Jews to be accepted in Sweden. And that is when, without government or king (since the end of August, Christian X had been kept under Nazi surveillance in his house), a whole people organized, often improvising but with exemplary success, the rescue of practically all the 7,500 Danish Jews taking them to Sweden on board an armada of little fishing boats: a whole people of Just men, or few who weren't!

To find the Just, a major difference from other countries: there is scarcely any need, here, to spend a long time looking—they are everywhere.

For a long time, now, I have admired the Danish for this exploit in the exercise of solidarity, generosity, and justice. I vow that I am going just to take in the legend without occupying myself too much with the deeds. I believed, I wanted to believe what I had been told. For example, that when the Nazis ordered that the Jews must wear the yellow star, the King and Queen came out of their palace wearing yellow stars, and that all the Danes did the same. In the postwar period, in the fifties and sixties, my dreams, as an artist imagining this scene, uplifted me, reliving the challenge . . .

My search for the Just cannot, therefore, avoid the country of the Just. I must, however, pay more attention to the hardships than the deeds.

And, first of all, the myth of the yellow star worn by all the Danes following the King had to be thought about carefully if, for any reason, it was not completely accurate.

This is the explanation of Jorgen Kieler, a Copenhagen doctor, who was twenty-one in 1940: ''The King never did that, neither did anyone else. And not a single Jew, it is true, wore the yellow star. In reality, a similar story appeared in a Swedish newspaper to illustrate the King's response to the Nazis: '*If the Jewish Danes must wear this star, well, we will all wear it!*' That is the origin of this imagery which attracts you so much. But it is clear that the members of the royal family did maintain real contacts with the Jewish people in Denmark: they had Jewish friends, and often went to the Synagogue."

"And the Germans didn't react?"

"No . . ."

"What's your opinion why the Nazis, contrary to what they did in the rest of Europe, did not force the persecution of Jews in Denmark right from the start of the Occupation?"

"They had their reasons, and Denmark was in an extraordinary situation compared with the other occupied countries. We had a government which, without a protest, gave in to the Germans. They lived in the delusion that we could stay neutral. It took the Danish people three years to demonstrate to the government that such a position, apart from any moral indignation, was not sustainable. During these three years, the Resistance was built up, bit by bit . . . To revert to the Nazis, we can say that Hitler, tactically, decided to accommodate Denmark. His troops and his political agents had to reinforce the illusion of 'cooperation,' the illusion that they were there to 'protect': their propaganda was 'friendly,' and the recourse to bloody repressions was not therefore put in place. This relative clemency also was sustained because they didn't have any networks, supported by the Danish people, as was the case in other countries: here, no large Nazi Party to fervently welcome them, but a population feeling very ashamed at having been invaded without even defending itself, without the authorities even calling them to battle. Equally, I would like to add this, which was going to be decisive when saving the Jews: the Germans were short of boats. They had not been able to lay hand on the Danish naval fleet, which was scuttled—a bit like the French fleet at Toulon. The patrol boats were too few in number, insufficient to allow them to control our coasts and the 500 islands with which they were faced . . . And then about the 29th of August 1943, after the government resigned, the Danish police had deserted, en bloc, to the Resistance, and they too participated in the evacuation of the Jews."

"How was the mobilization of the fishing boats, necessary for the general evacuation of the Jews, carried out?"

"We had to improvise everything: find hiding places, find boats, find money. My father had already arranged for two Czech Jews to escape to Sweden. We had contacts with the fishermen, and we were able to hire their boats. In fact, the difficulty wasn't the money nor the boats: it was, at least at first, to make contact with the Jews and to lead them to the embarkation points."

"The fishermen wanted to be paid to take the Jews?"

"The fishermen had different attitudes. Certain ones belonged to the Resistance and wanted nothing. Others were frightened, in case they would be caught by the Germans, that they would confiscate their boats: they therefore wanted the ability to buy another one . . . They forgot that if they were arrested, the Germans would also confiscate their lives! Other fishermen, finally, had simply decided that this situation constituted an opportunity to make money . . . Don't push! It is clear that the most honorable are among the first kind, those who acted without asking a penny. But, all the fishermen, it is true, were in the front line for that evacuation."

A curious thing, very far from that I had always understood, the fact of learning that certain Danish fishermen had not risked their lives for the Jews absolutely free of payment made me rejoice. They are normal, then, these Danes! They also have their faults, their pettiness, their small-mindedness.

*"All human beings have merits and vices,"* said Maimonides, that Jewish follower of Aristotle from Córdoba, in the twelfth Century, and he *"in whom the merits outweigh the vices is a Just man." "It even applies,"* he added, *"for one country": ". . . if the merits of all the inhabitants of a country exceed their vices, that country is good. If their vices predominate, that is a bad country."*

In this, perhaps too mechanical, appreciation, Maimonides

introduces an element of Jewish thinking which has always fascinated me: responsibility—responsibility of one towards others. *"Because he is the one man in which something good is found,"* says the Bible (Kings I, 14, 13). Or, on the contrary: *" . . . Even one sole fisherman destroys many good things"* (Ecclesiastes, IX, 19). The idea is simple: We are all in the same boat, and if one of us, one single person, makes a hole in it, we all risk drowning. Everyone depends on the individual and the individual depends on everyone. When I write about a man doing good, maybe saving all humanity, I am not talking about saving bodies but of a certain idea of Man and Humanity: that which allows for hope. And the fact that we hope gives us reason to live.

Primo Levi gives us this example in *If it is a man*. Apropos an individual, in a death camp, who shares his meager ration of soup with him, he writes:

> [It is because of him] that I am still alive today, not so much for his material aid as for having constantly reminded me, by his presence, by his simple and easy manner of being good, that there still existed, outside of our own, a just world, pure beings and things of integrity which neither corruption nor barbarity have contaminated, which remained strangers to hate and fear; something indefinable, like a far away possibility of goodness, for which it was worth the trouble of staying alive.

The stories of the Just, among which there are many about Danes, bring to us this *something indefinable, like a far away possibility of goodness,* for which one still wants to suffer, to hope, to live.

"When I think again about those years," emphasizes Jorgen Kieler, "I find them very inspiring and full of challenges. It was necessary to find the dividing line between Good and Evil, to know who were friends and who the enemies. I know: we cannot forget the persecutions, the extermination, nor Auschwitz . . . We cannot ignore them. But we must discover, even if it proves infamous, the positive side of those years: in this wave of massacres, there was, and justly, the courage of the Danish people who knew they must save 7,000 of their Jewish compatriots. The positive in such moments, is when someone takes the risk of sacrificing himself so that others may live."

He went quiet for a few minutes, in a thoughtful mood. Then he added this, which made me think of the secret resources of Good, capable of manifesting itself even in Evil's own obnoxious den:

"The Jews have had their saviors, but we also have had ours! You know, I myself was saved several times from the Germans. After a general strike in Copenhagen, I was arrested with all my family, and we were to be shot. We escaped the firing squad thanks to a Gestapo agent! Later (they sent us to a camp), I was saved again, by an SS doctor this time: I was beaten and stoned (yes with stones!) with a friend because we were not working hard enough for the camp. My friend died. The doctor, who picked me up in a pitiable state, not only cared for me, but, learning that I was a medical student, gave orders for me to work with him from then on; that's what saved my life! A kind of professional solidarity . . . Between doctors, we look after each other. There was also another doctor in Portovesfelica camp, a Frenchman, a detainee like me, and he also saved my life. You see: there are always more saviors than you think!"

Yes, perhaps. But, taking account of their extreme rarity, each time, they seem to take part in a miracle. In Denmark, it is the opposite, it is the large number of Just people, itself, which is the miracle.

Miracle? "No, there must be a willingness," said Henny Sundoe. And, like the Polish lady, Irena Sendler, she insists: "But you must *want to, want to!*" Then, why did some—and not others—*want to?*

I know I ask the same question repeatedly, but from different angles. Insomuch that I have not found a rational answer to this question, the word *miraculous* risks reappearing under my pen. Perhaps because *"miracles only appear to the miraculous, and not to mathematicians,"* as the American philosopher, Ralph Waldo Emerson, wrote.

# 31

# The Sundoe family

''**My** attitude, and that of all my friends, was simple: we could not admit that it had happened, that the Germans had occupied Denmark without encountering the least resistance. And we could not accept the persecution of the Jews. The Jews were our friends, they were Danes. We had never had the least problem with them. It was obvious that we must help them. The Protestant organization to which I belonged had been aware for some time of the danger that threatened them.''

Blond, a little scarf tied around her neck, Henny Sundoe tells of the action taken by her father and her family without raising her voice and without any harshness. However, under the calm, under the self-control, a blazing fire continues to glow. The intensity of feeling shows, and burns, in these passionate glances, giving out sparks of indignation and disgust. Yet another being who never succumbed in any way to the seduction of barbarity. An inflexible passion: quite simply, this is the force which motivated this Danish woman, who did not hesitate to brave the wrath of the Nazi occupation forces.

At the time, in 1943, aged twenty-three, she participated in the rescue of the Jews, along with her brother and her father: the latter, right in the middle of the Copenhagen docks, had a nineteen-ton mail-boat under his control (of which she still has a model). This boat was called *Gerda III* and carried several hundred Jews out of German reach, to Sweden.

"My father found a new quay where he could moor the boat.

This quay, on the other side of Copenhagen, was very close to Vilter's Place alongside a warehouse and he moored *Gerda III* there. My task was, every evening, about six o'clock, to go and look for Jews, to assemble them in groups of twenty, twenty-five people and to guide them to the warehouse, where we hid them. From there they had to cross the quay in the dark to get on the boat. The main difficulty was that they had to slip across in between all the comings and goings of the German patrols watching the Copenhagen port installations. This quay was no different from all the others . . . When I recall it, it was incredible, fantastic: In Copenhagen we weren't allowed to go out at night, it was forbidden, and I went all those times scorning the danger—with a sort of dread, and ardor. Five journeys every night, and the Jews we brought passed the night in the warehouse granary, watching for favorable moments to cross the quay. In the warehouse we left them something to eat and drink, and, also, sleeping draughts to make the children sleep, as it was essential that no noise could be heard by the German soldiers patroling outside.

"The boat was in the postal service, it couldn't lift anchor till seven o'clock in the morning. When it started its engine, the two Germans on duty came on board to check the papers, and the other official documents and authorizations. They never once thought to go down into the hold, where they would have found our Jewish guests. It must be said that, every morning, the crew offered drinks to the two soldiers: they toasted each other and talked about the rain and . . . good weather . . . Then the Germans went back on the quay, and the boat could weigh anchor and take our friends out of danger. We reckoned we evacuated between 600 and 700 Danish Jews on the *Gerda III*. Besides, after we saved them, there were others: the refugees from Poland, Danish Resistance, English parachutists. We clandestinely evacuated all of them to set them down on the Swedish coast."

"All the same, weren't you frightened during all those nights—those dangerous nights?"

"I think we were all very nervous, naturally, and tense. I

was always apprehensive of these nightly clandestine walks, leading Jewish families through the streets of Copenhagen. But, we were young, we had ideals, we considered we had a certain task to accomplish. When we were in action, we weren't scared. It was *afterwards* that we felt it."

"Do you often think of those times?"

"Without doubt, there has not been a single day, in fifty years, when I have not thought of the war. Of the persecution, but also of all that followed after, with the Resistance, where I lost many of my friends. You never forget such things. It was our youth—and it was the war. I think of it every day, yes . . ."

# 32

# Rabbi ben Melchior

Arriving on the invitation of King Christian IV in 1662, the Jews had been established in Denmark for 278 years when the Second World War broke out. They were originally Sephardis from Amsterdam and Ashkenhazis with a history in Hamburg. There were never many of them, and they stayed in Copenhagen and its environs. This geographical split up hasn't changed much with time. Very quickly they became . . . Danish. This will be a constant fact which their rescuers will confirm. One of them even said: ". . . the Jews? Danes like us, with their Sunday on Saturday, but that didn't bother anyone!"

Other than the beauty of its port nestling in the northern mists, Copenhagen appears a well-ordered city, very clean. The very beautiful old town has at its center a huge square with a surrounding wall: This is the Jewish Cemetery, with the tombstones leaning over, a bit like in Central Europe, but better kept, well maintained by the State authorities. On crossing through, I notice that the family name Brandes often reoccurs. I think about the Danish novelist and essayist George Brandes, who was one of the authors my mother preferred . . .

But how did this Jewish community in Denmark, with its much more enviable fate, compared to other Jewish communities in Europe, react to the news of the roundup scheduled for the beginning of October 1943?

"I remember," recounts the great Rabbi ben Melchior, "that after the woman who warned us of the imminent roundup had gone, we organized ourselves so as to warn as many people as possible. Because of the curfew, it was forbidden to go out at night. We telephoned innumerable friends, who, in their turn, telephoned others. We didn't know whether or not our communications were being tapped, but we had to move quickly! Next morning we went to the synagogue very early. That evening we were due to celebrate Rosh Hashana, the Jewish New Year. About a hundred people were there. My brother and I were sent to town: by bicycle. We visited neighbors and friends of neighbors to pass on the message. As a first thought we gave instructions to the Jews to leave for the country, as if for a walk or a holiday. But the country implied the seaside, the coasts, fishermen with their precious boats . . . As all the Jewish community lived in and around Copenhagen, we were sure that with the concerted effort of one and all, every Jew had been alerted of the danger. The Germans had to be blind enough . . . wasn't it natural, on a day like that, Rosh Hashana, that the Jews would go for a walk in the country? But improvisation is the Danes' strength, and it worked . . ."

Ben Melchior, who was forty in 1943, participated in those events. Today, he is an old man, still with a strong face and expressive mouth, whose smile and natural affability is tinged with melancholy, serious at the thought of that period of anguish.

"That evacuation saved my life and my family's, and it saved 7,000 Jews, who were transported, safe and sound, to Sweden. This collective rescue is, without doubt, much more important than if one only looks at the numbers on their own, because, of course, it only represents one per thousand of those who perished in the camps and elsewhere. But I think this event is capital for the future. There was a time when I was loath to speak of it; but now, today, I see that we must not forget: we must not forget the violence, the Nazi barbarities, the darkness of those far-off days. But also we must not forget what remained, in this Europe painted in black, forces which understood and who wanted to give fraternity, solidarity, humanity! . . . And the fact that these forces were able to exist and assert themselves in the middle of the darkness is decisive, if not the shadows would always win."

"And your crossing to Sweden, on this little fishing boat which smelled strongly of fish?"

"Many ideas cross your mind when you find yourself in the hull of a little boat like that, as if one is oneself a sardine in a sardine can, and one thinks of many things, but the prime preoccupation is always to know if one is going to come out alive. And that smell of fish, ah . . . ! I think that much of what I have done since—the fights for human rights, the campaigns for solidarity, etc.—I owe to that childlike anguish in that shell of a boat crossing the narrows with all lights extinguished so as not to be seen by the German patrols. Yes! We had to leave our homes, our country, and hide as if we were the criminals! It was so absurd! And, happily there were people to help us. Those hours then have many, many times over counted for me, towards my future existence: in a certain way, they have made me what I am."

# 33
## Boats to Sweden

The Melchior family was taken to Sweden by Niels Sorensen's father. So I am on my way to the port of Guillelai to meet that Just man's son. He is a fisherman, a true Danish fisherman, who practices his skills in the same way as his father before him. A corpulent figure, in his long overalls supported by thick braces, white hair escaping all around his sailor's cap. A large scarf tied round his neck disappears into the collar of his donkey-jacket, large spectacles on a round smiling face, Niels Sorensen is leaning with his elbows on the side of his boat, feet well anchored with the natural stance of a man well used to walking on a rolling deck. His smiling good nature, his humorous modesty, immediately awakens a fellow feeling.

"Did the Danish Jews cross over to Sweden on this type of boat, or on some other kind?"

"Yes," Niels Sorensen replies, "it was the same type. Not the same boat you see now, but all the same, exactly alike."

"What age were you when the Jews were evacuated?"

"Sixteen."

"How did you come to be involved in the adventure?"

"That's simple: I was working on my father's fishing boat. The local councillors, the doctors, the Protestant Pastors, and many of the villagers came to see if we could help the Jews evacuate to Sweden. Thirteen hundred Jews left from here, from the port of Guillelai."

"Your father, what was his religion, Jewish?"

"At the time, at my age, you didn't ask your father such awkward questions . . . It was our mother who told us children, that these people, these Danes, were going to be persecuted by the Germans and that they needed our help. It was she who encouraged us to take part in that evacuation."

"Were you afraid?"

"It wasn't then that we were afraid, but later, in the last six months of the war: my father had been arrested and sent to a concentration camp. Me . . . , I had to escape to Sweden, and the Germans confiscated our boat. It was returned to us at the end of the war."

"And where did you hide the Jews, on this little boat?"

Niels Sorensen, on the bridge, lifts a square trapdoor about forty-five centimeters across.

"They went down there, and disappeared in the hull. If they squeezed up, it could carry five or six. They could only take one little bag for the journey: all big cases or bulky packages would have taken the place of another person . . . Once they were all in the hold, we shut the trapdoor, and we stacked our nets and ropes on top. The Germans who inspected the boat never suspected that, under the nets and ropes, there was a trapdoor! We made many trips to Sweden, then, many . . ."

"How long did the crossing take?"

"An hour and a half—two hours, depending on sea conditions."

"Do you often think of those times?"

"Of course!"

Christian Algreen-Petersen is practically the same age as Niels Sorensen; he was seventeen at the time of the evacuations. For him, also, the Danish Jews were Danes, compatriots. He participated in these operations with his parents. He tells us that they continued until after the 2nd of October: until after mid-October, in fact. His father, like the majority of Danish doctors, is distinguished by an unfailing devotion towards the Danish Jews who had to flee. He was in touch with other doctors and with the hospitals to find the money needed to pay the fishermen.

"How did your father and you plan your actions?"

Christian Algreen-Petersen's answer reminds me of the words of Rabbi Melchior apropos the Danish capacity for improvisation: "We didn't plan anything at all!" he responds. "This threat of a roundup came so quickly, and in such an unexpected way! It was one of those situations you can be faced with all of a sudden. And everyone came to do what they could—or at least nearly everyone. But most of the Danish people opened their doors to the Jews and provided them with hiding places, then clandestine gathering centers to permit the organization of their evacuation to Sweden. It was . . . how can I say? . . . it was like an official secret that everyone knew, to gather information necessary to put the evacuation under way."

"What happened, at your parents house? How did the Jews you were going to save get there?"

"They came from everywhere! At home, the telephone never stopped ringing, and my mother had to understand, without having it spelled out to her, whether the calls were from genuinely sick people needing a consultation, or Jews who needed, well . . . , something else . . . The reception rooms, the bedrooms, all the house was full of people waiting until someone found them a boat. My mother looked after the administration of this exodus: she made lists of names and addresses, with an inventory of their possessions. They needed money and, besides the collections that we had organized, it was decided that the better-off Jews would help those who were poorer. I saw some very moving scenes of people who had to give up enormous suitcases and parcels which they had brought with them: there was not much room on the boats, and priority was not for baggage, but for humans. Several of them remained emotionally submerged, for ages without a break, as they could not understand why they had to abandon their personal belongings. I must say that they were all very upset, full of anguish during the event . . . We had organized a taxi rank in front of the house, safe taxis, drivers we knew, who would not denounce us—and five at a time, every three minutes, a group of Jews accompanied by a non-Jew (I made several of those journeys!) crammed into a taxi to go to the point of embarcation. On average each of the boats with which we worked could take about ten people. In the beginning they were stuffed with twenty. Other boats took more, but they were really taking too many chances.

"What did this action of helping the Jews signify for the Danes? What consequences did the rescues have for them?"

"When, on the 29th of August 1943, the cooperation between the government and the German authorities foundered, many people wanted to fight the Germans. And then, all of a sudden, the announcement of the next round of persecutions which were to be loosed on the Jews! It was that which acted as a sort of trigger—these persecutions almost came like a present from Heaven: with a single blow, we had something to do, a path of action to follow, a meaningful task! A present from Heaven, yes: we could help all these innocent people who were our friends, and, at the same time, work against the Nazis. All that prepared the way for the underground work which was carried out within the framework of the Resistance, which grew, and was reinforced after this event. Many of those who took part in saving the Jews kept contact with the Resistance . . . If the Jews have a liability to the Danes (and they never cease declaring that they have), then, we too, the Danes, owe a debt of gratitude to the Jews for the task we were given and for the opportunity which they offered us in being able to help them: they obliged us, by letting us save them, and, in so doing, safeguarding our self-respect."

# 34

# Generous? or Just?

I am reflecting on the stories that these Danes I have just left told me. One question comes to mind: What happens if there are no Just men, only generous ones? Another question emphasizes this latter: is there any difference between the two? Is generosity, itself, not a rare and marvelous quality?

To be generous, someone says, is to be capable of wanting to give. But, can one *want* at any time? Can one be ready to give to all? From the point of view of this consideration of Good a Just person does not have to want to do good: he does it. He doesn't choose those good deeds from which he will profit: he gives. He does. Naturally. In a banal way. Each time that a life is in danger. Because that is what he thinks he should do.

Others say to us that, if generosity was absolute and universal, she would dispense Justice to us. Perhaps this would be sad. True, it is preferable to be saved thanks to a generous gesture (or even simply one of charity) than to perish—but my dream, since the Just give us things to dream on, remains that one saves life because everyone has the right to life. That is Justice.

One can also maintain that there is no generosity without love. But I have already said: a Just person does not have to know, or even like the person he saves.

Let us take an extreme example: a river where someone is drowning. We hear the cries for help. A crowd gathers on the bank. Among the crowd present at the scene, there are two or three people who think about calling for assistance, to warn the Fire Brigade, the police. A few even take a few steps into the water. It is an anonymous individual, without any particular physical attributes, who, suddenly, pushes through the crowd, dives in, and saves the unfortunate person being dragged away by the current. But, having heaved the latter onto the bank, he disappears as he came. Modestly. Without explanations, without waiting for thanks or compensation of any kind. What one is left with despite searching to find it, as I have with those who saved Jews during the war, is to ask *why*—why he stretched out his hand to a stranger—and he won't reply. Or, at best, he will say: *because*. Reply (yet nonanswer) of the perfect Just man. But is there a single category of the Just? One single way of being Good?

With their collective rescue, the Danes introduce a new dimension to my research. This then obliges individuals who participate in the saving of others to give a rational explanation, over and above this famous *because*. The generosity which characterizes them is not, however, the sole motivation of their engagement. Perhaps it is no more a determinant than in other cases, those individuals who figure in this book. On the other hand, they express it in a very forceful manner in the explanations they give; this is how I met the Danish rescuers who were recognizant of those they rescued, of those they had actually saved, in that they had given them the chance to discover and become a part of the Good.

But the Danes still pose one more problem: that of the efficacy of collective actions against the Germans. In fact, I have noted, in the course of this enquiry, that each time a collection of people have had the courage to oppose an iniquitous decision made by the Hitlerian powers, they have won their case. Even in Germany itself, on the one time that they came together to take on a cause, the churches succeeded in making Hitler give up one of his objectives: the extermination of the mentally ill. In this regard, recent research carried out in the Gestapo archives show that the Nazi regime feared the activities of the church more than those of the Communist Party.

I have already told you, in my account of my meeting with Baron Loewenstein de Witt, of the collective German objection in favor of mixed couples and their children whom the Gestapo, in February 1943, had interned at 2–4 Rosenstrasse in Berlin with the intention of deporting them. Thanks to the week-long demonstrations organized in the streets by the families of these mixed couples, Goebbels had been obliged to liberate them. On the 5th of March 1943, he himself wrote in his diary: "The action engaged by the Gestapo against the Jewish husbands and wives has had to be called off because of the protests it created."

Another example of collective action is in Bulgaria. Under the pressure of public opinion and the Orthodox Church, and in spite of the alliance between Bulgaria and the Axis, King Boris had to interrupt the deportation of the Jews. And, unique deed in the history of Occupied Europe, the Bulgarian government, on the 25th of August 1944, abolished all anti-Semitic text from the country.

Even in France, when, upset by the great roundup of Vel'd'hiv', ecclesiastic personalities, led by Cardinal Garlier and Pastor Boegner, finally began to protest publicly against the deportations, the number of these slowed down. Furthermore, Laval was obliged to explain to his Nazi friends that because of the difficulties intervention was causing, from then on, it would be difficult for him to furnish Germany with regular contingents of Jews for deportation. The fact is that the two German generals in charge of the problem, Hohberg and Knochen, agreed with this advice!

But, while some massacred and others, very few in number, it is true, tried to save lives, what was everybody else doing?

# 35

# Ships of ill fortune

Yes, what was everybody doing while the Jews were being massacred? This nightmare of a question torments my mind each time I manifest my solidarity with the persecuted. I am not looking for reciprocity—do unto others what has been done to you. No, I want to understand: why the death of children in Rwanda today is insupportable, when, only yesterday, the death of Jewish children left world opinion indifferent?

*What was the world doing?* This interrogation is not addressed to those who were here at the time, in the shadow of the concentration camps, to our neighbors, to our compatriots. Among them, I have met men and women who opened their doors wide to the persecuted. We may remember that Dutch woman, Henriette Kroon. To the question: "When did you decide to save Jews?" she answers: "I decided nothing. A man knocked on my door. He said he was in danger. I asked him to stay, and he stayed till the end of the war. He was the first."

Henriette Kroon is a Just person.

Now, when I ask *what was the world doing* when they were massacring the Jews, I am thinking of people living far from Europe, as far as we are today from Rwanda or Somalia. Yes, to continue the battle for the respect of human rights which I and others have led for so long, I need to understand how the people of the United States, Australia, Latin America, the

Orient, and Asia behaved—everywhere where they were still free to react to echoes of the cries of the victims. How did they react, faced with these thousands of German Jews who, since before the war, fled the Nazi regime wandering the seas on all kinds of ships?

To make my film, *Tzedek*, I had to go through many files: kilometers of film newsreels of the time, sourced from these countries. From these sessions I came out in a state of consternation, thunderstruck. Let's recall the atmosphere and some facts.

The 9th of November 1938, in Germany, it is *Crystallnacht:* hundreds of synagogues destroyed, libraries burned, 25,000 Jews deported to the concentration camps of Dachau, Buchenwald, and Sachsenhausen.

One year later, German troops invade Poland.

The 20th of May 1940 Auschwitz camp was opened.

The 31st of July 1941 the most odious of projects, the *Final Solution,* was defined and put in process—that is the program for the complete, definitive, extermination of a whole people . . . the Jewish people, who were, according to the vows of Hitler and his associates, to disappear from the face of the earth.

Those who lived during that period in free countries and who did not manifest the least spirit of solidarity with the persecuted respond today: "We did not know," or again: "Television didn't exist then; we did not have any pictures which would have made these impossible stories credible to us."

These pictures did exist! Actual films, and one of the 'dailys' of the time are full of reports showing these Jews who, despairing of heart, attempted to flee from their executioners, and approached—in vain—the American shores. The terrestrial frontiers were closed to them. Stay at sea. Ships of every kind traveled back and forth, overloaded with thousands of refugees: the first boat-people this century, no one could have been unaware of them.

Ships of bad luck, of which some of the names are still known, along with their odysees: they were called the *Saint-Louis*, the *Struma*, the *Mefkura*, the *Pancho* . . .

In May 1939 the *Saint-Louis* left Hamburg, with 907 Jewish refugees on board. Arriving close to the American coast, the ship was turned back. It was redirected towards Havana: at the idea of having to return to Germany, several passengers committed suicide. For some weeks the boat wandered the oceans. No one wanted to accept them. In the end, out of compassion for his passengers, the captain, a German, made the British authorities accept them: by beaching his vessel voluntarily, abandoning it on the English coast.

At that moment, this changed public opinion. Holland, France, and Belgium agreed to welcome some of these refugee families. Alas, these three countries were soon to be occupied, and the survivors of the *Saint-Louis* who found refuge there were to be recaptured and sent to Auschwitz . . .

Several more boats, full of illicit Jews, desirous of reaching Palestine, then under British mandate, appeared out of Romania. These included the *Struma* in 1942, the *Mefkura* in 1944. They were turned away by the Royal Navy, and finished by sinking in the Bosporus . . .

Only the nearly 800 Jewish passengers of the *Pancho,* which scuttled near the Palestine coast, following the example of the *Saint-Louis,* were fished out of the sea by the English—the same English, after this forced rescue, didn't hesitate to send the unhappy escapees to internment camps built in Sudan and Kenya!

Desperate wanderers who were refused access to ports of call or welcome, persecuted, abandoned to the waves, and rejected by the world: here we are very far from the magnificent gesture of the Danes, who, conversely, in 1943, used the sea and their frail fishing boats to remove their Jewish compatriots from the Nazi persecution.

Yes, memory of the Danes, in regard to the indifference of the rest of the world towards the Jewish tragedy, is a slight comfort, even if the comfort is there to attest, over and above everything, to the presence of Good even in the depth of darkness.

Law, Good, Evil . . . No one has appointed me to think about them. I am driven by a devouring anguish. People, my parents, life itself, have transmitted to me a pessimistic, hopeless idea of humanity: nobody, no, no one is going to help us.

I continue in my search for the Just to be able to contradict this last statement, to contradict the categoric character of this astounding opinion, to prove it mistaken and, in fact, wrong. It is because justice does not exist that I must do it. And, to prove it true that the Just do come along to undermine the proposal that *no one* is going to help us.

However, the essential is not to know the past, but to establish an idea of the past which one can use as a base for comparison to understand the present. I ceaselessly review the information which I have gathered on the behavior of people of yesteryear, like a game of mirrors, against the reactions of people today. Each *idea of the past* can, in effect, *be used to serve as a comparison*. From this comes our concerns about the massacres of today being perpetrated in Rwanda, in ex-Yugoslavia, and Chechnya.

On the 6th of July 1938, on the initiative of the American president, Franklin D. Roosevelt, a conference was held in Evian, at which thirty-two nations were represented, with their objective, the solution of the refugee problem, of these Jews, of these antifascists fleeing Nazism. Now, at the inauguration of this conference, it must be accepted that every one of these States represented was disposed to welcome the persecuted . . .

In America, at least until the surprise attack by the Japanese on the naval base at Pearl Harbor, the general opinion was as hostile to the idea of intervention in Europe as it was to a mass intake of refugees. They talked about the "threshold of tolerance," and Charles Lindbergh, the first man to cross the Atlantic in an airplane, paraded on Fifth Avenue, New York, at the head of an immense demonstration whose objective ("nonintervention in Europe") and the slogan ("Don't fight the Jews' war") was all the more scandalous as numbers of these Jews were already rotting in the ghettos and the camps. There again, how can we accept the idea that all Americans at the time would have taken the same stance as Charles Lindbergh? But, for all that, what could they do?

We know that someone who plunges into a river to save a drowning man—and does it without asking for thanks or recompense—is one of the Just. Yet, what happens if the same individual finds himself on the opposite bank? This question was raised by Vitas Landsbergis, a past President of Lithuania. "This individual sympathizes," he often replied to me.

But, can we not be generous without feeling pity? We are not bound to take on the suffering of others to ourselves, but if we can, it brings us solace.

In America, those who tried to ease the pain of their peers in Occupied Europe did exist. Also, there did exist there those who risked their lives to assist the persecuted to escape from the Nazi hell. But they have kept quiet about these "humanitarians" from 'before the event,' as simple and modest as those Justs in occupied countries. Did they act thanks to the same love of life, to the same natural thirst for Good?

These questions have led me to abandon, for the moment, the path I have been following, since the start of this book, across Europe in the direction of Italy and France. This detour will take me via America, then through Switzerland: these two countries of which millions of individuals dreamed, whilst on the roads or the high seas, fleeing the swastika.

# 36

## New York, New York

"At the time, I didn't bother much about *what was going on*. I have told you: I was twenty-five, rich and American . . . I lived in Paris and Paris belonged to me. A bit like Hemingway's novels. We danced a lot. We drank a lot, we had fun. It was better not to think of what was happening in Germany . . . And America wasn't at war. In 1939, I was in love with a young man, a little fling. Because of him I found myself in Marseilles. But once there, he left me. Good riddance! I met Marianne Davidport, a friend, and all those refugees waiting for a miracle! . . . I understood, I was touched by their stories, by the fate of all these hunted people. I was available, I had money, I could help: this adventure attracted me. In the end the frivolous became serious . . . And then, little by little, we were all to meet again during 1940 . . ."

New York; 68th Street, between Park Avenue and Fifth Avenue; seventh floor. Mary Jane Gold sits in front of me in a black leather armchair: she has white curly hair, alert disposition, and is a fast talker. Elegant, slightly aristocratic, she is wearing a white jacket and her sophisticated makeup emphasizes the blue of her eyes when she laughs. She speaks excellent French, with a strong American accent. Bright eyes, round cheeks—Mary Jane Gold talks with conviction, in a serious voice, rooted in the memories which she is bringing back to light; here and there, a humorous point which adds sparkle to her story.

But this *what was going on* at the time, which Mary Jane Gold spoke of, what was that?

With the Occupation, Jews from the different countries concerned had to flee (or, for some of them, flee once more) through force of circumstances, in every direction still open to them. But the world is not all that big, and the refugees were going to find the escape routes, in turn, becoming cul-de-sacs, as in Lithuania, where the refugees from Poland, Czechoslovakia, and even from Holland were caught in a pincer movement between the Red Army and the advancing Nazis.

In their regions, the German, Belgian, and Austrian Jews, who, in the first instance, were able to escape to France, saw themselves forced by the Occupation to flee south along with the French Jews: very quickly, they reached the South of France . . . to find themselves blocked, backs to the sea.

At Marseilles, which at the time had a Jewish population of 15,000, these others who were arriving in their thousands, installed themselves in filthy small hotels. Among them the European elite: Marc Chagall, Max Ernst, Thomas Mann's daughters, Anna Mahler (who escaped with the last symphony written by Bruckner in her bag), Franz Werfel, Arthur Koestler, Hannah Arendt, Anna Seghers, Lion Feuchtwanger—without speaking of all those who stayed in the Hotel Terminus and others, who came to the town to visit their friends in danger: André Gide, André Breton, and the surrealists . . . A whole civilization in distress! All waiting, most often without money and in the midst of general indifference, to be able to gain a place on board some hypothetical ship.

The nongovernment organizations, as we know them today, did not yet exist. In America, there was not one framework within which a Good man would have been able to bring pressure to bear in favor of the persecuted. Then a group of universities created the Emergency Rescue Committee.

This group gathered money (several thousand dollars) for the refugees, but at first couldn't find anybody willing to take it to Marseilles. At last one volunteered. He was young, Protestant, he knew Nazi Germany, which he had visited in 1935 and

from where he returned horrified: his name is Varian Fry. It
was he who took the aid there and organized the departures to
America. Also, he knew how to build the indispensable networks without which an operation of this scale could not have
been accomplished.

Varian Fry, this other Just come from abroad, come from
America to save, apart from those in Marseilles, Jews and
antifascists from France and everywhere else, should he not be
one of those I must interview? Alas, he is no longer with us, but
his friends, members of his networks, of this *Marseilles channel*
are, at least a number of them, still with us.

"You know," Mary Jane Gold said to me, "Varian studied
Classics at Harvard. At first sight he wasn't cut out for this
mission. But, when at last, this organization was set up in
America, he had to take the money to Marseilles. Varian was a
liberal, that is, in American parlance, to the left of center. He
would say, laughingly: 'They could have found someone better
than me to do the work, but since, it appears to me they haven't
found anyone, well, here I am in Marseilles!' He arrived with
$30,000, I believe, and a list of 100 people to save: antifascists,
Jews, of whom a number were well-known artists and intellectuals who had found refuge in France up till then, and who
needed help to get them to the United States . . . Why did he
do it? Out of conviction, anti-Nazism. One day he told me
several things, which explained his disgust of Hitler and his
cronies. He had gone to Germany in 1935. In a cafe, sitting
close to him, was a fellow who looked Jewish. Two Nazis
arrived, SS or SA, I don't remember anymore. The Jew, the
supposed Jew, was a bit nervous when he lifted his glass. Then,
one of the Nazis went over, with one knife blow pierced his
hand! His hand was fixed to the table! He let out a cry, he
moaned with pain. The Nazi took back his knife, then went
away with his companion, and Varian heard them exclaim: 'It's
good to have Jewish blood on a German blade! Today, it's party
time! For us, it's a beautiful party day!' He saw all that, all that
infamous scene. I have always thought that incident that he had
told me about was a telling reason why, later, he took on the

Nazis. That is why he went to France. He understood what happened, what was going to happen. He kept himself informed. He told me about the terrible things that had taken place in Eastern Europe. And he revealed to me that some very important people, writers, painters, musicians, fleeing from the Nazis found themselves blocked at Marseilles, and that he had to help them."

"Did the American Consulate in Marseilles give you its support for this aid operation?"

At this question, it is Marianne Davidport who answers with vivacity and emphasis in her tone. She was the first to have been contacted by Varian Fry at the time. It was she who introduced Mary Jane Gold to him. She too is a white-haired lady, full of verve, and who forgets nothing. The American Consulate at that time? In a critical fashion, and with all the irony she can muster, dotting all the *i*'s and crossing all the *t*'s:

"Oh no! the Consulate didn't help us! Never! On the contrary: they didn't like our 'clientele,' they didn't like the work Varian was doing. They found us a burden, irritants . . . The American Consul General did not like the English. He thought the English were going to lose the war, that it was the Germans who would win!"

An elderly man intervenes. This is Jean Guimilip, also one of Varian Fry's group and a friend of long-standing of Mary Jane and Marianne: "No, it was in '41 . . . In '40, Varian created the Emergency Rescue Committee . . ."

As often happens in a meeting with several people who are all passionate about the same subject, the same common shared experience, everyone suddenly starts talking at the same time.

Marianne Davidport describes the circumstances: "When the Germans invaded France, I was in Montpellier where I was studying Rabelais. America was not at war yet. Because of the advancing German armies, I went to make contact with my consulate in Marseilles. In principle, being American, I had no cause for alarm. And it was there that I became acquainted with a young American university man like me: Varian Fry. At the time he was running a certain 'American Aid Center'. We talked about it . . . and he enlisted me in his adventure! There weren't very many of us: a few Americans, two or three French, and we had very little money. Now, to get these people out of this mousetrap that Marseilles had become was going to take a great deal of money . . ."

At this moment Jean Guimilip intervenes, and defines: "Yes huge amounts of money were needed. But, also, false papers and a network of smugglers and spies. And if our lodgers were to cross Spanish or Portuguese frontiers to travel to Lisbon, we also had to find visas. 'Cause everyone looked towards the ocean, sir . . . The ocean: their one chance to escape death . . . All these exiles wanted to reach the Atlantic and from there the other side of the Atlantic: the American continent, specially the United States. But the *Law of Quotas* of 1924 limits the number of entry visas into this country which, at its origins, was founded by emigrants, exiles, and outlaws from the world over. Protectionism, a certain diffuse and disdainful anti-Semitism: requests for visas were often turned down. Besides, candidates for emigration were not authorized to leave French soil until they could obtain a guarantee that an American would look after them. Over and above they had to have a bank draft drawn on the Banque de France. And finally, having complied with these two conditions, it only remained to find a place on one of the three or four American packet boats available, which were profiting from the situation by setting prohibitive tariffs."

Jean Guimilip explains: "The crossing cost a minimum of $5,000 per person. And you must imagine how difficult it was, in a city full of informers, patrolled by the Vichy police, to gather together and hold on to such sums!"

He was quiet for an instant. Then, above the loud wailing of the New York police sirens: "It was dangerous. Today, I can think about it. Besides, some of our crowd were arrested, and some deported . . . And then, here and there, we ran into some young thugs, apprentice gangsters, who tried thereafter to 'make us sing'—blackmail!"

"Where did you find all this money?"

Marianne Davidport intervened, this time: "That again was Varian's work. He knocked on every door, and some of them opened. Few, but important ones. The first to respond to his appeal was Peggy Guggenheim, the very rich collector who championed the artists; then there were Metro Goldwyn Mayer and the American Book of the Month Club. In spite of all this support, it was not so simple. It was necessary to pay off the French civil servants, to turn around the unwillingness of the American authorities . . . Also, to allow our proteges to work while waiting their departure, Varian hired a villa near Marseilles—a huge villa which he baptized 'Bel Air' . . ."

"Why did you do it? Why did you go to the aid of all those people?"

My question elicits general astonishment in my hosts.

"But, . . . what do you mean?"

"Well, why did you, Americans, spend so much time and energy to save people, far away in some part of France, . . . Marseilles?"

"Varian came quickly, yes. As for us, we were already there, and available," replied Mary Jane Gold. "And then, we had to help people in danger!"

I allowed myself an upsetting question, even insidious: "If so many of them hadn't been celebrities, would you have reacted in the same manner?"

"Do you doubt it?"

And Mary Jane, with a large smile, gave me the evidence: "Celebrities or not, people in danger, how could we not help them?"

I leave the old *Marseilles escape team*, Varian Fry's old network, thinking of an old debate, bearing on the application of the famous Commandment in Leviticus: *"Love thy neighbor as thyself."* It appears that a modicum of doubt persists on the object of this love. The order to *love thy neighbor,* is it referring to a member of the same people, the same family, or no matter what human being? In fact, the same word in Hebrew is used to designate a "friend," a "fellow-citizen," as well as sometimes for an "other." I am thinking also of the reaction of the

Just Danes: "The Jews were our friends, they were Danes," Henny Sundoe said.

And what if they had not been Danes? If they had been strangers? Leviticus (XIX, 33–34) replies: *"You must treat the stranger among you as if he were your own; you will love him as you love thyself."* And Henny Sundoe has, in fact, followed with her own evidence: "We think we evacuated 600 or 700 Danish Jews. But after we saved them, there were others: Refugees from Poland, British parachutists . . ."

And if they had not been *strangers among you,* but strangers come from faraway countries? Those who, like Varian Fry, found themselves far away but saw, in those dark times, people drowning on the other side of the Atlantic, what could they do? *"God created Adam on his own,"* replies the Talmud (Sanhedrin IV, 5), *"to make us see that he who saves a single human being saves the whole world and he who loses one man can be likened to he who loses the whole world."*

But the Psalmist does not yield: "What is Man to you for you to think of him?" he asks. Leviticus responds once more: Man is a *neighbor* for the man because both have been made in the image of the same God. From where the Commandment: *Love thy neighbor* . . . even if this neighbor is not always worthy of love. In this precise case, I will willingly replace the word *love* with that of *solidarity,* which appears more exact to me to qualify the behavior of these humanitarian Just people. The action of the *Marseilles escape team* having been accomplished in the name of—and in favor—of *humanity* suggests, by underlining the collective gesture of these young Americans, that it was humanity which drove them on. Humanity, that is to say, both the dignity of man and his sense of solidarity.

# 37

# Franco–Swiss border

In this Europe transformed into a gigantic concentration camp, the second country which millions, condemned to death, dreamed about was Switzerland. I think that, at that time, they dreamed even more about there than America because, being geographically nearer, it appeared more accessible. But along its frontiers were Nazi patrols, and ever watchful people ready to denounce them. To counter this, there were networks of countryfolk, priests, and pastors. Some of these paid for their commitment with their lives. Why?

"Because Abbé Reuze asked it of us. He said that we must help these persecuted people over the border. And then the Curé from Vegy brought them to the house and it was emphasized . . ."

"Have you any idea how many people you and your father helped in this way?"

"I don't know. Certainly more than a thousand. Yes, practically every night we sheltered several people, up to about twenty at a time, before taking them to Switzerland."

Thérèse Neury-Lancon is a large country woman, imposing stature with a sweet round face. Bringing back those years is not without distress for her, and tears often flow as she speaks.

The modest family farm, which, during the war, had ten cows and a horse was only a few meters from the Swiss frontier. Thérèse Neury-Lancon points out with her finger a line of trees, which stretches out for over a mile and is the border of the farm fields as well as the frontier.

"There were patrols. We always had to send someone ahead on their own, to scout, to warn us, to tell us the right moment when we could cross all the fields, make the woods, and pass the Jews through. It was hard work cutting the barbed wire. then lifting it so everyone could pass under it and cross the stream which ran at that point: The other side of the stream was Switzerland. There, there was a very nice customs man, Mr. Kurdi, who, occasionally, even gave a little money to these unfortunates so that they could pay for the tram into town."

Thérèse Neury-Lancon is the eldest of seven children. The youngest one was only eighteen months when her mother died, in 1937, and the young girl had, very early on, to face up to life.

When I asked why she and her father had helped unknown Jews escape the worst, she laughed

"Why? Well . . . I think that's normal, isn't it?"

"You knew what a Jew was?"

"Oh yes, in a Catholic environment, one couldn't not know that Christ was one of them."

And then, all of a sudden, as if to free herself from the burden of a secret, never shared before, she relates: "We were dealing with impoverished people, frightened, who were fleeing with old cases, badly tied up with string. It became very difficult, and much more dangerous, after the German Occupation replaced the Italians. Besides, the Germans were only here a fortnight when they arrested me. They kept me three weeks, and then let me go. We had been denounced. They only released me, on the 27th of October 1943, in order to try and trap my father, and therefore catch the whole network. However, he had gone into hiding, long before I was released . . . He was arrested in the end, yes . . . , on the 10th of February 1944, and I never saw him again."

Thérèse Neury-Lancon is crying.

I ask her: "Were you ardent practicing Catholics?"

"Yes," she says stifling a sob. "My father was a believer."

And then I learn that her father, François Lanson, in company with Abbé Reuze and his friend Perillat, were deported to Auschwitz, then transferred to Einsbruck, in Bavaria, where they met their deaths.

"François also suffered terribly . . .", she confided to me.

And this "also" bowled me over. Not "my family were not alone in their suffering," I knew that—but, equally, I know that they would so much have liked to have shared a little of the good luck with the others.

"And if it was all to happen over again?"

"I don't know . . . Perhaps, yes. You know, when one becomes old, you have less go, and you can see . . . you can see farther ahead than when you are young. My father was fifty when he died, he was still at the peak of his strength; that was hard to bear, it was so hard for him . . . But, . . . if it had to be again, . . . it would be the same."

I consider the distance which separates the farm from the border, beyond the trees. Over there, struggling through that rough ground, a thousand Jews passed by. I ask myself about this *"if it had to be again, it would be the same,"* that Thérèse Neury-Lancon felt. Why does this old woman, worn out by hard work, this peasant, daughter of a peasant, think she must do something for persecuted people?

# 38

# Education and Switzerland

I am walking along the Swiss border. In the distance, the sun sparkles on the snow-capped mountains. As in one of Hemingway's novels, and perhaps because of him, the chain of the Alps looks like a file of white elephants. Everything is calm and peaceful now. During the war, from place to place along the red barrier that marked the frontier, two armies were face to face.

"The one organized, disciplined, ranked—' in the Swiss fashion'," says another Just, René Nodot. This army, whose motto was: "the ship is full," then forbade access to one of the rare sanctuaries saved from the German Occupation of Europe. The other "army" resembled charity workers, unrecognized, without ranks, with the only password: *"You will choose life."* This army, this veritable army of the shadows, had sown, all along this Franco-Swiss border, clandestine stop-offs, assembly points, and setting-off points: Saint Julien-en-Genevois, Douvaine, Ville-la-Grande, Vegy, Jursy-en-Suisse, Saint-Cerques, and last of all Colognes-sous-Salèves.

I arrive there towards the end of the afternoon. The street climbs up to a little square that has a Protestant church to one side. Not far away, there is an old house, with a large cross on the top of the roof, next to a fountain. An old man, wearing a beret, comes to meet me. He supports himself on a thick walking stick, as if fearing that his thin frame will split in two.

We didn't waste time in reviving the period of the Second World War and its processions of persecutions.

"How was it able to happen? How could men like you and me let it happen?"

Gilbert Ceffa speaks: "It's our education. Yes, our education! As much in France as in Switzerland: at that time," he says, "it was an anti-Semitic education. For the 'religious' the Jews were the people of deicide. For others, economic parasites . . . Also, when Vichy and the Nazis rounded up the Jews pretending it was *for their own good,* to send them to work in the camps, everyone or nearly everyone was soon satisfied. 'Good riddance to bad rubbish!' they said—even in the left wing Swiss press! I think this is what explains the absence of reaction against the anti-Jewish laws issued by Vichy. This is what explains the quasigeneral indifference which followed the abrogation, by Petain and Laval, also in France, of the Marchandeau Law condemning all incitation to racial hatred. From that moment on, official hatred was maintained and it only reinforced the hostility toward the Jews which we had already inherited from our schooldays . . ."

Correctly, Gilbert Ceffa, pinned the problem on education. This had played such an important role in the choices which that generation had to make: "I was educated with the idea that you must help someone who needs it," said the Polish woman Irena Sendler; and the German woman Klara Munzer: "My mother repeated over and over: that which you do to the weakest of my brothers you do to me." Finally, René Raoul, shoemaker at Malzieu, in France, affirmed very simply: "It is because of my education that I did what I did."

Religious education teaches us that man was created in the image of God. That idea led to the concept of equality of man with God, or rather to the affirmation of the freedom of man in regard to God. This is the origin of the Humanist conviction, along which each man carries in himself all humanity.

The Lubavitch Rabbi tells: "On the first day of a festival, God invites us to enjoy a day of rejoicing; the second day, we invite

God to celebrate with us. The first day, it is God who orders us to carry out the observance; the second day, we instituted ourselves.

"Now this power of education, so dear to the philosopher Montaigne, does not explain everything. Did Cain and Abel not receive the same education, in the same environment? And yet . . ."

"You know," Cardinal Lustiger said to me one day, "there are two types of education. One touches upon mechanisms, stereotypes, and prejudices. The other, that is the education that gives courage. The mechanisms and the prejudices need to be respected, as they always reappear: our great democracies, lovers of right, defenders of the rights of man, constantly see the reappearance, like a kind of illness, in epidemic form, almost impossible to cure, this composite epidemic of hate, racism, willingness to exclude, to persecute, which more and more seriously disfigures the real world. Education, *efficient* education, will not, perhaps, only contain prejudices, but, above all, will awaken people to a sense of their liberty, waken them to their deepest internal liberty—but that they will not learn as easily as the multiplication tables. You cannot teach people how to be free like you would teach them to walk . . . And you will see that it is not enough to have been well educated: the anti-Semites with whom I mixed at the time, in Orleans, had received excellent educations—that didn't prevent them vaunting the 'virtues' of mass assassination! Education, then, is a most important task, but it is an infinite kind of work, since hate rears its ugly head incessantly. But, in the framework of this necessary education, I will come back to what I said a short while ago, and that it, perhaps, will be agreeable for all to learn, rightly: I wish to speak once more about the secret, stretched-to-the-limit link that unites all true believers, the real Christians, is the Jews. It, without doubt, results from a continuous history allied to the Messianic character of the two religions, but it has as a corollary the following observation: the persecution of the Jews by followers of the Christian faith has been resented by the victims as a doubly horrible crime since it emanated not from pagans, or people with no religion, complete strangers, but absolutely from 'cousin' populations, in principal using the same Bible, with the same values as themselves . . . Those, on the other hand, whom we call the *Just* and who have saved Jews clearly perceive this spiritual parentage, and it is by leaning on this that they have developed and gained strength, which for want of better words I will call *'religious love.'* They have seized on this fact: Israel is our source, our spring. You don't pollute your spring, you don't let it dry out. If someone does, if we accept that our spring can be polluted, we condemn ourselves to death, to die of thirst. We cannot not love our source . . ."

I come back to Switzerland: Calvinist, Catholic, Rousseauist, would it have also included Rabbi Lubavitch's paradox or Cardinal Lustiger's discourse in its philosophy? Fifty years ago, would it have even been possible, to postulate this discourse, in the time of Pope Pius XII?

The fact is that Switzerland, ostensibly neutral during the conflict, did not willingly allow foreigners to enter its territory; this virtual ban included refugees and victims of persecution. To be permitted to walk on Swiss soil, one had to obtain a visa which took a long time and was difficult to arrange.

In 1942 Switzerland defined her attitude: she declared that refugees of racial oppression could not be considered in the same way as political refugees . . . She did, however, allow for a few exceptions: pregnant women, people over sixty-five, children less than sixteen, and those with family in Switzerland. Thus, deserters and political refugees were admitted, but all the others and particularly the "racial refugees"—the Jews notably—were sent back . . . This is how, in the second half of the year 1942, 8,146 people were authorized to enter Switzerland, whilst 1,056 were turned back. In 1943 there were 13,452 admissions against 3,343 refusals. It was not simple, therefore, to gain access to the very neutral Swiss Confederation . . .

Gilbert Ceffa was not unaware of the difficulties that he would have to overcome in order that his persecuted refugees could find a haven of peace in this Switzerland which, by tradition, knew how to shield itself from the horrors of war. In sustaining this shield, its principal mission consisted in securing, and in making its frontier secure.

"At the beginning of the war," he said, "I was eighteen. I was being assisted by Abbé Gaston Desclouds, one of nature's strong men: they nicknamed him 'Abraham' . . . His Presbytery of Thonex, because of its favorable geographical location, quickly became a transit point for the French Resistance. I therefore helped pass hundreds of French Resistance into Switzerland . . . But, I didn't have much occasion to pass many Jews through—only two! And today, I am a bit ashamed. I could perhaps have passed more . . ."

Gilbert Ceffa goes quiet, assailed by thoughts, which, fifty years after the event, don't cease to trouble him. He explains: "When General Pierre de Benouville, one of the chiefs in the French Resistance, asked us to reserve our activities to only rescuing Resistance members, without bothering about the Jews, because he said 'they weren't really in danger,' the only one among us to protest was the Reverend Father Louis Favre who declared: 'I am at the service of those who suffer as well as those who fight.' But he was very much alone . . ."

As for Gilbert Ceffa, he is too modest. The network to which he belonged saved hundreds of children. All the parishes along the Franco-Swiss border played an essential role in these operations which were certainly not without danger. Abbé Maurice Jolivet, the Curé at Colognes-sous-Salèves, was shot by the Germans, and Abbé Jean Reuze, the Curé of Douvaine, died after being deported to Bergen-Belsen. At this point, it is worth noting the ecumenical dimension to this action, and therefore to this network, which contained many Catholics and priests who were in constant contact with Protestant organizations such as CIMADE, and with affiliated groups like the one from Lyons run by René Nodot.

I leave Gilbert Ceffa, but not the immediate vicinity of the Franco-Swiss border, to visit, on the French side, another of these *passers* who long ago helped so many unfortunates to escape the worst by 'passing' them from one country to another. Raymond Boccard is a Catholic monk: everyone in the monastery, which he has not left since before the war, affectionately call him "Brother Raymond." He is a very old man, fragile to the extent of seeming diaphanous. His hearing is poor and his voice frail, but his eye and spirit sparkle with a sort of perpetual joy. Occasionally, he makes me think of a happy elf or clown, who rejoices again, fifty years on, at having fooled the Germans. The monastery in which he lives is just on the border: outside the window on one side of the building is Switzerland; at the end of the garden, near a little stone wall, is also Switzerland—an ideal place then for passing refugees. Hundreds of Jews have crossed this garden, climbed that wall, jumped the Furon stream and the barbed wire, which is still there, ultimate slight obstacles before freedom.

"What did you do during the war, Brother Raymond? What was your role in this dangerous activity?"

Brother Raymond gives out a somewhat high-pitched laugh, goes to open the window, then scratches his head for a moment.

"There you are," he says, "That's what I did! You see, during the war, I opened the window!"

And he laughs again before adding: "Like that: I opened the window and scratched my head. That's it, my dangerous activity! Heroic, eh . . . ?"

The impulsive humor of this old religious man surprises and seduces me. All the same, I ask him to be more explicit. Brother Raymond, still smiling, consents to elucidate: "From this window, upstairs, you can see a long way: I therefore watched the German patrols who watched our part of the frontier. There was a small group of soldiers with guns on their shoulders. They always took the same route, and walked exactly along the border line, passing and repassing at regular intervals. We spent weeks studying their routines, timing their comings and goings with a stop-watch . . . When they got to the top near that huge pine tree you can see over there, that gave us three minutes for our proteges to run to the wall and climb the barbed wire without being seen by the men on patrol. So, when they arrived at the big pine, I scratched my head: that was the signal for our friends waiting down below, to run whilst the Germans were far away and had their backs turned towards us . . . There, my role was only a watchman."

"Who, in the monastery, took the decision to help all these people to cross the frontier?"

"Reverend Father Favre. He was in touch with the Intelligence Service to pass couriers and secret messages."

"When did you start to pass Jews across the border?"

"I think it was during 1941. Excuse my memory. Dates . . . you know . . ."

"Brother Raymond, when I talked to you just now about danger, you laughed, you joked about your 'heroism.' Your modesty and your sense of humor do you credit, but, all the same, what you did was very dangerous! Were you never afraid?"

Brother Raymond is still looking at me with this humorous look, but nevertheless answers me seriously: "No. I was never afraid. Not here. It could only have happened if I was caught outside by the Germans. When it happened—and it did happen—that our Jews, after having crossed the frontier, were sent back by the Swiss, they returned here to the monastery. Then, they slept in the barn, and we gave them all the necessities, food, drink, clothes, and the next day I would take them to Annemasse, with all their baggage, in my trailer: there I would pass them on to another network, who would try, in their turn, to help them into Switzerland. Sometimes they were afraid when we passed patrols en route. But, I wasn't afraid, and I would say to them: "Smile! Smile at me, *now!*" And we got away with it . . . If someone had asked us for our papers, you may be sure, we would all have ended up in concentration camps, but . . . , they smiled OK and the patrols passed by! Not one patrol ever stopped us to ask what was what . . . You say that I said this was not dangerous, no I didn't say that. But fear is not very useful. You know, our director was arrested at the time; he was six months in prison at Annemasse and they shot his father. How could we pretend there was no danger? But, danger or no, could I have stopped opening the window, looking all around, and scratching my head when the Germans had their backs turned?"

Brother Raymond smiles. He radiates a warm mischief—a false mischievousness—it is the mask of modesty that changes his face to hide his real nature, which is goodwill, stunning and jubilant goodwill. I know that very shortly, as soon as I will have left him, he will revert to his usual silence, he who today has talked much more than he is used to doing. And I remember one of those rare definitions of the word, which does not seem overdone, as it appears in one of Appollinaire's most beautiful poems, "The Pretty Redhead": "We wish to explore goodness, an enormous task when all refuse to talk about it."

Brother Raymond will not talk about it, but he will always scratch his head, while smiling out of the window.

# 39

# History repeats itself?
# (Rwanda)

While I was trying, with Brother Raymond, to unravel the events of over fifty years ago in which he participated, other events, sometimes just as dramatic, were being inscribed in letters of blood in the great book of history. It was then that I saw on television the first pictures of the massacres in Rwanda. "Familiar" pictures: decapitated bodies, adults without arms or legs, children, starving, abandoned.

*History repeats itself*, my friends soon said to me. To which Engels had said in advance: *"It does not repeat itself, it stutters."*

Now the ocean waves that break on the shore with a constant rhythm from time immemorial, are they identical? That is the impression they give. However, each one is unique. Each one is different from the other in size, weight, in its intensity and direction, as well as in its power of erosion of the coasts.

The most flagrant contradiction in history is, without doubt, to think that its objective is singular, unique, that each event only happens once—*"that its goal, like that of all the sciences, is to attain the universal, the general, the normal,"* as it is underlined by Jacques le Goff.

The massacre of the Armenians in Turkey as with the Tutsis in Rwanda both have the objective of eliminating the other because they are different. Now the reasons for these two massacres, the one at the beginning of the century and the other at the end, are not the same. They are not the same, neither were the methods used, nor the historical and social environment. Also, each one of these events will take a unique place in the history of humanity—in the long list of its assassinations.

What then are the reasons for this curious sensation of déjà vu?

From whence comes the idea of history repeating itself? Does it not come from within ourselves, from our attitude when faced with a dramatic event or an injustice—when we look back at the behavior of those who preceded us and whom we have discovered thanks to our studies of the past?

All of a sudden, things appear clearer to me. That which repeats is not History, but *us* in History. *We* with our violence and our cruelty. *We* with our generosity and our sense of justice. In short, *us* with Good and Evil who live in us.

There were certainly Just men in Rwanda. As there were murderers. The fact of finding a Just in that country, would that confirm the correctness of my theories? Perhaps. Now, I have found several—and, among them, Laurient Ntezimana: he is a fifty-year-old teacher, who lives in the town of Butare. Tall, bald with smooth features, he traveled through the nights over the deserted roads carrying supplies to needy families on his old motorbike. This Hutu could never resign himself to admit that his brother Hutus could wish to exterminate the Tutsis with whom they have shared the land since time immemorial.

"I refuse to accept that ethnicity should become a battle horse," he says. "'Struth, I have the large Hutu nose, and that gave me some protection when faced with the warriors, the militants who have the same nose as me. But the question of humanity, surely, cannot be reduced to an affair of the nose!"

In Rwanda nearly a million men, women, and children have been exterminated. Sometimes killed with a machete. And no less troubling is the name which has been given to the places where these murders were carried out: the synagogue. Now, like Irena Sendler in Warsaw, Laurient the Hutu, rescued more than sixty Tutsi children from one "synagogue" and hid, nourished, and protected them. At the peril of his life:

"Is a Hutu capable of accepting that the *other*, the Tutsi, is a man like himself? That he exists as much as himself? That he also has a right to live?"

And Laurient Ntezimana added: "During the war I attempted, from day to day, to stay where I was. I am no hero. I can be frightened like everyone else. But I think there are still means of reaching the heart of a man, even a killer, on condition that you can show a little love."

Even spread among thirty-six Just men, this *little love* capable of touching an enemy's heart, could it change the world? Surely not. It serves only to maintain it. A modest specialty? Yes, but reasonable. We are entering an age of modesty, of modest philosophies. Compared to the two preceding centuries marked by nonsensical collective hopes, in the belief of changing the world—and even of changing man. But these infinite hopes have been shrouded under infinite suffering. Now, at the dawn of the third millennium, with new diseases menacing a humankind which does not know how to defend itself, when new wars, deceitful wars, tribal wars, ravage continents with no one knowing how to stop them, when new fears will take hold of man without his having the slightest means of dissipating them, there remains nothing else, it seems to me, but to oppose these new manifestations of Evil with a positive idea of Good.

# 40

# The Curate's network

"By Good," writes Spinoza, "from now on, I understand those means by which we know with certainty that we can approach more and more closely to the model of human nature we talk about; Evil, on the contrary, is those means which we know with certainty will prevent us reproducing this model."

Marie-Louise Lefebvre knew Thérèse Neury-Lancon well, and like the latter, has her own idea of Good. And above all of Evil, for which she wants to hold up its expansion and reproduction. Both of them worked in liaison with Abbé Jean Reuze, the Curé at Douvaine. According to Marie-Louise Lefebvre, this man bore witness, in saying, while speaking of the persecutions against the Jews, that he "could not remain doing nothing in the face of such abominations." The two women's parents were agricultural workers whose farms nestled on the frontier. You can see immediately that the geographic situation would enable hunted people from the Maquis as well as Jews to pass over the border to Switzerland.

I am beside Marie-Louise Lefebvre, in the family house where she was born. She lived there with her parents during the war. In 1939 she was sixteen; that is, just a young girl when she faced the situation.

"In fact," she says, "I always went there every summer, after I started training to be a housekeeper in a small family hotel near Annemasse. My parents were smallholders. We were a very united hard-working family."

"Were you a member of any youth organization?"

"I was an ardent, very active *Jaciste*, that's to say a militant member of the JAC, the Jeunesse Agricole Chrétienne, and Abbé Reuze placed much confidence in me. It was he who began to make us understand that we had to help the Jews. At that time, in our country area, we scarcely had occasion to meet a Jew. I don't think there was any anti-Semitism. Abbé Reuze, like most of the people here in that era, was very traditional, right wing. But, with him, the *deicide people*, and arguments like it, did not go down well. He was really a very intelligent man who had the love of others in his heart. One never knew just how many, or when he helped them . . . He saved hundreds from death, perhaps even thousands of people. He was the soul of the people here. When I think that he finished up in a concentration camp, in that horror which he had helped so many to avoid, I think to myself that sometimes the good God has some very odd ideas . . ."

"This help for the Jews, how did he give it?"

"Members of the Christian faith would bring people here, where we would take them in before taking them on to the Curé at Vegy, who, in his turn, took them to two farmers, François Lanson, Thérèse's father, and his friend Perillat, who were in charge of this clandestine *passing* of Jews. They cut the barbed wire at the frontier and passed the people, with their children, their sick, and their baggage underneath . . . They were magnificent, true heroes. They did it with great courage, total selflessness. Later they were deported and killed after having been denounced."

"But, before you passed them over the border, you had to feed these people you welcomed? How did you do that? Ration cards . . . ?"

"Oh, it was relatively easy to find food in the country where hens lay eggs, cows give milk, and there's bacon in the pigsty! Generally, our 'guests' slept the night at our house. Here, in this house, it was especially children that came. There was one girl, Rolande Virgie, a Scout leader, who dressed the little Jewish children up with their neckerchiefs and berets, and made them take the train as far as here, where they were handed on to the *passers*. She also worked with Abbé Reuze and the Lancons."

"Were you ever frightened?"

"All the time! I was permanently frightened to death. Villages were burned, hostages taken, people shot, arrests . . . You were constantly on the alert. The least noise, the least thing . . . We lived in a climate of anxiety, yes . . . But, what could we do? For all that, we weren't going to let those people die, let those children die because we were afraid! Less at twenty than at seventy, but unless you were an idiot, you knew that what we were doing was dangerous. One day I remember, Mum, who was ninety at the time, said to a man who had returned much later to thank her: 'But, sir, all I did was totally natural. There could be nothing more normal than that.' And this man replied to her: 'Madam, this was not as natural as all that . . . There are many people who did not act in that way. What you did was supernatural!' Then, let us say that perhaps it was a little . . . supernatural—but how could we have done otherwise? When we saw these groups of infants arriving . . . I'll never forget one little scrap of four, maybe five years old, who I took to the border, one evening, with Rolande Virgie; he only had one shoe, and he walked as best he could, hopping on one foot—it was absolutely poignant . . . You couldn't leave them. What should we have done? Send them back where they came from? Send them back to their deaths?"

"If, alas, it was to start again? If it happened again, would you do it again?"

"Yes; it isn't a matter of heroism, you see. It is just that we must do it, and then, there we are. It's a real peasants' attitude: there's something to do, OK, perhaps it's not too easy, maybe even dangerous, but it must be done! And then, all those people, all those refugees, we loved them. The little Jewish girl we kept here for three years, we loved her like our little sister. She never saw her mother again, poor child, but she cried with us, with the same sadness, on her mother's death. We loved her, you know; we were poor, not well-educated, and we loved her. I believe that, then, there was more love in the air and in the hearts of men, than today when they are richer, more self-centered, and perhaps, have less need of others . . ."

". . . the good God has some very odd ideas," Marie-Louise Lefebvre said, while speaking of the deportation and death of Abbé Reuze, who saved so many Jews. This remark set me thinking about the reflections of the German Jewish philosopher, Hans Jonas, apropos of *God after Auschwitz:* how was God, in essence good, generous, and all-powerful, able to have this "odd idea" of allowing those who had saved men *made in His image* to be tortured and killed? Why, after having heard the cries of the supplicants, did He not descend to earth, as he did in the time of Sodom and Gomorrah, to see if some individuals *had not given themselves up to the ultimate licentiousness* (Genesis, XVIII, 21)? However, the cries which rose up to Him from the *bottom of the abyss* (Psalms CXVIII, 5) could not have left Him indifferent.

According to Hans Jonas, the disciple of Heidegger, the very existence of God only matches the excessiveness of Evil to such an extent that God is powerless in the face of human distress. The question remaining, to clarify this matter, is to know whether this divine powerlessness results from choice or necessity. The sages of Hebraic tradition often resigned themselves to the first hypothesis.

For the two great Cabbalists of the sixteenth century, Isaac Louria and Haim Luzzato, the choice of not intervening at these grave moments proves the necessity for God to limit himself, to hold himself back from time to time. This idea of the *"retreat of God"* has found a specific name in the Cabbala, the *Tsimsoum:* God retires some way to give men a little freedom, because without this respite, without this retreat, nothing could exist outside of Him.

But, there it is: when God holds Himself back, Evil quickly takes His place, remarks Hans Jonas. Several questions assail me: what if God does not totally retire during His "absences"? And, what if, before he limits himself, He leaves a need for Himself in Man's heart, as a sign of His presence? And if, finally, in the course of withdrawing (or, in the words of a Master Hassid, Rabbi Schneour Zalman de Liady, *in turning away His face)*, He commands certain individuals among us—unknown, modest, humble—to continue to maintain the idea of Justice and the desire for Good?

Perhaps, this is the explanation of the mystery of the thirty-six unknown Just men who, according to the Talmud, are never missing from the world. For its survival. For its perpetuation.

Yesterday, then, were there Just men in Sarajevo?

And, today, are there Just men in Sarajevo?

# 41

# Bosnia

In Jerusalem, one day, while talking to a Jewish woman, Tova Grinberg, née Kabilio, I learn that during the Second World War, she and her family were saved by a Bosnian friend.

Therefore there are Just people in Sarajevo!

Heartened by this news, I leave for Bosnia, as soon as possible, to look for this Just woman, Zaneiba Hardaga.

Ground covered in rubble, walls pitted with bullet holes, burnt out cars: this is the scene that greets my arrival in that part of town where the old lady lives. When I finally enter the hall of her block of flats, I see that as there is no electricity, the lift is off. Earlier on, someone had told me that she lives on the top floor, the ninth. Evening is coming on, the whole block is plunged in darkness. Suddenly, like a miracle, points of light appear and sparkle on every level. Someone is coming. I introduce myself. I learn that all the neighbors, warned of my visit to see Zaneiba Hardaga, the Just of Sarajevo, decided to light the way for me, with candles all the way up the lift shaft . . .

Zaneiba Hardaga is a Muslim. She is seventy-seven years old. Her husband, Mustapha, the carpet merchant, gave up this world five years ago.

Dressed all in black, her hair covered with a long black shawl that went right down over her shoulders, this woman's face had the look of an Icon, almost diaphanous, with deep dark eyes. The way she carried her head, well-groomed, and her clear speech, bore witness to an obvious vitality and lucidity. She is delighted that I am bringing news of her granddaughter, Amra, and of her friend Tova Grinberg-Kabilio.

"During the Second World War," I say to her, "did you live here in Sarajevo?"

"Yes."

"And the Kabilio family?"

"They were our long-time friends. Our friends and our neighbors. We didn't care about religious differences. We each respected the other's. They had respect for us and vice versa. From the start of the war we all shared what we had. And during the whole war—a period of exile for them—we kept in touch. We were happy to be able to help them. And then, happier still, in 1945, when they came back to the liberated region of Kordun. They all came back, Yoje, his wife and their children, alive and well. So few families all came back . . . Why did we do it? But . . . it's normal: they were our friends . . ."

"All the same, it was very dangerous for the Hardaga family to hide a Jewish family, the Kabilios, wasn't it?"

Zaneiba Hardaga sighs. Under the black shawl, her expression suddenly darkens—and yet becomes more alive at the same time.

"In fact," she says, "in 1941 we lived in the district between the Gestapo headquarters, the Commandant's office, and the prison! . . . All the posters said: 'Anyone saving a Jew will be executed.' Yoje was condemned to death, then we hid him until he could get to Mostar thanks to the Partisans. His family had to be separated from him."

"Were you afraid?"

The old lady shook her head with a smile of defiance.

"No," she said simply.

Then she quickly leaned over towards me, to add this astonishing sentence: "Humanity knows no fear."

Solidarity, spontaneous charity knows no fear—or, at all events overcomes it. This is what confirms Zaneiba Hardaga as one of the Just, finishing her life, today as yesterday, under the bombs in Sarajevo. *We did not care about religious differences:* that is the secret of this Muslim who has saved Jews.

What was the Jewish community in Yugoslavia before the war? We know that the first Jews to reside in Sarajevo arrived around the year 1465. The first Synagogue was built in 1581. That community was mainly composed of Sephardis who had fled from Spanish persecution. Before the Second World War, there were 12,000 Jews in Sarajevo, 20 per cent of the town's population.

The Nazis invaded Yugoslavia in March 1941; they came in from Austria and Hungary. The Italians profited from this by occupying a part of the Adriatic coast, including the town of Mostar.

Hitler soon partitioned Yugoslavia into two provinces: Catholic Croatia and Orthodox Serbia. Anton Pavlovic, the chief of the fascist Party, Oustachi, became President of the Croat State and participated in the extermination of Orthodox Serbs and Yugoslav Jews, after more than five centuries in residence.

On the arrival of the Germans, a group of young Muslims went and set fire to the Great Synagogue in Sarajevo. It was in Bosnia that the Grand Mufti of Jerusalem, Hadj Amin el-Husseini, created the Muslim Division and promised Hitler to fight, beside the Nazis, against "Communism and the Jews."

Despite that shameful connivance, this Muslim couple, Zaneiba and Mustapha Hardaga, protected and saved their Jewish friends, the Kabilios.

And it is here that the miracle perpetuates itself, from generation to generation, *in order that the world may survive,* since, at present, here in Yugoslavia, it is the saved family which brings help to its old rescuers.

Just come from Sarajevo, here I am, now, in Jerusalem, in the house of Tova Grinberg-Kabilio. Amra Hardaga, Zaneiba Hardaga's granddaughter, is with her. Both of them, sitting in front of the verandah of the apartment, full of plants and flowers, answer my questions.

"I was born in Sarajevo in 1938," Tova told me. "When the Nazis invaded Yugoslavia, I was three years old. Naturally, I don't remember very much about the first year of the Occupation. My first memories are linked with an apartment which was not our own. It belonged to neighboring Muslim friends of my parents: Mustapha Hardaga and his wife Zaneiba . . . From the time when the Nazis, aided and abetted by the fascist Croat Catholics and the Muslims, began to hunt out the Jews, Mustapha and Zaneiba took us to their house, under their protection."

Tova Grinberg-Kabilio is a woman with composed features, a round face and a calm air about her. She exudes a strength of character, full of goodness, which is underlined by an affectionate smile. She gives off a feeling of maternal generosity, a sense of protection.

She shows me a photograph which is well used, stained with time. "This is one of the rare photos I have left from those days. You can just recognize Zaneiba Hardaga, although she is veiled, like most Muslim women. Beside her, that's my mother hiding her yellow star with her handbag over her chest. The two young girls are me and my best friend, Amra, Mustapha and Zaneiba's granddaughter . . . When the situation in Sarajevo became dangerous for us, because of the denunciations, Mustapha Hardaga took us, that is, my mother, my brother and I, to friends of his in the Italian zone . . ."

"And what about your father?"

"He had problems, he didn't know where to hide: finally he went back to our friends, the Hardagas. After the Liberation we were all reunited in Sarajevo and, as our flat had been totally devastated, we were once more installed with Mustapha and Zaneiba. It was only later, in 1950, that we left for Israel."

"Did you stay in contact with the Hardagas over all these years?"

"Indeed, yes. But in the course of time the contacts grew less. However, whenever the Yugoslav authorities permitted, my brother visited Sarajevo."

"And now, since the civil war began? . . ."

"Yes. As soon as I learned about the events and saw on television the first deaths in the Sarajevo streets, I telephoned Zaneiba Hardaga and asked her what I could do to help them. She told me of the horrors of this war, and begged me to help her granddaughter Amra and her two children leave Sarajevo. Then, I had them come to Israel. That wasn't too complicated . . . We had to obtain visas and money for the journey. I organized the whole thing in a day; the plane tickets, the visas, everything. All by myself, very quickly."

"Tova, why did you do that?"

"I don't know; I felt I should. They were in difficulty. Therefore, it was natural to help them. I didn't need to think very long about it . . . I don't think there was a choice. There was no way I could leave them there with the bombs! How could I look in a mirror later?"

I turn to Amra Hardaga: "Amra, do you think it was natural for Tova to welcome you into her home with your two children, here in Israel, as if you were family?"

Amra Hardaga looks towards Tova: "Tova is more than family . . . She was my mother's best friend. Without her . . ."

Amra, whose brown hair floats around her face in time with the vivacity of her gestures, puts so much warmth and tenderness in her answer . . . Her hands speak at the same time as her voice; it is very clear that she is overflowing with affection and appreciation for Tova.

"You know," she carries on, "for me, there are two kinds of men: those who prove their humanity, and the rest. I believe that friendship is a sacred thing, the most wonderful thing in life. You love your family with a natural love; with friends it's much more. We grew up with the idea that we have friends in Israel, and when our friend, Tova, decided to take us in, the image I had of these friends, the Kabilios, was reawakened in me in all its goodness. On her part, it was such a spontaneous reaction, so humane!

"If the situation was reversed, I would have welcomed Tova in Sarajevo. God willing that there is no more war! But, if it did start again, I would welcome her without thinking twice.

That's humane, normal. Once here, to my great joy, I found that all the images I had of Tova turned out to be true. She has helped us tremendously. I don't know how I can thank her enough . . ."

Tova Grinberg interrupts her: "I did nothing special!"

And Amra: "Oh, yes you did, Oh, yes!"

Tova blushes. She is overcome. She leans over to Amra and gently holds her arm so that she stops saying these words of praise which are embarrassing her. They exchange looks, burst into tears.

# 42

# Istanbul

Since my discussion with Tova Grinberg-Kabilio and Amra Hardaga, I have not really hurried to think about this somewhat unusual story of a Jew rescued fifty years ago by a Muslim, who, half a century later, saves that Muslim's family. I would have been able to continue my reflections on this—this exchange of generosity, this *sharing of goodness* which has something rare and precious—if the telephone ringing unexpectedly had not reminded me of the urgency of my enquiries, of this search for the Just which I have not yet completed, which I don't know when I shall finish. On the telephone is the President of the Jewish community in Istanbul: he invites me to join the festivities marking the fifth century of the arrival of the Jews in Turkey.

Istanbul: here is another town that I have dreamed about . . . At the time when it was still called Constantinople, at the end of the fifteenth century, she received and integrated the Jews fleeing from the Inquisition in Spain and Portugal. This Muslim city had even welcomed one of my forbears, the Jewish printer Abbakhou, and his son, Abraham, escapees from the great fire of Salonika. And before him, his father Mechoulam, whose tomb was in the cemetery of Egri-Capou, near the port of Kalligaria. At least, it was there centuries ago. At that period, it was, it appears, a very ancient burial place, now covered with scattered tombstones, eroded by time, carrying Hebrew inscriptions, much of them indecipherable, like time itself and like the history of the Jews.

But nearer to our times, during the Second World War, had Turkey made any gestures of support for these poor Jews fleeing from the Nazi persecution taking place in France and Italy?

Here I am, now, in Istanbul, on the Bosporus. The room I have been given is spacious, with windows opening out onto the Golden Horn and, from there, the arsenal and the naval dockyards from whence the smell of tar sometimes blows in on the breeze.

"I believe in God, I am a Muslim, and I did nothing but listen to my conscience. My conscience pricked. I am a Muslim, yes, but, above all, I am a man who believes in humanism, in humanity. I put myself in the place of those who would have been the victims. My conscience told me to do what I could. That's what you can describe as my 'motivation.' "

My interviewee is a frail little man, gentle but inflexible. I detect in him a resolution, a power to make decisions, that nothing, once made, will make him change his mind. Silvery hair, smiling face, elegant manners: Selahattin Ulkumen is my image of a retired diplomat who will never lose his calm control. He is wearing a wine-colored suit and a T-shirt with a rolled collar, and apart from some stains down his shirt front giving away his age, he still has the figure of a young man. In 1943, scarcely aged thirty, he was appointed Consul General of Turkey on the island of Rhodes.

Rhodes, like the island of Kos, both in the Aegean Sea, belong to Greece, but early in the war these islands fell to Hitler and Mussolini.

"At that time," explains Selahattin Ulkumen, "Rhodes was under the joint control of the Germans and the Italians. Under this regime there were no persecutions affecting the Jews. But, in September 1943, the 8th to be precise, the Italians withdrew and the Germans became the sole masters of the island. It was about that time that the arrests started, and the Jews were rounded up to be sent for deportation. There were 2,200 Jews, in all, on the island of Rhodes."

"What was the situation of the Jews on the island at that point?"

"They had to stay in a specially determined area, but they never had to wear the yellow star . . ."

And Selahattin Ulkumen describes the curbs on communication that prevailed then on the island. Fear prevailed everywhere, then a greater and more real unease, then desolation— an atmosphere of strangeness, almost unreal: since 1941 the Italians had confiscated all the radios so effectively that the Jews knew nothing of the fate reserved for their race on the continent.

It was, therefore, with the advantage of total surprise and without the slightest difficulty that the Germans arrested all the men of the Jewish community on the island to send them to different sorting centers, in Rhodes town, in Trianda, in Crementon, and in Villanova, before having them deported to the concentration camps on the continent.

That was the time when the very young Turkish Consul General, Selahattin Ulkumen, intervened. The scenes of utter distress that he witnessed overwhelmed him, and he decided to act.

Without delaying, he organized a census of all the Jews on the island who were in any way of Turkish origin, and distributed Turkish identity cards to their wives. By this action, he put himself in a position to be able to negotiate, and so, in an official capacity, he would demand, from the Gestapo, the release of all those Jews who, with legal proof in their hands, were well and truly Turkish citizens. But he had to do it very, very quickly.

"I went to see the Commandant of the island, who was a Gestapo general. He told me he had orders to transfer all the Jews on Rhodes to other places. I guessed what he meant by this: to make them disappear, evidently . . . I made the objection to him that these people were Turkish citizens of Jewish religion, that the Turkish laws and the Turkish Constitution establish no distinction between Turks of different religious persuasions . . . and that, in consequence, my duty and mission was to protect them, to safeguard the human rights of these Jews who were, above all, Turks, citizens of Turkey, that is to say a neutral country with which Germany does not entertain hostile relations, but more a benevolent . . . After all, didn't Von Papen, Hitler's grand official, establish in Istanbul, with the agreement of the Turkish authorities, a whole network of surveillance and spies to control the narrows of the Bosporous where the British submarines and the Russian fleet passed? Did that not prove the goodwill of the Turks towards Germany? Why therefore risk spoiling such good relations by arresting and then deporting Turkish citizens just because they are Jews? And how could the Turkish government allow the German government to take Turkish citizens to foreign territory? As you see, under cover of being a good diplomat, I argued, I pleaded with all my strength, the case for our friends the Jews. I had to listen to much that was bad. After the first interview, I had not succeeded in convincing this Gestapo general. I had to return to see him the next day, and the next day, and the following days. Without result! . . . He refused to give me an answer, a hope. And then, at the end of four or five days he sent his aide de camp and he addressed several words in German to me . . ."

A little emotional, Selahattin Ulkumen interrupts himself for a few moments, then: "At last he gave me his agreement! I felt, at that instant, a great joy! Think about it: forty-two men were going to escape death . . . They were not going to be deported!"

"This is how you saved forty-two Jews in Rhodes. Do you know if, in other countries, any Turkish Consuls acted like you?"

"I believe that Necdet Kent and Yolga Namik did. But I am not a direct witness to their actions. The first was in Paris and the other in Marseilles while I was working in Rhodes . . ."

"Have you ever seen any of those you saved since?"

"Yes, some of them. It gives me great satisfaction to know that these men are alive thanks to my obstinacy when I was faced with that German general."

"Today, Mr. Ulkumen, when you look back, how do you see your reaction? How do you feel about the decision you took then?"

Selahattin Ulkumen smiles. He closes his eyes for an instant, then addresses me with a quotation I would never have expected: "As the Chinese proverb says it: *Instead of complaining of the dark, you can light a candle.* That's what made me act. I said to myself: if I could light a sort of candle, that would give me the greatest pleasure. Then I lit that candle . . ."

Still in Istanbul, I take my leave of this Just man to go and meet the wife of one of those Jews from Rhodes whom he rescued in 1943. She is Mathilde Turiel. Now a widow, she remembers Selahattin Ulkumen very emotionally, and she is going to tell me, from her side, some things which from modesty he did not.

"When the Germans rounded up all the island's Jewish men, I went, with many of the other wives, to the gates of one of the camps where they were shut in. Someone had told me that my husband was there. Soon after I arrived there, a car stopped: a young man, a Turk, Mr. Ulkumen (whom I did not know yet), got out and told me to go away from there, that it was a dangerous place, and that he was going to try to save my husband . . . The next day, a decree concerning the wives and children of the detainees was posted up all over the island by the Germans: we were to present ourselves at the camp before ten o'clock; if not, all the men would be shot. We all rushed there. And we stayed there several days. Then, thanks to Mr. Ulkumen, my husband was freed! What joy, if you can only realize, what a joy that was! Mr. Ulkumen had done something extraordinary, yes, extraordinary! And in addition to the Turkish Jews, he succeeded in saving twenty-five Italian Jews, whom he passed off as Turks, whom he had in some way transformed into Turks!"

This last point, this supplementary rescue, Selahattin Ulkumen had not judged worth mentioning at my meeting with him. The marvelous discretion of the Just, once *led to do good* by their understanding of *Good!*

I ought, however, to find out about the general situation of Turkey during the Second World War. This position of neutrality, and, above all, not having discriminatory measures in regard to the Jews, which permitted the decisive intervention of Selahattin Ulkumen. What was the position of the Jews in Turkish society at that time?

# 43

# The Turkish Consul in France

*"Pharoah searched for Moses to kill him. Moses went far away; he went to the country of Madian and sat down beside a well . . ."* One could easily transpose Turkey with this country of "Madian" as the Bible describes it (Exodus II, 15). But we know, in fact, that the first meeting of the Turks with the Jews was at the beginning of the Ottoman Empire: this historic gift substantiates the true age of the Jewish integration in Turkey. Is it not significant that the first synagogue built in this country was in 1324, while the first Mosque dates from . . . 1325, one year later?!

In Istanbul, by the middle of the sixteenth century, an important Jewish community was already flourishing, composed of Byzantine Jews and, above all, the Jews recently expelled (1492–1494) from Spain and Portugal. Four centuries later, at the declaration of the Second World War, there were 84,000 in Turkey, of whom 50,000 lived in the capital.

In fact, from the Turkish point of view the Jews had always been part of Turkey. In Istanbul I have a meeting with two of these Jewish Turks: Nedim Yahya and Harry Djalvo. We are talking over all the points of this question that they know well. For them, the attitude of the Turkish officials—and in particular those diplomats who were inspired to help the Jews during the Second World War—is not very surprising: they correspond to this country's traditions.

"All the same," I say to Harry Djalvo, "Turkey's neutrality

during the war was a sort of one-sided neutrality, rather more goodwill towards the Germans, a 'pro German' neutrality, was it not? Tell me why these Turkish officials openly risked going against the Nazis on the Jewish question?"

"For the same reasons which we have just been talking about: the Turks, throughout their history, have always appreciated the Jews' support, and have never entertained a policy of their segregation in one place. The neutrality towards Hitler had no basis at all on his racist theories. There was never any ambiguity in that direction."

"Do you know the story of Raoul Wallenberg, the Swedish diplomat who invented Swedish passports for the Jews, to be able to save them?" interrupted Nedim Yahya with this other question. "Well, the Turkish officials did other things like that. Among the Jews, who sought them out in their embassies and their consulates, some of them said: 'My uncle Moses lived long ago in Istanbul' or 'My grandfather Isaac and my great grandfather were citizens of the Ottoman Empire.' Then the Turkish officials had the pleasant idea of inventing a document: the *Application for Naturalization*. Every Jew, from then on, who wished it, could, on the base of a nonproven Turkish origin, become a Turkish citizen, and, with this simple *Application for Naturalization* in his pocket, was protected from German roundups. A great many Jews were given shelter and were saved, thanks to this famous piece of paper. Thus, these diplomats were not only helping to save their own countrymen (Turkish Jews), but any Jews (including, therefore, the non-Turks) who could gain access to a Turkish Embassy or Consulate: it was enough for them to fill up this *Application for Naturalization* to become citizens of this country."

I don't know what to think. I will explain myself a bit better, how, at the same time, and in the same way, Selahattin Ulkumen was able, apart from the forty-two Turkish Jews in Rhodes whom he saved from deportation, to also save twenty-five Italian Jews . . . Harry Djalvo, inexhaustible, brings me other precious information on the atmosphere reigning in Istanbul at the time. It is true that Von Papen had established his teams of informers and spies there, but the capital remained open to every current, to every opinion.

"You must understand one important thing; that is, that all the great Jewish institutions, who were doing their best to save the Jews, had their headquarters here, in Istanbul, during the war, under the benevolent eye of the Turkish authorities, who practiced a policy of 'laissez-faire'! And the Germans were never able to counter this convenience. The Jewish leaders chartered ships to take them illegally to Palestine (illegal, because to satisfy the demands of the Arabs, the British forbade them to land there): the Turkish Government, itself, always closed its eyes to these activities . . ."

In truth, a strange climate pervaded Istanbul during the war. I also learn that here also, at the time, the representative of the Roman Church, Cardinal Angelo Roncalli, spoke out loud and clear for the Jews. In 1942, profiting from the distance between himself and the Vatican, from where, at that moment, emanated a heavy pall of silence on the Jewish question, he did not hesitate: in his position as Apostolic Nuncio in Turkey, he used all his influence to bring assistance to persecuted Jews in Bulgaria, Yugoslavia, and later, in Italy itself. In 1943 he protested against the projected deportation of Bulgarian Jews and demanded that the Italians, in their zone of occupation along the Yugoslav Adriatic coast, protect them . . .

This Cardinal Angelo Roncalli who, from his base in Istanbul publicly supported the Jews against the Nazis under the nose of Von Papen, is the man the world will discover later under the name of Pope John XXIII . . . No one, in Turkey then, dreamed for a single instant of keeping him quiet . . .

"Besides," reinforced Nedim Yahya, "Turkey knew, well before the war, from the thirties, and signaled her distance by telling the German government that she would accept the Jewish and antifascist intelligentsia who were fleeing Germany or banned therefrom. It was Atatürk who launched this movement. Between 1930 and 1938, we thus welcomed 230 teachers: 150 Jews and 80 who were either half-Jews or antifascists, or of the left wing—all teachers, professors, and renowned researchers. They were of great use to us here in Turkey. They were the foundation of our teaching University . . . In 1943, the German Ambassador in Istanbul received an order from Hitler, urging him to expedite the extradition to Germany of the 150 Jews in question. Franz von Papen himself then demanded the Turkish President to give him these people: he came up against a brick wall, 'No,' polite but firm."

"There were other Jews who came as refugees to Turkey at that time. How did that come about?"

"We were very young, but we lived through it all with passion, thanks to the Jewish institutions which were based here and in which we participated. For example, when someone said such and such a boat was about to arrive, overloaded with Jews from the Danube area, we went to the port to wait for them, come rain or come hail, with whatever we had to welcome them. And, we fed them, gave them shelter, sometimes for several weeks, while they waited to go to Israel."

"And . . . you never had any difficulties with the German secret service? Did you have to play the game of cat and mouse with them?"

"No, scarcely at all. In fact, there were also British secret service here. And they were both so occupied, the Germans and themselves with counterespionage, that they tended to neglect us a bit; that allowed us to help our coreligionists who were in need of us."

This discussion brings Turkey closer to me, more familiar than I have felt it up till now. I understand better how certain of my own ancestors were able, long since, through the centuries, to live in this country, to be Turks. And it is with a light heart that I stroll once more through Istanbul before going to meet two other Just men from this country: two other diplomats, mentioned to me by Selahattin Ulkumen, and who, for their part, saved Jews in France, when they were Consuls in Paris and Marseilles respectively.

Yolga Namik has a long career as a diplomat behind him. At twenty-six, in 1940, he was in Paris holding the post of Third

Administrator in the Turkish Consulate—a sort of treasurer. It was his first overseas posting. Later, after the war, he was, over the years, Ambassador for Turkey in Rome, Paris, Caracas, Teheran, etc., and he became, because of his age and experience, Foreign Minister of Turkey. He describes this brilliant career with a touch of irony, when he adds, as his gaze becomes more intense:

"It is an honor for any mortal to represent his country like this, isn't it? But, I am only telling you this to arrive at the following conclusion: I consider that the period during the war when I was Vice Consul in Paris was the most interesting, the most productive of my life. I swear to you I remember it very happily, and, excuse me for saying it, with pride: with a moral satisfaction which, still today, gives me confidence and hope for the future."

I understand this man's feelings. With his friends, during the war, he helped 400 Turkish Jews . . . or pseudo-Turkish, escape from France, using the same method of the *Application for Naturalization* that allowed any Jew to present himself at a Turkish Consulate and obtain the necessary papers to protect him from the German or French roundups. When I talk with Yolga Namik, the most astonishing part of what he regards as his greatest reason for pride seems to be less the fact that he saved 400 Jews, but that while they were in France, thanks to his intervention, they did not have to wear the yellow star.

"From the time that these Jews were Turkish citizens (or were obliged to become so), I was empowered to ask the German authorities that, in their case, the yellow star should be forgotten: in fact, why should a Turk wear a yellow star?"

He repeated the next words, several times, with great insistence: "In spite of pressure from the Germans, in spite of pressure from the French Collaboration Government, I never accepted . . . never . . . that 'my' Jews should wear the yellow star!"

Yolga Namik drinks his coffee a sip at a time. Short hair, bleached with age, a neat mustache, face deeply lined in the manner of his race: the old diplomat had aged, but had never lost his calm, well-constructed eloquence which always and without hesitation framed his arguments. As he had emphasized it himself, those moments of his life, during the war, still filled him with a sort of exaltation. He returns to the problem which led him to establish the famous safe-conducts more or less "arranged," thanks to which those Jews had been able to escape:

"I was in Paris for the German invasion, and then, in October 1940, Petain promulgated his first laws of segregation, the anti-Semitic laws. For a Turk such persecution aimed at the Jews was inadmissible! We had endless discussions with the German and French authorities of the period reminding them that racial discrimination was condemned by worldwide public opinion. And we looked to our own Constitution to intervene in favor of the Turkish Jews, and any others we could claim. Our Constitution forbade all forms of discrimination be it race, color, language, or religion between Turkish citizens. We therefore could not in any way accept that a foreign country could take upon itself to decide the fate of our citizens: Jews or not, the Turks respond to Turkish authority and no other. These arguments carried because Hitler had no intentions, in the immediate future, to attack Turkey. It was therefore possible, with these documents invented by our caring people, to partly counter the German persecution."

"Mr. Yolga Namik, these 400 Jews that you saved, where did they go?"

"Oh, they had to go on a real odyssey by rail! Think of it: we had to organize eight convoys (three in 1943, five in 1944) and in those days when millions of Jews were stuffed forcefully into trains that took them to their deaths, . . . anyway ours were sent in the opposite direction, as Turkish citizens, with Turkish passports. They had to cross right through Germany, then the Balkans, to finally arrive in Turkey."

"They went through Germany! . . . In a train? They must have nearly died from fear!"

"Without any doubt, yes. But legally they were Turks, they had nothing to be frightened of. Besides, as I have already told you, they arrived unhindered in our country . . ."

"When you were in Paris, did you know what Necdet Kent, your colleague in Marseilles, was doing, also to save Jews?"

"We knew that the Consulate in Marseilles were doing their best, as we did in Paris, and that they did well. But we did not have direct communication with Marseilles: France was cut in two, with a demarcation line. It was not until after the war that we were able to reconstruct all that had happened. You see, it was after I discovered that he too had helped the Jews that I realized how much Necdet Kent and I had in common . . ."

"For instance?"

"We were both young! That presupposes lots of energy, great enthusiasm, doesn't it? The enthusiasm to do something, to serve others . . . We were happy, Sir, happy to serve life!"

"Mr. Namik, are you a Muslim?"

"Yes, thanks be to Allah, as you say, I am a Muslim. But that does not at all signify that I feel differently from you French, or Jews, or whoever. That didn't hinder me from saving Jews, on the contrary! It is the humane qualities in a person that are important. If a man is good, kind, God—be it the God of Allah, of Jews, of Christians or other religions—God, then, will take you into His Paradise. Then, on this Earth, you understand . . . it goes better for you if you begin at once to show love, to help one's fellow man . . ."

*"It is better to be two than one—in case of trouble, the one supports the other,"* affirms Ecclesiastes (IV, 9–12), and adds: *"There, where one man is overwhelmed, two survive, and the link between three is not easily broken."*

# 44

# Train ride to Nimes

Fifty years on. Time for two generations to be born. Time for witnesses to disappear. Today, now, has the time come to bring together the memory, all the memories, of the past? I want to talk about it: Good and Evil.

I know that the law punishes crime and is supposed to protect people in danger. But what if one finds oneself far from the crime and with no connection between those who kill and those who are being killed?

Does distance, physical or temporal, dispense with the need for memory?

There, in Istanbul, Necdet Kent, a Turk, who knows France well, does not think so.

In fact, he is the first Just man that I was introduced to, in Istanbul. I met him on the occasion of the five hundredth anniversary of the Jewish community in Turkey. The festivities, which were presented with great panache, had for their setting an old castle illuminated with thousands of candles in the maze of paths bordering the gardens. Besides the official personages—such as the Presidents of Turkey and Israel—there were more than a thousand guests participating like well-behaved children in this modern reconstruction of pomp and ceremony from the days of Suleiman the Magnificent. Some-one told me, during that evening, that "hidden among these guests is one of the Just men you are seeking, a former Turkish Consul in Marseilles . . ." And this is how, in the middle of the splendor and the noise of the party, I made the acquaintance of Necdet Kent.

This very elegant octogenarian, flower in his buttonhole, hair black and shiny, was the epitome of the oriental aristocrat. You sensed in him the ease, the high moral stance he took, the complete discretion. At first, he was somewhat disturbed at the idea of telling about his actions as a rescuer during the war. He would have preferred to have the survivors of these actions near to him. He had scruples and was very exact.

"You must understand," he said to me, "I would not like anyone to hawk around such important things without taking adequate precautions about the images I will leave for my children, grandchildren, great-grandchildren and my country-men. With witnesses to hand we will reduce the risks of error, approximations . . ."

I didn't dare reply to him that time was very short (from all points of view—the brevity of my stay in Turkey, his great age, and that of the witnesses) to find these people, but Necdet Kent, a very sensitive man, had picked up the nuance of what I thought and agreed that actually it was more sensible to tell me his story immediately, even without the witnesses.

"I was appointed Vice-Consul in the Turkish Consulate General in Marseilles in 1941. Following that, I was promoted to the rank of Consul and I remained in that position in Marseilles until 1944. Like many others, the Turkish Jews, fleeing from the occupied north of France, were arriving in the free zone, at Marseilles. They were therefore arriving there, into the area assigned to our Consulate; according to us, they then came under our jurisdiction. Now many of them were arrested in the great roundups in August 1942. We could not remain unmoved at such suffering. We, perhaps, had the means to make clear to the Germans that Turkey intended to protect her nationals, *all her nationals,* including the Jews. Then we moved into action . . ."

And Necdet Kent gives details of his methods: "If a Jew, Turk or not, asked for assistance from the Consulate, I immedi-ately gave him a certificate attesting to his Turkish citizenship and delineating his place of work as being under Turkish protection."

"How did the Germans behave in the southern zone of France, at that time?"

Necdet Kent stiffens. With an expression of disgust, he replies: "Ah, every day they found new ways of persecuting the Jews. For example, they didn't hesitate in stopping a Jew in the middle of the street and making him drop his trousers, to make sure if he was or was not circumcised. And then, when the Nazis invaded the southern zone, during eight days, with the aid of 12,000 French police, they organized an immense roundup. One evening, Sidi Iscan, a Jew from Izmir who worked at the Consulate as an interpreter, came to see me. He was very upset: the Germans had just arrested about eighty of these Turkish Jews. They had taken them to the station with the obvious intent of sending them to Germany. Sidi Iscan could hardly hold back his tears. We left quickly by car, he and I, to go to the station, Saint-Charles at Marseilles."

"What did you find there?"

"What I saw was incredible: cattle trucks full of people, hundreds of women and children, sobbing and screaming! I was never more sad or angry. The most striking memory I have of that night is the plaque I noticed on one of the wagons—with an inscription that I cannot wipe from my memory: 'This wagon can carry 20 large beasts and 500 kilos of hay.' And in each one of these wagons, there were eighty people pushed in one on top of the other! . . . When the Gestapo officer was warned that I was there, that the Turkish Consul was interested in this convoy, he came toward me and asked me in the most arrogant tone, what was I looking for. Courteously, I told him that these were Turkish citizens, that their arrest was erroneous, and that he should correct the mistake by releasing them. But the Nazi officer answered me, saying he was only carrying out his orders, that these people were not Turks but Jews . . . I then called Sidi Iscan: 'Come on, get on the train!' I shoved aside the SS who tried to bar my way and I climbed into a wagon, Sidi Iscan at my side. The officer began to shout, but in vain, since the train started to move. When it stopped at Arles or Nimes, I don't remember exactly which, some German officers came up to me in front of the wagon. I received them coldly, I refused to salute them. They apologized for the train's departure from Marseilles when I was aboard: it was a mistake for which those responsible would be punished. They put a car at my disposal for the return to Marseilles. I retorted that this was no mistake, and that it was scandalous that these Turkish citizens of the Jewish faith had been shut up in these cattle wagons! I pushed my luck: one Turkish Consul could chance it, faced with these most beastly Nazis. I told them that it was out of the question for me to leave these people on their own; as they were citizens of my country and I represented their government whose policy with regard to religious beliefs would not in any way allow such treatment and indignity, I refused to leave for Marseilles without them. Doubtless, by now, the officers had received orders of a conciliatory nature. They asked me if all the people there, in the wagon, were Turks. I remember the looks of these men and women, and the childrens' eyes watching my lips. All of them, petrified, observing the discussions on which their lives depended. I confirmed that all were Turks. Finally, the SS made us get down from the train and left us there. I will never forget it: the people we had just saved threw themselves around our necks, Sidi and me, they took us in their arms, they shook our hands with looks full of tears and gratitude, with stifled sobs . . .

"We all went back to Marseilles; Sidi and I hired a car, deliberately refusing the Mercedes Benz that the Germans had put at our disposition."

Necdet Kent remains pensive for a moment, with a faraway look in his eye, then: "In my whole life, I never experienced again that interior sense of peace and tranquillity which filled me early that morning, that day when, at last, I slipped between the sheets of my bed . . . All through the years, I have received letters from many of my companions on that strange journey. Today, who knows how many of them are still in good health and how many have died? I always think of them with affection, with some emotion, even those who, perhaps, don't remember me any more . . .''

Why has this Just man waited fifty years before speaking out?

Why had I to wait fifty years to question him?

Do we realize that we are the last witnesses, he and I? That our years are nearly done? That we can hear the dying breaths of the century?

More serious still: do we realize that, under our very eyes, the memories are already being blotted out by history?

What if it all happens again?

What if it has already started?

# 45

## Cardinal Lustiger explains

There have been, there still are horrors occurring in the whole world," Cardinal Jean-Marie Lustiger observed to me, "but, in my opinion, they are not of the same type as the Final Solution invented in the heart of Europe by the Nazis to annihilate a people, to make them disappear. In the *heart of Europe:* That's to say in this geographic region of Judaism, Christianity, and the rights of man. That is in this area which gave to the world something to be held up as the ideal civilization for the human condition and then spawned and developed this evil for which we must find a remedy! . . . In fact education . . . I think that the categories (My God, what an abstract word to use to say this!), maybe . . . the *latitudes* of pardon, of reconciliation, so hard, so difficult to live out but so important, so decisive, make part of the apprenticeship of love thy neighbor. *Love thy neighbor as thyself,* yes, it is in the Bible—and The Gospels go even further, as far as recommending to *love your enemies!* Every man is the brother of every other because they were all created in the image of God. It is very difficult, I know. It does not sound as if it is asking to forgive torturers. It sounds as if it is talking of other things. Perhaps to work towards Utopia, towards an impossibility: as if to find a brother in the enemy camp, as if to stop Cain's hand before he kills Abel, as if to overcome the innocent destruction of the history of humanity . . . When one looks at what is happening today, one remains somewhat skeptical. But we can

do it, we can carry on to the very end, even while thinking that
we will never achieve it . . ."

I cannot remember either when or where we first met nor
how we became such good friends. Neither can I remember
when we started to use the vocabulary of close relationships. It
seems like forever. Right from our first meetings there was a
feeling of kinship between us, and it has never left us.

Our story is, in fact, slightly banal: we are both Polish Jews,
now French and "saved ones." Except that one chose to follow
the tradition of his fathers whilst the other decided to go along
another path, albeit parallel. Since our first meeting, our views
of the world, so alike from our history yet so different from our
choices, have engendered a love of our interminable discussions together.

There is a saying, 'you do not really know a friend until you
have eaten a lot of salt with him.' Jean-Marie Lustiger and I
have done more together: we have eaten the salt of our
common memories.

"To the Civil authorities, to this very day," he confided to
me, "my name is Aaron. That I was a Jew was nobody's secret
in Orléans, where I found myself during the war, and where I
was denounced. I had to escape a few times. At first I was
hidden in a Catholic school on the outskirts of Paris: I sat my
Baccalaureate there. But I had to leave and hide in Orléans
after my mother was arrested, sent to Drancy and then
Auschwitz . . . As for my father, for a year he had been in the
'free' zone in Decazeville. Like me he survived with 'real false
papers.' Mine, which had been given to me by a Mayor in the
Orléans region, established my surname Lustiger, and invented a new Christian name, Jean-Marie. In spite of these
correct papers, my father and I were both found out. It was
then that we set off for Toulouse. I went straight to a house for
Catholic students, where I met Abbé Reuze (whom I did not
know at the time was an important member of the Resistance).
I put myself in his hands and those of the other religious
people I found there. I told them the whole story of who I was
and what a situation I was in: I had nothing, no money, but I

was full of hope and trust. I knew from experience that these
people would welcome me in. And, also because I was a Jew
converted to Christianity, and because I found myself in a
position of being persecuted, from their point of view, that
gave me the right to be defended, sustained and protected by
them. Somehow, instinctively, I knew the difference between
men of hate and the others . . . And, in fact, they did welcome
me. We were able to find a gardener's job for my father, in a
horticultural college. This was now the end of 1944. I was
sixteen, seventeen years old. We could feel that the end of the
war was near, but that situation only made the Germans more
violent, more vicious in their persecution of the Jews. It
therefore became necessary for me to go into hiding. Abbé
Reuze gave me new false papers so that I could go and hide in a
holiday camp for underprivileged kids from Toulouse. And so I
spent three months there, at Saint-Sulpice-sur-Leze, until the
Liberation came, among dozens of other kids, all hideaways
like me, who came from the poorest areas of Toulouse and had
been sent there to be away from the bombardments and the
roundups.

"Why do you think that these Catholics, who were part of
the Christian Witness movement, decided to help you?"

"I have already told you: they were not on the side of hate.
At that time, to the extent that I could understand such things
as I saw then, there was one thing which was obvious to my
eyes: that was hate. I say, strongly, *hate*. It emanated from
those, who since my childhood my people had called, with
dread, 'anti-Semites'—those who despised us, those who humiliated us, those who persecuted us, those who killed us.
Having listened to the stories of my father and grandfather, I
knew that there had always been hatred. And for us Jews at that
time, we had to face hate for the first time—hate and humiliation, a permanent, incredible humiliation! For me, who had
been brought up as a little French Jew, very proud to be Jewish
and very proud to be French, French culture was mine with its
principles of liberty, dignity, and respect for all men. Besides
all that was mixed up in my eyes with love: love of goodness,

love of truth, love of man, and service to others. You know, the first criterion, thanks to which I have stayed alive, is that used by the Just, to use this word love *justly*, like this: the Just were those who believed in these same values, in this love, who believed in it sufficiently to act as they believed—who crossed the frontier of their personality to reach the other side: to side with others, the side of the heart, to help the persecuted, to do them service. They had to face this hatred, with its people and its agents: collaborators, denunciators, traitors of all kinds, by 'conviction' or for money . . .

"Then, where was I going to find those who loved truth, justice, respect of others? Fear was all around. There was no right anywhere, and I had no rights. How then, was I to know whether I should knock on this or that door? . . . Doubtless, and even with certainty, only by founding my intuition on a base of love which some radiate from inside and all around themselves, at a time when the world is full of hate, when men are permanently invited and incited to hate. I saw all that: the force of prejudice and the stereotypes of anti-Semitism (above and beyond the most deliberate atmosphere favorable to racism offered jointly by the Occupation and the Collaboration in France), this violence and inhuman negation of others, however, gave way in some, to an interior force, a sort of essential conviction which made them risk their lives for the love of truth, the love of justice—in a word: the love of thy neighbor. Between these men of hate and those of truth, there is a difference . . . How should I say it, a little secret ingredient, which binds the Christians to the Old Testament, that's to say to Israel, to the Jewish people of Israel . . ."

"Sister Ludovica in Poland had said to me that, for her, *'to save a Jewish child, is like saving Jesus Christ'* . . . Another Just, Madre Sandra, in Italy, said to me later: *'I love the Jews. Without them we would never have even known Christ . . . We adore the same God as them, we are one with them, we have our roots in Judaism . . .'* And John Paul II when he visited the Chief Rabbi of Rome, declared: *'I have come to salute my older brother . . .'* Is that what you have in mind?"

"Almost, yes . . ."

"At heart, true Catholics are, for you, those who find very much of their moral source, their ethics, in Israel: in the Ten Commandments. It is a bit like putting Pascal's reasoning into practice: *'If God is always in communication with men, it is to them that He must turn to learn the tradition.'*"

"I think so, yes. That is tinged with the secret ingredient I told you about. Among those at that time whom I called the true believers, the authentic believers, I noticed they all had a love . . . I don't know what other word to use: a real love for the Jews, the people of God, a *religious* love. Those men and those women prayed, read the Bible and the great Jewish Prophets. They had, then, in some way received into themselves, in the most intimate recesses of their being, a graft of the Jewish people, a graft of liberty, a thirst for justice, a sense of right, of love of God. When they found themselves face to face with a persecuted Jew, it was a shock: they had to choose immediately between barbarity and hate on the one side, and, on the other, justice and love. And, other than being schizophrenics, they had no option than to recognize the most profound truth in their being, and reach out to help the Jew . . . When I was under their wing, I was never humiliated: and when I asked for help, I never once had to beg. I was penniless and without any means, but I had this instinct which enabled me to recognize these people who hated, and to avoid them. The Good people, as Catholics, became part of this love: part of this religious love of liberty of which the Jews were the symbol most flouted, most humiliated . . ."

"Did you ever find out who denounced you in Orléans?"

"Yes, I learnt who it was."

"Did you see him after the war?"

"Yes."

"What happened?"

"There are still some members of the family alive today. I don't want to go into details. Besides its much more complicated than that: in fact, I was warned in advance that I was going to be denounced by people who were themselves members of the denunciation system. You see how complex these things are . . ."

"All the same, how was it possible for Christians to collaborate with the Nazis, or even to close their eyes and do nothing—whilst an infinite minority among them had the courage, even the audacity, to go to the aid of the Jews?"

"Indifference, apathy . . . You know, experience of life shows us that great events are often received that way initially. It takes time for men and women to wake up, to finally realize what is going on around them, and most often it needs others to take the lead and say to them: 'Listen, Look, Think!' But that has no effect because they have not yet realized that they can do something; that, alas, is almost inevitable. You can be sure that this time lost in not understanding creates new victims every minute. And then, time is always short. In reality, to the question to those who have *done nothing* one can find answers—of the type which I am going to outline. But first I am going to ask a more difficult question, even a cruel one: why did some of them go over to the side of the assassins in all good conscience, having the feeling that they were acting in accord with their Christian, national, and even patriotic convictions? What went on in their heads? What went on in their souls, in their hearts? I have discussed it, over many long years, with anti-Semites; I have tried. I have tried to understand them. I think I have seen by what mental mechanisms they arrived at such extreme, horrible conclusions, to satisfy themselves— but I never understood why, in themselves, something gave way to such a point in coming to this total absence of feeling, to this emptiness, that they imagined they would be able to cope with the massacres. The true mystery, after all, is not the relative laxity of those who were killed and did nothing . . ."

And after that statement a moment of silence. "The mystery, it seems to me, is no longer the compassion and the courage of those people, who with intimate self-awareness, stretched out their hands to help Jews. No: the real mystery is the denunciator, the traitor, the torturer, the executioner, the agent of extermination, his system. How can men, on the few occasions when they are given the opportunity, how can they wish to play these roles? How can they feel at peace with themselves?"

When working on my research on the Just in France, I often recall this discussion with Jean-Marie Lustiger. To arrive at the conclusion that the Jews were very much more realistic than their fellow Christians, Jean-Marie Lustiger was horrified by the manifestations of hate. Myself, I am surprised by those of love. Could that be because they are rarer?

*"Remember of what you are made, Amalek . . . Do not forget . . . ," the Bible has repeated to me 169 times. And even if I wanted to, how could I forget, me whom history has never let forget?*

*Why, then, have I thrown myself with such passion into this research of the Good? At a period when, in fact, Evil is king? Perhaps it is because I have also learned from the illustrious Joshua ben Hanaiah, witness of another disaster in Jewish history, that of the destruction of the Temple in Jerusalem in A.D. 70 that "don't all mourn, for you cannot," and that, "too many cannot mourn either."*

# 46
## Occupied Paris

Here we are in France. The Jews have lived here for more than 2,000 years. My family arrived in Narbonne in A.D. 722. It was there, some years later, that a Jew became king (Natronal bar Habibai, sometimes called Makhir)—recognized by Charlemagne himself.

Here nearly 1,600 years ago the Jews arrived in Paris, where the synagogue, described by Gregory of Tours, was built almost on the exact spot where Notre Dame now stands. The *Cour de la Juiverie*, the Jewish Quarter before their expulsion by Philippe Auguste in 1182, occupied the area which became in recent centuries, in turn, the Gare de la Bastille and then the new Opera House. In the Middle Ages, the rue de la Harpe was called the *rue de la Harpe juive*. Under Saint Louis, the famous Rabbi Yehiel established his Yeshiva.

In those days the Jewish cemetery extended across today's Boulevards Saint-Michel and Saint-Germain. The Great Synagogue used to be in the Rue de la Cité, where now the Church of Saint-Madeleine is to be found. It was destroyed in the Second Expulsion by Philippe le Bel in 1306.

It was only on the 27th of September 1791 that the Jews were finally emancipated by the Revolution.

For me, France began at the Gare de l'Est, one winter's morning, in 1950. With my parents, I had managed to survive to the age of fourteen, after having lived under two totalitarian systems: Nazism and Stalinism. In fact, however, I knew Paris well before coming here. My guides were called Hugo, Dumas, Flaubert, Balzac, Eugène Sue . . . And that is where I learned about liberty—at the same time as learning French.

But I had also learnt about the great roundup of Vel'd'hiv', in 1942, which cost the lives of thousands of Jewish children— the roundup organized and executed by the French police.

For my friend, Cardinal Jean-Marie Lustiger, the mystery resides in this agonizing question: how could men who look like us and who live alongside us, all around us, here, in France, have been able, as if it was the natural thing, to become denunciators, traitors, torturers, and executioners?

The Cardinal's astonishment astonishes me: because, if these permanent leanings towards Evil did not exist, if they had not manifested themselves from the dawn of time, would we have had need of religion? *"God created Evil,"* says the Talmud, *"and its antidote: the Law."* In fact, without the presence of Evil, what do the two Commandments mean: *You must not kill* and *Love thy Neighbor?* Why should man have to remember them always?

*"It appears to me,"* wrote Karl Jaspers, *"that we must consider all things in their complete* banality, *in their prosaic triviality, for this is what distinguishes them."*

I, too, believe that since Hitler, Evil is well installed with us and in us, permanently. And, in spite of protests against todays' crimes, protests arising from our education, our culture, we have resigned ourselves to its natural and banal presence. That is why, to rebut such a resigned acceptance, I wanted to take on this search for Good, its manifestations, its acts. Hoping, in the absence of global response to contemporary distress, that these *acts of Goodness* could at last, like all exceptions, become the rule.

*"I am convinced now that Evil is always simply there, but never radical,"* wrote Hannah Arendt, in January 1964, in *Encounter. "Evil has no depth or other devilish dimension. It is capable of devastating the whole world precisely because it can expand its surface area like a mushroom. Only Goodness is profound and radical."*

It is from Pierre Saragoussi's story that I have drawn the elements of this next reflection. Pierre Saragoussi is not a Just, but a *'saved'* one, an escaped Jew from that period. Adviser to the Director General of the Treasury, he is a sweet and gentle man. With a young face but a smooth bald head, little by little as he is overcome with emotion his speech becomes more and more excited. Often he joins the tips of his fingers together, although holding his hands mainly open while he tells his tale.

"We were taken," he says to me, "on the 5th of November 1942, my parents, my sister, and me, in Paris, at 11 rue des Islettes, where we lived. It was late evening, about eleven o'clock. Two uniformed French police, accompanied by a third in civvies. In fact, they came to arrest my father, a Greek Jew who had volunteered to join a regiment of 'foreigners' in the French Army in 1940. My father held France in high esteem and that is why he joined up, to defend the country and to combat Nazism. When he saw us all together, the man in mufti (French militia? Gestapo? We never found out) said, 'Oh well, since all the family is here, take them all!' I remember the screams, the tears, the supplications. Aroused by the noise, our neighbor, Elise Caron, came. She tried to intervene. The man in civvies threatened her: 'If you interfere again, we'll take you too!' The police took us to the Commissariat in the 18th Arrondissement. Dozens of people, all arrested like us, were waiting. One of the uniformed policemen who brought us there asked my parents to go to him, then he looked at my sister and me for a long time. She was eight and I was five. The policeman, perhaps moved by my parents' reactions, took their papers and then called out: 'Couple Saragoussi: Jews without children . . .' I can remember it well. He said: 'without children.'"

Pierre Saragoussi is upset. He has to take a minute before proceeding with his story in a more assured voice.

"You must understand, that declaration by the policeman: 'Jews without children,' that still echoes in me like something very powerful and very destructive at one and the same time, since it saved us, my sister and me, and because at the same time it signified the negation of our family, because it tolled the death knell: from that moment on we were never together again."

"And your parents?"

"I never saw them again . . ."

The tears, in the eyes of this man, begin to flow again . . . I leave him time to gather himself and then he goes on:

"Afterwards, and it really is extraordinary, this policeman crossed Paris once more to go to the rue des Islettes and presented himself, at dawn, at our neighbor, Elise Caron's door, saying to her: 'If you want to take these children, come with me.' And then imagine this irrational courage of the woman, to leave her home at such an early hour, to go to the Town Hall of the 18th Arrondissement, to collect me and my sister. She kept us several days at her house but forbade us to go near the windows because she was frightened of a grocer, whom she mistrusted, who lived just opposite. It appears that I cried all the time, calling out for my parents. Elise Caron, for her part, prepared to send us to a safer hideout. She had contacted her sister-in-law, Lucienne Guyollot, who lived in a village in the Yonne valley, between Auxerre and Joigny: at Appoigny. Mme. Guyollot had therefore taken a train from Migennes to come and look for us in Paris . . . There again, when one imagines what that could have meant, in that era, to dare to go from Migennes to Paris by train, in order to take back with her, to her house, two Jewish children . . . It was an act of unbelievable courage! I have often thought about it. It was also a natural courage, an ordinary courage, because Mme. Guyollot like Mme. Caron was not a politically active person or somebody who campaigned against Nazism, anti-Semitism . . . I think they acted out of a sense of revulsion, a spontaneous revolt against inhuman actions. We stayed with her, at her house, at Appoigny, up to the end of the war and a little after. Everyone in the village knew we were Jews, and nobody said anything. What is especially puzzling, if one thinks about it, is that in Appoigny there were collaborators, active collaborators (who were eventually killed by the Resistance after the war)—

but everybody observed a kind of silence, a *passive complicity*. A sort of chain of silence was built by them, where each one played a role in our protection. Also we were baptized, thanks to the village Curé's complicity, after he was approached by Mme. Guyollot: with baptismal certificates, we were somewhat better protected. It was my father who wrote, just before he disappeared, to Lucienne Guyollot to recommend her to proceed with this strategy . . . And then a strange thing happened: great danger followed from a bit of unforeseen bad luck. Lucienne Guyollot ran a cafe-restaurant which had many German customers. One day, one of them, an officer went upstairs and entered my room. He saw, there on the mantle-piece, a photo of my parents. He went back down to the restaurant:

"'That photo, the one of the children's parents: they are Jews,' he said to Lucienne Guyollot, 'Why are you doing this?' My aunt (for that is what me and my sister called Lucienne Guyollot) tried to put together an explanation without giving the whole game away. Then the German officer appeared satisfied and replied to her: 'That's humane, it's humane . . .' He never denounced my aunt. You see: there was a sort of chain of solidarity, made up of unforeseen links, like the discretion, the understanding of this German."

What would have happened, Paul Ricoeur and I asked ourselves, if this officer had found, in Lucienne Guyollot's house, not a photo of the Jewish couple whose children she was hiding, but a revolver used by the Resistance? He would have taken out his own revolver and shot Lucienne Guyollot, along with other villagers. For he would then have found something in a language he understood well: that of violence. Knowing his own and unjust code, he would have replied, to this supposed revolver, with violence in the service of justice: just violence, truly in his eyes, but violence all the same. By reflex action, out of habit, he would have countered violence with violence.

But here, confronted in a language for which he doesn't know the rules—a language which is aimed at that part of his being totally buried in a thick layer of ideology, education, and the natural propensities of Evil—he is taken off guard. And under his Nazi uniform, in the heart of the man he is, there lights for an instant this spark of humanity, this eternal knowledge of Good which, from the start of my adventure, I have been trying to flush out.

That German officer did not eat that day, nor any day since, in Lucienne Guyollot's restaurant. He never came back. As if he feared that, in spite of himself, he would be tempted to fall back into his Evil ways, and do what he "should" as a Nazi.

Pierre Saragoussi carries on: "Those two women, Elise Caron and Lucienne Guyollot in particular, made such great gestures, in truth, such beautiful gestures, that I have always retained a huge admiration for them. Because, in fact, you know, in these cases you can ask yourself the question: 'And you . . . what would you have done?' It's true: in fact, you can never be sure of yourself, of having been able to accomplish such great acts of strength, of capacity, in those terrible times, to risk your life for others, as they did." Pierre Saragoussi is nearly crying, a photo of his parents in his hand.

"There is something which has been on my conscience all this time," he added. "When my sister and I climbed on the train for Yonne, Appoigny, towards the south, towards life, at the exact same time my parents were on a train in a convoy which was going in a completely opposite direction: towards death . . ."

Pierre Saragoussi is quiet.

A little later, he again answers my questions: "Did you ever again find that policeman who saved your life by handing you over to Mme. Caron after falsifying your parents' papers by declaring them 'without children'?"

"I did not return to Paris until 1960. Alas, no . . . I never found him . . ."

"Nowadays, what is your relationship with Lucienne Guyollot?"

"You know, at Appoigny, Lucienne became our mother, . . . even though we called her 'aunt' . . . She is still alive, although quite old. My sister and I fixed her up in Nice, where we often go to see her.''

"Pierre, you mentioned the role of the French police in the successive roundups of the Jews. Your parents were victims of these roundups, and you yourself were, though thanks to a Parisian policeman you were saved. Do you think there were many policemen like him? Many policemen capable of taking such risks to save two Jewish children from death?''

"In fact, I find it admirable because it is exemplary. Very often, too often, one thinks that one can do nothing, that one belongs to a team in which before everything else you must *obey*. And yet, that man, whom we do not know, took the risk, of being reported by his colleagues, by his superiors, for saying '*no*' in secret, and acted. It is a gesture that gives hope.''

# 47

# Police station of the Just

Pierre Saragoussi is right: the police, the officials who carried out orders and those who did not expose a problem that is still very real: that of conscience.

Is a man bound to disobey, and even oppose orders from his superiors when these orders flout all human rights?

Does a state which, by use of force, abrogates the laws and regulations of the constitution on which it was based still merit respect?

These are questions which are still worth asking today, but to which a country like Denmark, during the war, gave an unequivocal answer. Her police played a determining role in the rescue of the Jews, in October 1943, when the population helped all the Jewish members of the community to escape to Sweden: the police were the ones who directed the people towards the clandestine points of embarkation.

I am going to find police of this kind, in Nancy. There were seven of them. Two of them are still alive today: Pierre Marie and Charles Bouy, the only survivors of the "Police station of the Just."

Charles Bouy is no longer young. This policeman with a rebellious streak and a mischievous look is ninety years old. Often supporting his chin with his fist while speaking, he delivers an unequivocal message about his feelings at the time:

"I was never able to accept the Nazis . . . Never . . . My grandfather fought in the 1870 war. He was at the front . . . I never liked war. Then, on that day, the 17th of July 1942, the telephone rang at the police station. Someone asked for Inspector Marie. I said to Pierre, who was next to me in his office: 'It's for you.' It was a friend talking, a Parisian policeman, and he told us about a terrible roundup of the Jews in Paris, and warned us that very soon there would be another one in Nancy. Then Pierre called us together: 'The situation is very serious,' he said, 'in Paris they are rounding up the Jews. Rounding them up, they are rounding them up . . .' And then he explained what his friend had told him: that in Paris they had taken the Jews to a large sports stadium before sending them east, to concentration camps. We immediately visited all the areas of Nancy, the four arrondisements, to warn all the Jews in our town and to tell them to go away. Because in a few days' time they also risked being taken away from here and sent on their way by the Germans. We said to them: 'Go and visit friends, hurry!' Most of them went—but about thirty did not believe us, they said: 'It's nothing, Mr. Bouy, they only want to send us to Germany to work.'

"On the 18th of July 1942, the day after the roundup in Paris," Regine Jacubert, one of the rescued, remembers in her turn, "the policeman Pierre Marie, whom I knew well, came to see me and said: 'You can do as you please, but warn your coreligionists that there will be a roundup of Jews in Nancy tomorrow evening. I am one of those who have been given the duty of organizing the roundup, and I hope to goodness not to find any Jews at home!' Then I ran from door to door to warn everybody. Pierre Marie had told me that we must hide for several days, and that afterwards he would give us a packet of false identity cards. He was as good as his word. Unfortunately, a couple of Jews who fled were arrested at the border. The Germans must have tortured them because they talked, and Commissaire Vigneron was arrested; he spent three months in prison."

"Do you think it normal," I say to Regine Jacubert, "what these policemen Marie, Vigneron, and Bouy did for you?"

"At that time, I was young, naive. After the war, I began to understand what an exceptional, aberrant thing these police-men, Vigneron, Marie, and Bouy, had done here in Nancy! A whole police station helping Jews . . . But these were people we had always known. I think they held us in a certain position of esteem. They knew we had had to fight to obtain French nationality—that no one had wanted to grant it to us before the war . . . You must not think that things had always been easy!"

Pierre Marie is not much younger than his friend Charles Bouy, but he is alert. Neither the white sparse hair nor the glasses made him look old. He lives with his wife in three rooms on the third floor of a sort of inexpensive apartment block.

"I am eighty-five," he says. "The roundup in Nancy took place on the 19th of July 1942, two days after the one in Paris. When we learnt that we were going to have a roundup in Nancy, we all got together. In our section, there were seven of us: two secretaries and five inspectors. We decided to go to the help of the Jews, and each one of us took a list and went round Nancy to warn them. Some of them refused false identity cards to enable them to get away . . . Alas, 30 of them were arrested by the Germans, but on our side we had been able to warn over 300."

"And were they saved?"

"Yes . . . A while ago you asked why I acted as I did. Well, from humanity and patriotism. I had been in the police since 1935. I knew a lot of the Jews by the wartime: Poles and Italians. They had come to France to work. They were good people and respected our laws. As we often saw them at the police station, we knew them well, we had a certain sympathy for them. We were like friends. For example, Jerome Sorin, who is here with us, . . . I have known him and his sister Regine Jacubert since they were very little . . . And from then on things got worse. When, through the police organization, the Vichy Government gave the order to carry out a census of the Jews, we were very upset. Following that, when in 1941, we had to give them the yellow stars from the police station, it was really painful. The men, women, and children were all crying: they were treated like animals."

"In 1941–42, did you already realize the danger they were in?"

"We had our suspicions, but we did not know they were going to their deaths. The Jews from Nancy thought that they were going to a work camp near Vittel where French and allied nationals were being interned."

"In which year did you learn the truth about the death camps?"

"Very late. Vichy propaganda never spoke about such things. We didn't know until the liberation."

"Of your group of seven at Nancy there are only two still alive, correct?"

"Yes, Charles Bouy and me. I joined the police on the 1st of August 1930, and Charles the 1st of February 1930! We have known each other for more than sixty years . . ."

Charles Bouy stays with his daughter and grandchildren in the same house he was living in during the war.

"How were you able to make the false papers?"

"We made them here, with Edward . . . , Edward Vigneron, one of our good friends at the police station. It was at night, by candlelight, when the children were in bed—we had to make sure they didn't see what we were going to do, that they didn't know. We finished about midnight. As it was very late, I asked Edward to stay the night with us. To be sure, like every policeman, he had a night pass, but if he had run into some Germans with the false passes in his pocket, he would have risked everything. Yes, we made our seven or eight cards with the light of a candle, so as not to be seen doing it."

"Did you have genuine cards on which you wrote false names and fixed real photos?"

"Yes. I borrowed a seal from the police station. One day, I arrived about noon: two of the men were out and the duty man wanted to go for something to eat . . . I told him to go and get something. There was nobody left—but there were two pads of forms on the Commissioner's desk. I took them and went

straight to my house with them. I didn't want to go around
with them in my pocket. Next day the Commissioner com-
plained; there was an investigation—without result . . .''

"Weren't you afraid?"

"Oh yes, once: when they arrested Edward Vigneron. Need-
less to say, the Germans were furious that their roundup in
Nancy had given no results! In his defense Edward Vigneron
commented that with all the publicity given to the Paris
roundup, two days previously, it was clear that the Jews in
Nancy had been suspicious and cleared off. As there was no
proof against him, the Germans finished up by letting him go. I
had a hiding place for the false identity cards, the hutch,
behind the rabbits.''

After this, Charles Bouy, Pierre Marie, and I go down to the
yard where the famous hutch still stands. Charles Bouy leans
over, opens the hutch door and shows me, in one of the lower
cages, where he put the false identity cards to hide them from
any likely search made by the Germans: "I hid the papers here,
in the evening, between eleven and midnight, when we finished," he said in a mischievous and friendly way.

Another Jewish escapee from this adventure in Nancy,
Henri Krischer, remembers:

"On the 18th of July 1942, around midnight, I arrived back
in Nancy, from Strasbourg. And, you can imagine my surprise,
when, as I came into the railway station with my young brother
who had accompanied me for the first time, I was accosted by
two men who showed me they were police inspectors and then
said to me: 'Listen, Mr Krischer, the Gestapo is looking for you
and your parents. We were able to warn them and they have
managed to hide in a place we know: we'll take you there.' And
they took us to the friends who were sheltering my parents, M.
and Mme. Mouton ('sheep'), who at that time had a horsemeat
butcher shop (an amusing coincidence!) in the fashionable
quarter of the rue Saint-Nicholas in Nancy. As we were
escorted thus by these policemen to the Moutons' house, and
very happy to see my parents again, the inspectors advised me
that sometime in the next two days they would come back and

take us to the railway station where we would take the train for Dijon. They asked me for photos so they could produce normal identity cards, without showing the word *Jew*. I must say that at that time I was a foreigner, of indeterminate nationality. And that's how it happened. My mother prepared everything very quickly, washed the clothes I had brought back, and two days later the same two inspectors came and took us, my brother and me, to Nancy Station. They bought our tickets for us, didn't let us wander out of their sight for a minute, a little bit like we were under arrest . . . They put us on the train and, just before the train moved off, they gave us our tickets and our famous identity cards. I must tell you something: that card saved my life, and if I am still here, it is because I had one very important and precious thing: that genuine false identity card!"

"There must still be time," sighs Regine Jacubert, "to tell this story."

Soon there won't be anybody left, only memories. It won't be any use advertising in a newspaper, making an appeal for witnesses. The only evidence will be that which the nations will have voluntarily retained and that which will be found written in the big book of the ills of the world. Now, among those who will come after us, who will want, or have the courage to feature in such a book? Between the Gulag and Hiroshima, Stalin and Pol Pot, who will find it necessary to dedicate more than fifty pages to Auschwitz? Nobody—only, perhaps, the Jews.

# 48

# Good neighbors

Steven Spielberg tries, while there is still time, to recall the stories of the thousands of Jewish escapees of the Holocaust. Of the survivors.

On my part, I am trying to log and transmit the stories of their rescuers. The Just.

"Whatever horrors are still to come in History," writes Paul Ricoeur when considering my film *Tzedek: The Just,* "I hope there will be, forever and always, Just men as well as artists capable of preserving the perishable traces of their actions."

So, pushed on by the urgency, I am trying to hurry, after my return from Nancy, to visit Lucienne Guyollot, Pierre Saragoussi's savior. But . . . I am late: she is in the hospital, and the doctors advise against me interviewing her. That leaves Giselle Caron, Elise's daughter, Saragoussi's neighbor.

At the time of the arrest of the Saragoussi family, in 1942, Giselle Caron was a young girl of eighteen. However, she remembers those events very well. The Saragoussis lived on the floor below them at 11 rue des Islettes. They maintained good neighborly relations, even excellent, one could say. Giselle Caron, serious-looking under her white curly hair, remembers this period in a melancholic way:

"We knew that they were Jews, of course! They were good people, very kind, a lovable family. Mr. Saragoussi, the children's father, went to work every day in a material shop in Boulevard Barbes. He had no problems with anyone, he always had a cheery greeting for us when we met. When the French police came to look for him we couldn't believe it: we had already had the roundup of Vel'd'hiv', and our neighbors hadn't been involved. Then we thought the problem must be sorted out. We heard shouts, crying, and my mother went down. She forbade me to follow. She stormed and protested, but the police sent her back home in tears and led the Saragoussi family with their two children away. Following that, you know the story, with the policeman coming back at dawn, and my mother going with him to the police station to bring back little Pierre and his big sister Eddie. By the time my aunt, Lucienne Guyollot, took them to Appoigny, Eddie had been crying silently for three whole days in our apartment; she cried quietly, nonstop. It was pitiful. Pierre was younger; he cried and moaned. By good luck, my Aunt Lucienne, at Appoigny, was able to do everything for them later. In fact, she brought them up."

"Your mother and you, why did you decide to collect these children when the policeman came back?"

"You know, I can still hear the cries of that desperate woman, of that family, ringing in my ears! They were not from our family, but how could we let these babes we were offered go to their deaths in that way? My mother was forty-two at the time, and she felt just the same as I have explained to you today. We had to save them, whatever! It was a natural thing to do because, I think, its a question of heart. If such a situation ever presented itself again, in the same way, I am sure I would do the same as my mother did: without hesitation."

"Were you afraid?"

"Yes, I was. I was very afraid. Especially when that police-man came back very early in the morning, about 5 A.M. I said to my mother, 'This is it! This is it! They are going to take you away because you helped the Saragoussis a little while ago when they came to arrest them! They are going to take you away!' We half-opened the door, not very sure. And then it was the swallow (you know that is what we called the police because of the capes they wore). He was standing there, with his bicycle, and he said to my mother: 'Mr. Saragoussi has told me that you will take the children. If you want to, follow me . . .' I was not at all sure. I let my mother go with the policeman saying: 'Is it true? Isn't it really a trap?' I waited, dying of anguish. And then, after six o' clock in the morning, my mother returned with the two little ones. After that I remember, we went down into their parents' flat to collect the childrens' things, their clothes, etc., before the police came back and sealed it up: it was a shock to see all that was left of the apartment. One felt . . . *one felt that life had ceased there.*"

"Today, fifty years later, you are telling me that, on the one hand, you saw French police arresting a whole family, and on the other, one of the policemen came back to give you the children from this family: How do you differentiate the two?"

"There was a terrible dichotomy. We were surrounded by so many French who had taken the German silver! We never knew in whom or in what we might place our confidence. That is why, when I saw my mother go away with that policeman, I said to myself: 'This story, it's not possible, it's not true: she'll never come back!' But, the policeman had not lied. She came back. I knew then that there were still men with souls. Men who could, themselves, be parents, with children, who saw how distressed they were . . . It is a period of my life that I can never forget!"

# 49

# The Auvergne

Neither had Lea Radacz been able to forget those roundups of the 16th and 17th of July 1942, designated under the administrative code name as "the Spring Wind," organized and executed by the French police, who, by deploying about 900 teams, had arrested on those two days 12,884 Jews, of which 4,051 were children.

With an oval face, hair cut short, anxious to remember accurately about the events of the time: Lea Radacz, following my questions, evokes these memories:

"During the Occupation," she says, "we found ourselves in a village in the Lozere area: Le Malzieu-Ville, close to Mende. That was in 1942 after the roundup in Paris where we lived. I was fourteen. My parents had acquaintances, friends, down there, near Saint-Chely-d'Apcher."

"How many of there were you?"

"There were nearly 100 Jews."

"To how many inhabitants?"

"Nine hundred, counting the little hamlets around Malzieu—little hamlets where we had to go to find food."

"And nobody denounced you? . . ."

"No. Everybody in the village took part."

"Other than the cost of rent, did you give any money to these people who sheltered you?"

"No, no. We never tried to bribe them."

"A hundred Jews in a village of 900 people could hardly pass unnoticed!"

"That's true. There had to be total solidarity, a solidarity without fail! Later, you know, when we went back, after the war, we were received like local countryfolk, like members of family . . ."

A peal of bells welcomes me at the edge of the village. On this narrow, twisting country road, bordered by walls of old mossy stone which seem to support the fields and the woods, the car suddenly has to give up all pretensions of movement: we must stop to let the sheep past. There are several hundred, en masse, bleating, jostling each other a bit, filling the whole road, hassled by dogs and shepherded by a young man in no hurry. When finally the flock disappears, I find we are practically there. An arrow with the name Malzieu on it points the way. I pass through the main gateway to the heart of the old, medieval-looking village. In the traditional central square, a no less traditional fountain is pouring out fresh, clear water. Under a high canopy, the window of a shoe shop: this is where I am going. Mr. René Raoul, the shoemaker in Malzieu, is expecting me.

Thin-faced, bald at the front but head framed with white hair, he greets me kindly. His words, tinged lightly with the local accent, reveal his good nature. René Raoul is a Catholic—one of those Catholics for whom to save Jews was an absolute necessity in that period dominated by hate.

"About when," I ask him, "did the first Jews arrive here?"

"Difficult to say. The first to arrive was a Mr. Kuper. I don't remember anymore when he came. He was very old. That was before we were occupied by the Germans, here in the South. Mr. Kuper lived in the rue du Puy; unfortunately, he was taken and deported. He has never come back . . . It was after that when the other Jews arrived in Malzieu. The Poles were the most numerous. Among them were the families Radacz, Bromberg, etc. There was also a Hungarian family and a Dutch diamond merchant. There were also other families, but naturally, I best remember those with which I was directly involved.

"Who were they?"

"The Radacz family, of course. My father put them up in the villa that my sister lives in today. The Jews loved to meet them again, there were great ties between them: they partied and partied! I often went there because our garden, where we raised rabbits, was attached to the villa. In fact, I was there practically every day. From there you could see everything and who was coming. There was a little road leading to the house, and, at the back, you could run away as fast and as far as necessary. Later, that is the way our friends, the Jews, left when the Germans tracked them here!"

"All that was very dangerous!"

"Yes, but we didn't think so. They left when it became very serious. One day Mme. Radacz, Lea's mother, arrived here in a real state. She told us that the Germans had organized a roundup in Malzieu, but all the Jews were saved and that she would have to flee while she was able. She came to tell me where she was hiding with her family; she asked me to take news to her in the days to come. I agreed willingly. They went to hide in Vilard, an old manor house, two miles from here. The Bromberg and other families were also there. But they weren't able to stay there as the situation worsened. They had to leave the country. Mr. Radacz then came to see my father, before leaving, to ask him to keep all the possessions he couldn't take with him, and, in case they didn't return, to make him a present of them. However, we did have the pleasure of seeing them return, he and all his family, at the end of the war!"

I come back to the question of risk taking, of danger incurred: "Were you frightened, during all that time?"

René Raoul responds very sweetly: "In such moments, you know, you are thinking of others and forget yourself: I think that is the reason you're not frightened."

# 50

# Doctor's cure

*When you think of others, you forget yourself and are not afraid.* There you are, simple—and just. René Raoul does not show generosity towards others to beat or overcome his fear, but he forgets to be afraid because, first of all, he feels solidarity with others. Like Irena Sendler, in Poland.

Thus, fear—the main excuse, most often used, for our noninvolvement in favor of individuals in danger—disappears thanks to the involvement itself! What then is generosity? *"A desire by which one individual, with no other reason than right itself, makes himself help other men and establishes a bond of friendship between them."*

Spinoza, like Freud later, could not conceive of an act of generosity without a desire for reciprocity. Rene Raoul would, in these circumstances, have helped Jews to gain their friendship, perhaps also their love, or other advantages of an affectionate kind. Now, as much with the shoemaker from Malzieu as with other Justs that I have met, I have not detected in their gestures of solidarity with the Jews any other reason than simple and plain goodwill. Throughout this inquiry, perhaps I have even discovered, in these modest self-effacing beings, a category of humanity which we often look for in vain: free men.

I am impatient, therefore, to visit other Just people in this fortified village. Jacqueline and Marc Monod welcome me with warmth and kindness, both of them exchanging the lead in the conversation, as old accomplices do. Seated in large armchairs, they present an image of a couple united in complete harmony. The memories which we are asking them to revisit unite them even more, as it takes them back to the period of their youth as well as the war. Jacqueline Monod's right hand plays with the large pearls on her necklace. Marc Monod, bald, has a slim moustache and an angular determined-looking face. His eyes sparkle behind his glasses. I sense that, today as in wartime, this Protestant couple is absolutely resolute in their adherence to the path of righteousness, to justice and fair play.

"My father learnt through a friend in Mende that the doctor at Malzieu, having been widowed, wished to leave the country practice. There was, therefore, an opportunity for a young doctor to take over. I came and had a look. That was in February 1942. I arrived in a huge snowstorm. It was grim . . . and I got stuck! That's it."

Marc and Jacqueline Monod burst out laughing.

"Did you know about Petain's laws of exception?"

"Yes, indeed. Everyone knew about them."

"And how did you react to them, at the time?"

"With indignation and horror! How else could one react?"

"When you arrived, were there already many Jews and their families in the area?"

"A good number of them were already here. But I very quickly got to know what went on. In fact, when the first Jewish couples arrived, they found the place so nice, with a welcoming population and provisions available, that they thought it much better than in a town. They settled in, and word of mouth soon did the rest. Many of their friends, and friends of their friends, originally from Holland and Belgium, little by little came to live in Malzieu."

"Did these new, and numerous, arrivals not risk, from one day to another, being spotted or denounced?"

"We dreaded it. One day, these Jews would be trouble. It

was foreseeable. There were some who were hidden in the vaults of the Church, thanks to the Curé, Mr. Beraud! Thinking about the risks of denunciation, we had a word with Pastor Gourdon about how to warn them and protect them. He was worried, like us, about the threats which hung over us, but had access to friends in the police station in Mende. He knew what was happening and what was going to happen. And we were already aware of the roundups which had taken place in the Cevennes area. We had to have a warning system for any new trouble, especially a roundup. What you have to do when you have to . . . For our part, my wife and I joined the Resistance at the end of 1942, with an introduction from Gilbert de Chambrun, the regional chief of the Resistance in the Lozere area."

"Was it the fact of being in the Resistance that led you to help the Jews, or was it personal conviction?"

"Ah, not at all! It was from personal conviction, as much my wife's as my own. We were Protestants, and the Protestant position in France is to be as little anti-Jewish as possible. And I was from a family who supported Dreyfus in the famous case. There was a very pro-Jewish tradition in my family which was never talked about, but was always there. Even if by chance we had been anti-Semites, which was not the case in our house, then the fate which was imposed on the Jews would have made us *pro-Semites* and help them all the more. It wasn't a case of love, but . . . How do you say? These Jews were martyred, hunted: they had to escape capture . . . In fact, that had nothing to do with the Resistance, it was our commitment, inevitable . . ."

"But, weren't you doubling the risks you ran by working for the Resistance and an organization to support the Jews?"

"At that time I didn't even think about that! It is possible, yes, it is possible that the risk was doubled. But, you know, after the war, someone found a packet of letters of denunciation naming me and my wife, in the files of the police station in Mende! At least one every week . . . In fact, those that we protected from the Gestapo, were lucky that the Gestapo did not like traveling far from bases, into isolated parts of the country like ours. Since the Decree of the STO of the 2nd February 1943, about compulsory working in Germany, many young men were taken as they went about. In our region this stimulated us to create a large force of armed Maquis which made it very dangerous for any Gestapo car to risk venturing into our countryside."

"Mr. and Mrs. Monod, did you know that there were other people here helping the Jews during the war? Like René Raoul, for example? When I talked to him yesterday he gave me the impression that he acted all alone in his neck of the woods, without saying anything . . ."

The couple exclaim in concert: "But that's right! That's exactly right! Everyone had to be very discreet, one to another . . ."

I tell them about René Raoul, his supporting the Radacz and Bromberg families. Marc Monod listens to me with a broad smile on his lips. "And to think that I never knew, right up to this minute, that René Raoul was also active!"

"That is extraordinary, because you know him well: you were his doctor, you met each other often . . . and you didn't know, each one of you that the other . . . ?"

"Yes! It was very important! The organization of all that kind of thing had to be very well guarded to minimize the risks. I knew that the secrecy was really remarkably tight."

"Who else do you know at Malzieu who helped the Jews?"

"There was Mr. Souchon, the infants' teacher. There were the Pages, the hotelier Pages who helped them a lot, who took them in with him . . ."

"How was this aid transmitted to the refugee Jews in Malzieu?"

"There were about 100 of them, spread out all over the area, in Malzieu and round about, dispersed in farms and hamlets."

"Among how many inhabitants? Eight hundred? Nine hundred?"

"Yes."

"But they represented more than 10 percent of the population! Was the tolerance threshold not broken? . . ."

Jacqueline and Marc Monod laugh. "At Malzieu, the people helped them, with or without 'tolerance threshold.'"

"How did you get on with them?"

"At first, as doctor, I cared for them free of charge, because I knew that their resources were limited. In fact, they lived, they survived in very poor condition. But everything seemed more or less OK until the roundup in 1943."

"Did Pastor Gourdon still have his contacts at the Police station? Didn't he warn you of the imminent roundup?"

"Yes. Beforehand, he gave us this signal arrangement: 'If I telegraph you that *the packet has arrived,* that signifies that there is going to be a roundup. You can warn the Jews to hide.' That is what happened: we received the telegram. But Father Gourdon had been obliged to send several, to eight different contacts. The censor's office was suspicious, and the roundup was rescheduled for two days later. The Jews from Malzieu, who were in hiding, wanted to return to the village, seeing that nothing was happening. *And that's exactly when the roundup started . . .*"

Jacqueline Monod intervened: "That could have been dramatic, if this roundup had taken place two days later, because on the day—the French, the French police!—scarcely found two or three people."

"Two, and they were able to escape!" fills in her husband, who asks to tell this part of the story in which they all participated.

"One of these Jews, when he reached the village, learnt that the police were only a few steps away from arresting him. He immediately went to bed and sent for us, my husband and me, so that we could give him a medical certificate saying he was too ill to travel. All the women in the block were there, as well as the neighbors. They kept guard round his bed. A young policeman watched the room. At a signal, the women all charged at the policeman scratching with their nails, and the Jew ran off, he escaped at high speed just as my husband was writing out the certificate declaring him unfit to travel!"

The Monod couple laughed heartily at the memory of this scene, even if its ramifications were not without worry.

"Our fugitive was well hidden. The police searched everywhere without finding him . . . But that event brought us much unpleasantness, threats, and implied threats on the telephone. For example, shortly afterwards, my husband received a call purporting to be from Marvejols, where a violent individual summed it all up by explaining the facts to the doctor about this poor impotent who ran so fast!"

"The strange thing was," Marc Monod speaks again, "that I had the impression that the man on the other end of the line was forcing himself to appear angry . . ."

"Were you frightened?"

Jacqueline Monod lets out an exclamation. "Yes," she was frightened. Her husband hesitates: "Frightened? My wife was frightened. Me . . . I was so busy I didn't have time for fear! That's what I told myself. But later, yes, we were frightened. At home we had organized a little passage so that we could escape through the loft, in case when . . ."

"One evening," Mme. Monod remembers, "someone telephoned my husband to advise him not to sleep at home as there had been some arrests in Marvejols. My husband was tired, he had a temperature and a boil which was giving him a lot of pain. We went to find some friends—people who had always been our friends and whom we loved greatly—to ask them if my husband could sleep at their house. They didn't dare refuse, for sure, but they were a bit reluctant, a little reserved, in a way we did not like to impose on them. My husband said: 'Too bad . . . ! Come what may, I'm sleeping in my own house!' "

Marc Monod watches his wife speaking, with tenderness, a light smile on his lips.

"That night, we were like the Jews. We felt abandoned, we had nobody else . . . Oh, if we were frightened, I must say that all around us were *very* frightened!"

A laugh without resentment, a calm laugh, ended this last

observation. I will never tire of the fact that my interviewees never seem to cultivate regrets.

"Fifty years after? Those were the most beautiful and the most passionate years of our lives!" exclaims Marc Monod.

"If it happened again, would you do the same again? Would you take the same risks?"

"Oh yes! Yes, certainly! You know, we weren't members of the Resistance from the surrender, from 1940, only for the one good reason that the Resistance did not exist yet. But from the moral point of view, we were 'resistants' ever since the armistice. Pétain's collaboration: we were revolted by it, we were against it, absolutely!"

I leave Le Malzieu-Ville with sentiments close to those which I will experience in Chambon-sur-Lignon where, there too, a local population took huge risks by fearlessly taking a key decision: to welcome, protect, help, and to save those whom Nazism threatened with extermination. In these French villages, on the contrary, they did everything so they could live.

This type of collective silent pact, which no one is going to give away, fills me with admiration and leaves me equally gripped with a certain bitterness. Why if it was possible there, did it not happen everywhere? The same disposition towards Good exists, one can be sure, in other villages, in other towns—but ameliorated, without doubt, by the forces of barbarism. It is true that the geographical locations of Chambon and Malzieu, very isolated in their outlying environs, favored action which was none-the-less more risky—as we will see in Chambon.

What I have also seen is this ecumenical element of the religious, Catholic and Protestant, engaged in these affiliations of aid for the Jews—with, on the Protestant side, an obvious leaning to identify themselves with the people of the Old Testament, also perceived as the older brother in God—tinged with folk memories of anti-Protestant persecution—like brothers in misfortune. These pacts of solidarity seem to grow of themselves, but we will see that they are reinforced, revived by the exemplary action of men like Pastor Trocmé.

This leads to the thought of what would have happened then if across the whole of Europe, in all the churches and meeting houses, there had been, every week, a committed engagement comparable to that of the Curés, Pastors, and other religious leaders in all faiths?

# 51

# Pastor Trocmé's Plateau

Le Chambon-sur-Lignon is a small village of the Haut-Loire, nestling in a mountain niche, at an altitude of over 3,000 feet, between the Velay and the Vivarais, on the eastern flank of the Auvergne. About thirty-five miles from Saint-Etienne, not far from the town of Puy, Le Chambon is typical of this mountainous region of Velay which opens out onto the high plateaus overlooking the Rhone valley to the east and, plunging down through the Cevennes to the south, leads to the Mediterranean slopes of France. From the mountains which dominate the village, and which everyone here calls the *Plateau*, benefiting from clear air, there is an incomparable view over the Alps to Mont Blanc as well as over the Ardeche and the Gerbier-de-Jonc, at the feet of which is the source of the Loire, as every French schoolchild is taught. We will see that this famous Plateau has been, over the centuries, the theater of numerous actions witnessing a regional tradition of welcome and hospitality accorded here to the hunted of every origin. The Lizieux, an old volcano of the kind whose outlines have been softened and rounded by erosion, is near to the summit of the Plateau: it is the mountain, the haven nearest to the village.

Why make this journey, in my quest for the Just, to this stop at Chambon-sur-Lignon, small town on the edge of the world which, at first sight, would appear inaccessible to the tribulations of History?

Well, just because History has never ceased passing by,

stopping here, leaving deep scars—not in the form of clarion calls to arms, but of a discreet nature, silently. Here wars and persecutions have met and created their antidote: the collective solidarity of a whole community as regards another, hunted throughout Europe.

With Chambon-sur-Lignon, like a little time ago with Denmark, I am faced with a people of the Just. This "people" of Chambon (a few hundred souls) behaved in an exemplary manner in offering welcome, shelter, food, and protection to about 5,000 Jews during the war. In very large measure, it was by referring back to its traditions of hospitality that it was spurred on to organize and offer its aid. Again, it is necessary to understand that the impetus, the profound impulsion of this tradition comes in a straight line from its Protestant base.

The region of Chambon and its Plateau was, in fact, taken over by the Reform movement at its very inception. Evangelism here is not just words. The whole village attempted to put it to work, to apply the precepts relating to the love of a neighbor. Without ostentation or the least spark of pride. To a great extent, they succeeded.

"It is a link which comes from long ago!" says Gerard Bollon, the youngest of the direct witnesses who lived through that period of the war. "The history of Chambon during the war results from the general history of the community, the parish, during the centuries preceding the Second World War. We are in a region where the vast majority have been Protestant since the sixteenth century, with people who themselves have been persecuted since the revocation of the Edict of Nantes, and who have therefore known deprivation of their civil and religious freedom. When the Second World War broke out and exposed the problems being experienced by a persecuted religious minority, the Jews, we Protestants understood clearly the feelings of these people, that there were clear points of similarity between the persecution that they were suffering and that which we had faced long ago. In some ways you could say that similar destinies make us brothers. In coming to stay with us and living among us, many of the Jews, while remaining Jewish, were sensitive to our world, to our way of life: In some way, they 'became Protestants' living beside us, as we 'became Jews' in consideration of their troubles. And then, the Plateau at Chambon, over the centuries, has a real tradition of welcoming refugees, persecuted people of all kinds: during the Revolution the antirevolutionary Catholic Priests were hidden here by our Pastors. At the end of the nineteenth century, because of our excellent climate, thousands of children from the mining areas of Giers and Saint-Etienne were sent here for their health, under the auspices of the 'Workers for Children to the Mountains,' an association formed by a Pastor Comte in 1893. In 1936 we also took in refugees from the Spanish Civil War. After 1939, the antifascists of Central Europe, in their turn, found refuge on the Plateau. And then, in 1942–1944, this time it was the Jews, a large majority of whom were runaway Jews being searched for, who arrived. But, think of it: we had a large number of small hotels here, and in the immediate area. There was Le Coteau Fleuri, La Pension Beausoleil, La Joyeuse Nichée, l'Hotel des Acacias, Chante Alouette, Bel Horizon, etc."

"Charming names to face a historic reality that was not . . . But, it is a complete community here, who all help one another: the Protestants went to the aid of the Jews. Everyone here talks about the exemplary figure of Pastor Trocmé: does this movement for solidarity really owe him so much?"

"Ah, Pastor Trocmé! A great man, for sure! He died in 1971, but he has left his mark on our souls. He and his wife Magda were so clear-sighted, so enterprising! This welcome given by a whole community was, in fact, mainly made possible thanks to the Pastor, and his friends. André Trocmé was the Pastor at Chambon-sur-Lignon since 1934, and was supported by the actions of thirteen other Pastors in the parishes surrounding our own. All together they formed what they called one 'pastorale', and their sermons, in the meeting houses, always came back to the same theme: help the persecuted! The impact of these sermons on the inhabitants of the Plateau was very powerful, and the local tradition of welcoming the hunted was once again reinforced and revived in this way."

"Were there any difficult moments?"

"You couldn't say that we had anything here touching on the spectacular or heroic. No, there was a sort of *method of welcome,* with coded messages from one Pastor to the other, of the kind: 'I am sending you two Bibles . . .'"

"But, all that, I imagine, required a serious organizing of this Protestant community. Because to help all those people during the war, that would require ration cards, false papers, a capacity to feed these huge numbers of people! The estimate is that 5,000 Jews were made safe, here in Chambon."

"They say 5,000: as a round number. But we don't have any statistics or exact census. In actual fact, we think between 3,000 and 7,000 refugees were welcomed on the Plateau. But the organization, the welcoming structure . . . It wasn't as structured as all that, apart from, to be sure, the extreme care taken and the perfect conduct of Pastor Trocmé and his wife, as well as that of his thirteen Pastor colleagues and their wives.

"The Pastors seemed to have a total vision of what was going on in Europe. They were conscious of the persecution to which the Jews were subjected from the beginning of the Hitler regime. And they kept their parishioners informed, preparing them to accept refugees: they had no doubts about the Jews having to flee. From 1938 they put in hand a liaison with the American Quakers in Marseilles, a kind of system, a series of financial links foreseen to be required to welcome all comers at Chambon. From before the war the area around us was prepared with a multitude of small hotels and childrens' holiday camps being opened. And then, in 1938, the École Cevenole was founded—again by Pastor Trocmé!—which had everything required to lodge and educate young people. Finally, a multitude of institutions were involved in declaring that the Plateau and village of Chambon interested them as charitable retirement centers, and that they were prepared to support this charitable enterprise: among these institutions were, certainly, the Quakers, but also, for example, the Red Cross, the European Social Fund, the CIMADE (Comité inter-mouvements auprès des évacues), the Jewish association OSE (Organisation de secours aux enfants). All these groups supported action which would allow shelter for Jewish children and adults to be provided in our area, at Chambon and on the Plateau."

"All the same, this help, this rescue—these series of rescues, in which each and everyone in the region would have participated—this prodigious dedication and the risks taken have an exceptional character! The only comparison which comes to mind, where a whole community also came to the aid of another, is that of Denmark. There also, there was an affair involving collective solidarity, and a whole Just population!"

"Oh, you know, the old people on the Plateau say: 'There were no heroes.' Everything we did was normal. They just tried to obey God more than other men. It's a most simple message. Besides, there were other regions, in France, which adopted a similar attitude: the Cevennes, a traditional area for acceptance of refugees, or Dieulefit in the Drome; notably Protestant areas. Chambon certainly has been considered a symbol of such actions, but I don't think that these people here sought for glory. From their point of view, what they did was no more than any normal person would . . ."

# 52

# The Minister's reception

Marie Brottes has a country accent, a long face with an aquiline nose, white hair tied back in a chignon: a typical woman from the Cevennes. Despite her age, her memory doesn't give her any problems, and her lively spirit says a lot about her faith. She thinks she did nothing more than respond to what appeared to her, at the time, as "the will of God."

"You were thirty-four in 1940. When exactly did you become aware of the persecution of the Jews?"

"From the beginning of 1940 when they started arriving. For instance, at our house, we were asked to take in Dr. Motener, an Austrian, with his wife and their little five-year-old boy. We found them a room at the top of the village. Later they had to move elsewhere. They had nothing. We had to take them a little to eat, a bit of bread, potatoes, some fat—anything we could manage with our ration coupons. We must share, mustn't we?"

"A Jew, what did that mean to you?"

"Well, the Jews, are . . . well, God's people. We respected that then. The Old Testament is for the Jews, and the New Testament is for the others. Then Jesus Christ came to save the people and the Jews as well. But when He came, many things happened . . ."

"Madam Brottes, are you a Protestant?"

"Yes. I belong to the Evangelist Church."

"Does that mean that, as an Evangelist, you hold any particular feelings in regard to the Jews?"

"Yes indeed! All the same, at the end of the day, it comes as the word of God! He said you must love thy neighbor . . . Then, this 'neighbor,' that means the Jews more than all others. And there were all the other things Pastor Trocmé and the other Pastors said. And then again, when you saw the persecuted people, you know . . . Remember, before the war we had already taken in Spanish refugees, the victims of Franco's war. They weren't Jews; simply persecuted people, and we took them in, you see."

"By your reckoning, how many Jews stayed here, on the high Plateau, during the war?"

"That's a controversial question. Some say 3,000. I think there were more. Many of them came without staying very long, and there were very many! All through the war they never stopped coming. Sometimes we had to hide them only for one night by taking them to the barns about two or three miles from here, at midnight . . ."

"And how did you do it?"

"With the greatest secrecy! My neighbor, on the other side of the bridge, never knew what went on in the village. That's not to say that they were gossips!"

"Tell me about the visit of Pétain's Secretary of State: what happened then?"

"Ah! At first it was thought that Pétain himself was coming, but he went to Puy without passing near Chambon (well, we didn't take offense at that!), and then, a little later Pastor Trocmé received a letter from the Chief of Police, announcing that, as a 'consolation,' we would be having a visit from Georges Lamirand, his Minister for Youth."

"How was he received?"

Madam Brottes takes her time answering. She is once more savoring the situation, there, during wartime. She smiles and even laughs a little.

"With an official reception, the Minister had the right to expect a reception! You mustn't forget such things . . . It was

in the morning of the 15th of August. The Chief of Police and
he arrived, both in very grand uniforms; parked their cars in
the main square where the Town Councillors were to greet
them, and . . . nothing. Nobody. Not a flag to be seen—at a
time, when, in the delirium of the Vichy people, the Tricolore
was flown at the least excuse . . . They were quickly led,
without the least ceremony, so it wasn't possible for them to
give any speeches, to the banquet organized for them.

There again, the Minister and the Chief of Police were in for
a great disappointment: hardly anyone—just the Municipal
Council, the Pastors, the teachers, a few worthies from the
district—but not a flower, no decorations, no poster of Mar-
shall Pétain . . . and a most austere meal, totally and only
consisting of foods available under the rationing regulations!
An ambience, as you may guess, absolutely glacial; not at all
spontaneous cordiality! For a reception, that was a great
reception! Following the meal, they all went to the Church
where Pastor Trocmé carried out his duties. At first, he and his
friend Pastor Theis refused to say a word. It was Pastor Janet, a
Swiss who practiced at Mazet, not far from Chambon, who
gave the sermon. At the end, Lamirand shouted out: 'Vive
Pétain!' Pastor Trocmé said 'Vive Jesus Christ!' At that instant,
Pastor Janet called on everyone to sing the *'Cevenole,'* and
everyone, as loud as they could, sang the *Cevenole.* It's a
magnificent song, you know. I can still sing it for you today,
every word. With that song the Minister was dumbfounded!
The end for him came with the letter from the schoolchil-
dren.''

''A letter?''

''Yes, written by a dozen of the oldest pupils from the École
Cevenole, which Pastor Trocmé had founded. They gave it to
Lamirand and the Chief of Police, asking them to read it there
and then in front of everybody. In that letter they declared
their horror at the Vel'd'hiv' roundup in Paris. They pointed
out that it was contrary to the teaching of the Evangelist
Church to make distinctions between Jews and non-Jews, and
they announced that if such anti-Semitic persecutions were

ever to take place in the Southern Zone of France, they would disobey Vichy's orders and do everything possible to help the Jews. You can imagine the faces of the Minister and his entourage! The Chief of Police was furious and threatened Pastor Trocmé as he left. He told him that he was aware of his activities, and that he would send him for deportation. Five days later, we were raided by the police!"

"Vengeance was not long coming! What happened? It must have been dangerous with all those Jews in the village, in the hotels, and in farms around the district!"

"It was . . . in fact, it was really bad! You have to understand that, because of the height of the area, we could see visitors coming from a long way off. That day, there was a veritable convoy: one limousine followed by several police vans; one of them was full of policemen, the others were empty—proof that they were destined to take a lot of people away. They called out Pastor Trocmé and ordered him to tell all the Jews that he had hidden to present themselves to the police station the next day. They were to be taken to a country in Polish territory, specially prepared for them, thanks to the kindness of Adolf Hitler, so caring for their welfare. Because that was how it went, the propaganda of that type of men! Extermination camps: a country! What ignominious lies! . . ."

"What did Pastor Trocmé do?"

"As usual. He told them that he didn't know who were Jews and who not, as for him there were only men, and, as shepherd of this country parish, he had no reason to tell them where they were nor to give up any of his flock . . . At that, the gendarmes casually gave him a twenty-four hour extension. The next day when they went to look for the Jews, they didn't find any: only Christians were to be seen in Chambon! The Jews had had time to go and hide in the forest and back-country of the Plateau. For safety, they stayed there several days: in the village we were frightened of a new roundup, a surprise one, in the dead of night—of reprisals, to spite us for the collaborators not having been able to find anything in our village.

And then, about a week later, all our refugees came back.

Chambon is not easy of access, and we finished, in Vichy, by forgetting about roundups . . . but not for very long. Towards the end of the year, still in 1942, the Germans came to stay in the village, and then, in 1943 . . ."

"Why did you help the Jews? You ran huge risks, didn't you?"

"Absolutely formidable, yes!"

"You could have been arrested! You and all the others in the village!"

"Yes."

"And shot!"

"Yes."

"Then why?"

"Because they are the people of God. Because we had to do it. We had to protect them, shelter them, hide them . . . As we had to warn them to hide in the woods when there was that roundup. We were constantly finding them new homes, food, and comfort. We *had* to help them!"

"Were there any patrols?"

"Yes, to get food to certain Jews in their hiding places, we often had to go across the fields."

"During the war were you ever frightened? Frightened, running all these risks?"

"We were sometimes very close, too close to danger, but deep down we weren't at risk: we occupied ourselves with helping hunted people, who happened to be Jews; we knew that we were acting in God's will—how would we have been able to be frightened?"

"Fifty years after, if it occurred again, would you react the same? Without the least soul-searching? Without hesitation?"

"But, of course, how could you leave someone who is hunted to be hungry, thirsty, without trying to help him? But, that's God's word: Love thy neighbor as thyself! Your neighbor, you understand? Your neighbor . . ."

# 53

# Culpability

Le Chambon-sur-Lignon and her Just people once more raise questions about that inseparable couple, Good and Evil, and about our individual and collective responsibilities.

The German philosopher, Karl Jaspers, reflected, in a series of public seminars held shortly after the war, on the different degrees of culpability which the Nazi crimes should face. Could his analysis, if one transposed it to apply it to the Good, throw some light on the phenomena of the Just, allowing us some understanding?

Jaspers distinguished four types of culpability—criminal, political, moral, and metaphysical—in the crimes committed by the Third Reich.

*Criminal culpability* encompasses "acts, objectively established as being against unequivocal laws," and in this case the philosopher noted that only individuals could be punished: "The criminal" he said, "is always an individual." But, he also added, "Each citizen is responsible for the acts of the State to which he belongs."

*Political culpability* adjusts the previous observation, since, here, Jaspers talks of "acts of men of State," true, but that every person in that State must assume responsibility. There is no case for him here to cite collective criminal responsibility, but of a collective *moral* responsibility: "A crime is still a crime even if someone has ordered it to be carried out."

And Hannah Arendt, in an article which appeared at the

same time under the title "Organized Culpability," adds that every individual is also morally responsible "every time he fails to call out, fails to seize the slightest opportunity to call for protection of those under threat, to reduce injustice, to resist" . . .

Jaspers and Arendt speak here of the third category of culpability: *moral culpability*.

Jaspers, then goes on to evoke a fourth and last form of culpability, which he calls *metaphysical*. It seems to him to be the responsibility of everyone "for all the injustice and all the Evil committed by everyone": if you do not do something to avoid it, then you are an accomplice to it.

By listening to Jaspers and Arendt, one perceives that the rare individuals who escape from all these different degrees of culpability are very exceptional people: in reality, the Just. This exceptional characteristic, of conforming to our moral codes, makes them exemplary—not because they are made differently from others, but exactly because they are made in the same way as other men, yet they appear, in the midst of worst events in history, to preserve the universal Laws of love, justice, and truth.

These Just people are also exemplary because they prove, by their very existence, that it is possible to take such a course of action. And it is with regard to this possibility that the four degrees of culpability talked about by Jaspers can, and must, be taken into account and avoided.

In the twelfth century, in the *Guide to the Lost*, an indispensable book for the thinking Jew, Maimonides goes in the same direction when writing: *"God does not change the nature of man by miracles. Because of this important principle, it is said: Oh, if only they had this same faith and belief in Me!"* (Deuteronomy, V, 26). And Maimonides explains: *"If we accept this principle, it is not because we believe it would be difficult for God to change an individual's nature. On the contrary, that is possible and depends solely on His will. However, according to the principles contained in the Five Books of Moses, He has never wished to do it and will never want to, for if it was His will to*

*change the individual's nature each time He wanted to obtain
something from the individual, the mission of the Prophets and all
the legislation would be of no account."*

I discovered Lyons at the time of the Klaus Barbie trial. An
anguish hung over the city, an air of great tension, as if the
echoes of past events, with their loads of contempt, wished to
stifle the town. In the cafes, in the streets, in the schools, no
one talked of anything but 'the case.' Around the Courts, the
young people apprehensively watched a film of the past in
reverse.

But in a bar close by, other young folk were cooler about it:
according to them, the Jews had invented these deaths with the
aim of playing on humanity's guilty conscience.

I know that there are always those on the fringes who try to
negate the evidence of history. But I would never have believed
that those stories, those images, the witness statements given
there could generate such hatred.

And I said to myself that Jaspers situated his metaphysical
culpability in *space*, but it is also necessary to deal with it *in
time*.

I have been nourishing a senseless hope: that light would
triumph over the darkness of Evil, that the human species
would go from one progress to the next. Beaten by force of
arms, that Nazism would disappear. Now, here it is reappearing ceaselessly, under diverse guises, under various flags, as if
it had never stopped existing since the 1930s.

And, has no one really studied it, understood and judged it?

At the High Court in Lyons, it's a nice little man on trial, an
old man with an open inexpressive face who has to answer to
accusations of *crimes against humanity*. It takes a serious effort
of the imagination to picture this man at the time when he was
at the peak of his powers, when he held the power of life and
death over others.

René Nodot, he remembers it. That time, he lived through
it. The schemes of the Nazis and their accomplices, he saw
them. He even did the impossible, with his friends, to counter
the effects and save many of their potential victims from

Barbie and the other persecutors of the Jews. Round-faced, wearing glasses, René Nodot is now seventy-seven years old. He is in possession of all his faculties and does not mince words.

I listen to him with great attention, hoping his sole testimony will give back a more authentic, real air to this city of Lyons, which is oppressed by the Barbie case. Above all, he brings me back to reality: he is a Protestant, and he tells me right away that his spiritual belief has been the determinant factor in his personal attitude during the last war.

After my investigations into the Catholic Church, I am now being faced with these other Christians, the Protestants, whom we already met in Holland and Denmark. How did the French ones behave in regard to the persecuted Jews?

"I was twenty-four in 1940," says René Nodot, "I was a sergeant in the Medical Corps. I was demobilized in the South of France, and then I went back to my family, in Bourg-en-Bresse. When I arrived there everyone was talking about nothing but Pétain. He was their savior, the French acted like lost orphans who gather round a grandfather. It was an atmosphere that was difficult to overcome to let the young people know what was happening. Pétain was going to save France, he was going to be their shield . . . Unfortunately, this myth about Pétain still exists!"

René Nodot lets out a disapproving sigh, then takes up his story again: "Being a Protestant, I worked with the Pastor of Bourg-en-Bresse. I was the leader of the Christian Youth Union, better known in the world as the YMCA."

By the contacts with their coreligionists in Berlin, Munich, and Hamburg, the French Protestants, like René Nodot, were among the first to know the scale of the Nazi persecutions in Germany itself, from 1933. And they were also the first to react against them.

"I believe," he says, "that it all stems from our past, as persecuted Huguenots. In 1941 in Lyons an association called Christian Friendship was created on the initiative of Abbé Gasper (who personally saved many Jews), Father Chaillet, and

Pastor de Pury. If it had not been so dangerous, this society could well have called itself 'The Christian–Jewish Friendship,' as many Jews were also involved . . . It was an organization dedicated to helping anyone threatened with death . . . My resistance was primarily aimed at helping Jews. I helped others later, notably people in the Resistance. But the Resistance people were in danger because they had taken up arms—while the Jews were killed just because they were Jews! We learned, thanks to Pastor de Pury and Pastor Deson, from Bourg-en-Bresse, that there had been a terrible roundup in Paris. We didn't know any details, and, for sure, there wasn't a whisper of it in the Vichy press. We did learn, from Protestant messengers, that thousands of Jews, many of them children, were arrested in order to be sent to the Nazi extermination camps. The Christian Friendship had friends just about everywhere: even in the police and the police stations. That is how we were warned of a roundup in the South Zone of France in August 1942. With a friend, Rabbi Schonberg, we immediately decided to act. Thanks to the Jewish community and the news from the police station—obtained thanks to Jeanne Brousse, who worked there and who also saved many Jews herself—we were able to have lists. I knew that the Germans were expecting to arrest 4,000. They did succeed in arresting between 1,000 and 1,200, of whom 500 never came back after the deportation. As in Paris, there were sick old folk, pregnant women, and children. We were able to warn nearly all of them, but some of them didn't appear to believe us. The following year, on the 9th of February 1943, a new roundup hit Lyons. Klaus Barbie profited from it by having eighty-four people transferred to Drancy."

"But how did the first roundup go, that in August 1942? Who organized it?"

"Oh! The French police! It was the French police, like in Paris, who were covered in glory (if you can say that), on that August night in Lyons! It was between two and four o' clock in the morning. The police had chosen the poorest areas, where there were many foreign Jews. Black wagons, very characteristic, with very big wheels blocked the streets. Then the inspectors climbed the stairs of the apartment blocks, knocked loudly on the doors, and brought out the people to take them to a military camp. It was so shameful for us to watch the French Police coming to arrest the Jews!"

"Were they sent to a French camp?"

"Yes . . . Pastor de Pury, like all the Pastors then, knew of the existence of internment camps under Vichy control, nearly all situated in the south-west: Gueyze, Rivesaltes, Noe, etc. I know there were never any lists made. Many foreigners were interned, but mainly they were Jews. They often died. Pastor de Pury thought we were governed by a totalitarian regime and that, as in Germany, the Vichy people were going to take terrible measures against the Jews. From that moment, I was convinced that we must get ready to help them. Between August 1942 and February 1943, I think we saved more than 3,000 people. In the early days, we told them of some social services and people who would hide them in Lyons. But the town became less and less safe, and we had to take the Jews to other hiding places."

"How did you find Switzerland?"

"Yes, we had to cut through two layers of barbed wire . . ." René Nodot sighs, his face full of nostalgia.

"That was a terrible time, but also exciting. We had to do something for those unfortunates! Surely, we had to protect them from barbarity? Long ago, weren't we also, as Protestants, the hunted ones?"

"If you had to, would you do it again?"

"I cannot see how I could do otherwise . . . Yes, I would do it again, as you say, but," he added smiling humorously, "I know I will not be supple enough now to pass under the barbed wire!"

# 54

# John Paul II—the Pope

In Italy some 170 priests paid with their lives for having helped and hidden Jews. Many convents served as refuge against the German roundups in the Autumn of 1943, as, for example, the Convent of Saint-Sebastian, in the Catacombes. There they were fed and kept away from the curiosity of the SS. Father Lorenzi, who is giving me this information, has me visit several of the hiding places where the monks hid their proteges when the Germans were searching too close nearby, or showed themselves noisily outside the windows of this or that convent to intimidate the occupants.

Thus, in spite of the silence of Pope Pius XII, many men and women of the Roman Church were not afraid to give their aid to the hunted Jews. But what if this Pope would have spoken out? If he had called on all the Christians, but essentially his own, the Catholics, to help the Jews? Among the European community alone, would we not have found a much greater comprehension of what was happening to the Jews? Would the turn of events taken by the Holocaust not have been modified?

I have always had two images of Italy. The first of these faces, full of color and contrasts, bathed in art and the Mediterranean light: this is humanist Italy, that of Dante and Petrarch, Italy of the invention of perspective, Italy of the Rennaissance, of Giotto, Leonardo, and Michelangelo.

In the second century A.D. Rome was the most populous town in the world, and there were about 15,000 Jews organized in eleven congregations, each one with its own school, a synagogue, and social services. Five of these synagogues were in Transtevere, an old indistinct area of the right bank of the Tiber where Emperor Augustus had cleared out all the prostitutes and thieves two centuries earlier, to make the fourteenth district of Rome. Up till now, the Jews have never left the peninsula. And since the pontifical abolition of the Ghetto in Rome, in 1870, right up to the first anti-Semitic laws of 1938, emancipation of the Jews was almost perfect in Italy. On the eve of war, the community had 50,000 members, including refugees, some of whom had crossed the frontier with Germany, relying on the "flexibility" of the Italian administration.

In regard to this Italy, the other face reveals places, which, since my childhood, never cease to waken in me a dream tainted with anguish—mysterious places that have, I don't really know how to describe it, something to do with the destiny of the Jewish people: the walls of Vatican City, that's to say, the seat of central power, the supreme authority of the *Catholic Church, Apostolic and Roman*. Enigma, disquieting puzzle that these four words are!—followed by a fifth, nonetheless troubling: there in the Vatican Palace lives someone whose title alone gives off an impression of power—the *Pope*.

To understand these feelings, you must remember that I was not born in France, where the separation of the Church from the State is a fact: since the Revolution, the Church has not weighed so heavily on the life of men—on their daily lives, on their thoughts, on their behavior, on their commitments, on their reactions—as it did in Poland in the time of my childhood. At the time, it was unthinkable that a Pole, even if he were a communist, could miss Sunday Mass! At the same time, each Pogrom, each anti-Jewish demonstration could not have been organized without the knowledge of the Church, nor without its agreement and the support of its hierarchy. At such times, the bells rang as loudly as possible and my mother forbade me to show myself on the balcony. The Jews had to hurriedly close the steel shutters on their shops and go home quickly. Soon afterwards you would see one of these processions preceded by a gigantic cross and, as this procession moved on, anyone could hurt a Jew in all good conscience. Unfortunate Jew, if he was out late or had lost his way and bumped into the procession!

> Why are they ringing,
> Why do they keep on ringing,
> these arrogant bells that terrify us?

I first heard this Yiddish song in the yard of an apartment block in Warsaw, where my Grandfather Abraham lived. I was a very young lad starting to learn about the world, and this song, and only it, says everything about how a Jew from the Ghetto can look on these symbols of Christianity.

For the child that I was, these two major symbols of Christianity, the cross and the bells, were the emblems linked to an implacable enemy, an enemy that has hunted us for all time and whose inaccessible and shadowy Head Priest has his headquarters in the Vatican. For me to come to such a place is then for me to penetrate in the sanctuary, in the holy of holies of this childhood memory of a Jewish child.

It is also to bring back more recent memories: The picture of Pope Pius XII, cold, aesthetic, refusing to intervene in favor of his brother Jews. Even in favor of those arrested under his windows. However, the pressing calls of the Church hierarchy and the Catholics in high places, who asked him to denounce the anti-Jewish persecution, were many and varied. And they came from all over. I am thinking notably of the President of the Polish Government-in-exile, Wladyslav Raczkiewicz; Konrad von Preysing, Bishop of Berlin; the doyen of the Catholic Chapter of the Cathedral of Saint-Edwige in Berlin, the priest Bernhard Lichtenberg, who was later arrested by the Gestapo and who died on the 5th of November 1943, when he was transferred to Dachau.

The German Ambassador to the Vatican, Ernst von Weizsacker, reported to Berlin that numerous high-ranking churchmen were scandalized by the anti-Jewish persecution. "They say," he noted at the time, "that the Bishops of the French towns have produced similar objections and have condemned such actions."

These pressures were, nevertheless, useless: "The Pope," wrote Ambassador Weizsacker on the 26th of October 1943, "although being pressurized, they say, from many quarters, is not going to allow the slightest protest to be raised against the deportation of Jews from Rome."

Can one imagine the effect on the Catholics of Occupied Europe if, in Rome, at the Head of the Church, he had, in an official manner, solemnly, called on everyone to fight against Evil? Or, at the very least, condemned it, would this not have made people think?

In the absence of such a word of command, the churchmen at all levels of the hierarchy had therefore to act in line with their own conscience, often manifesting, and not without courage, the reality of their compassion and thus justifying, on an individual basis, their engagement to the Faith.

To believe Hannah Arendt, Pope John XXIII would have replied to anyone, when discussing what one could do to rebut the famous piece by Rolf Hochhuth, *The Vicar,* in which the German dramatist accuses Pope Pius XII of having, without any objection, allowed the Jews, including the Italian Jews, to be deported: *"Do? What can one do against the truth?"*

To enter the Vatican is not a natural act for me. Escorted by the Swiss Guard (whose famous and anachronistic uniforms were thought for a long time—and wrongly so—to have been designed by Michelangelo and haven't changed for four and a half centuries), I cross the famous square, called "Cour Saint-Damase." The Pope's secretary, Stanislas Dziwisz, is a subtle and cultivated man. Man of omnipresent confidence, he organizes everything, arranges meetings, revues the speeches, and makes me take the private lift to the rooms of John Paul II. It is he who fixed up this latest meeting. He understood what it means to me, in my search into the Just, makes it come nearer with every footstep through the Church. He knows that it is impossible for me to avoid this meeting, as he knows that it raises haunting pictures in my mind . . . And yet, here I am, invited to the Pope's table, where I learn that he has decided to lunch in my company!

Stanislas Dziwisz bids me enter the Pope's personal library. We wait for a few moments, and John Paul II arrives.

"Well now," he immediately says in Polish, "shall we eat? Are you hungry?"

"Very, . . . Holy Father, " I stammer, inwardly very excited.

"You are hungry, aren't you? Follow me . . ."

We enter a vast dining room, with a very large impressive table, covered with a white tablecloth. Three places are set: beautiful plates, silver and crystal. Dziwisz sits at the end of the table, and the Pope facing me . . .

The two-meter width of this fabulous table is quickly going to pose us a slight problem. The Pope's hearing is not good; he places his hands over his ears like a little trumpet to understand what I say when I speak. Result: he will eat nothing if I continue to shower him with words!

"Holy Father," I say to him, "eat! I will shut up while you are eating!"

"If I eat," he smiles, "I won't be able to speak. We will be forced to be silent. You won't talk, neither will I: what are we going to do?"

We laugh, and still find ways of eating. An old servant brings us a vermicelli stew, just like my mother's, years ago. Then we eat little breaded escalopes with cauliflower, all followed by lemon tea served in very tall glasses a la polonaise. This menu would only be anecdotal if it did not awaken in me a scarcely controllable emotion. Not being able to hold it in any longer, I sigh and: "You know, that was just like mother's."

"Ah, was it? Tell me about your mother."

I tell him: my mother, a Yiddish poet, has been dead for fifteen years, and in fifteen years no one has made me a meal like that: like hers, in her style, with her favorite ingredients. And I see him suddenly moved at the idea that he has, without knowing it, served a *maternal* meal, an atmosphere lost to me forever, and which has, literally, been recreated at his table.

Once the meal is over, we talk about everything, from

Russia to the Middle East. And he tells me something that, apart from the directly interested parties, no one yet knows: he is going to recognize Israel.

And, then, after a detour around the general subject of the spirit of man at this end of a century and beginning of another millennium, I say to him: "Holy Father, you know as well as me that man cannot live without hope. The great universal secular hopes have disappeared: only you are left and the Churches."

John Paul II takes his head between his hands: "That is dramatic, what you just said there!"

"Why, Holy Father? Here is a situation where everyone has to turn to you: that must please you."

"Please me? . . . Definitely not! Religion should be man's last recourse. If religion becomes the only recourse, then a war of religions will set itself ablaze . . . Listen: when you are ill, you first call for a doctor. If you call the Priest, you are already certain you will die . . . The Church has to maintain morals, ethics, hope—if not, man will become mad with thoughts of death; he will become mad at the thought of having to live forever with this idea. But if religion is all that's left, like the last rampart, faced with the problems of the world, then, yes, it is dramatic. If what you say is true, if the great secular hopes have gone, there must be, outside the Churches, something else to support man's belief."

Yes, but for something in which man can believe, first of all, does it not have to be credible? Now, to the contrary of what the philosophers say, the period of the Holocaust is not notable for the absence of God, but for the absence of Man. This last observation is perhaps even more agonizing. And I ask myself: is it this question, this problem above all others, that sends me running in search of the Just?

Today, before I leave him, I ask John Paul II if he will allow me to film an interview for my film, *Tzedek*.

"Ah," he sighs, "it's not simple to be the Pope! There are rules which I must respect . . ."

In fact, the Pope has never had interviews published in the press. He has never been in a film. When he moves around, the television companies from practically everywhere follow him: when he addresses the whole world, it is the televisions that transmit his words. When he gives an Audience, the Vatican television service records it and arranges the necessary showings. As for texts, or speeches he gives, you can't have them, other than by reading the official organs of the Vatican, *L'Osservatore romano.* As for the rest, have you ever read the Pope's declarations in this or that paper?

We cannot see any way through this mass of restrictions. But John Paul II is smiling.

"Our friend Stanislas Dziwisz will find a way," he says, "we will do something . . ."

We separate on this note of optimism, and the next day Stanislas Dziwisz calls me: he has an idea. He is going to talk to John Paul II. He is going to organize an Audience for people who escaped the Holocaust, tying it together with the fiftieth anniversary remembrances. The Pope will tell them what he thinks of Auschwitz and the anti-Jewish persecutions. He will take advantage of the opportunity to talk about the Just. Then he will say a few words to each person, as usual. And, as an exceptional favor, I will be allowed in with my camera team and equipment. Toward the end of this Audience, I will be given four or five minutes to talk to him while the camera is rolling.

The day comes, almost three months later, I arrive with my technicians. Unfortunately, the night before, Stanislas Dziwisz has had an accident: he is in hospital, one arm in plaster. I am concerned that his absence may create some slight difficulties.

Many people are there, representing various organizations of survivors, the majority coming from America and France. Access to an Audience with the Pope, in sumptuously decorated surroundings but in the middle of the crowd of people present, is not really very easy. Especially if you don't want to raise the suspicions and be handled (maybe even pushed) by the stewards, who willingly push more visitors out through the exit than they allow to enter. To each row of officials in elaborate habits and to the close guard at each stage, well muscled in their fancy uniforms, I have to be so careful without the help of Stanislas Dziwisz that would have been so useful in these circumstances.

Each time, I have to explain: "His Holiness is a friend . . ."

"His Holiness is your friend? And you, who are you?"

"Me, I'm the Jew, Marek Halter!"

Our arrival with cameras in hand causes a quiet chaos. They draw the suspicious attention of these very zealous men who scrutinize us without a break, almost as if they are looking at a cactus introduced by the devil's hand into a delicate floral arrangement. Finally, we have managed to make ourselves understood, and, after crossing through some different magnificent rooms decorated by some of the greatest Renaissance artists, we are in the Audience hall.

The ambience there is extraordinary. Little golden chairs in neat lines await the visitors. They face a platform, on which is a sort of throne, with two smaller thrones attached lower down, destined for the Pope. The right side of the hall is reserved for modern scribes, that's to say, for technicians from the Vatican television services, who record all actions of John Paul II. When he arrives, escorted by two cardinals wearing their sumptuous red brocade and their red skullcaps, everyone stands. This ceremony, which hasn't changed since the time of the Borgias, does not lack grandeur, and its hierarchic character is very noticeable.

When at last the Pope starts talking about the Just, the microphone of one of my men develops a fault. It takes me all my time to remain outwardly calm. When the microphone is fixed, John Paul II has finished talking! He rises and starts talking—for a few seconds, sometimes a few minutes—with each of the people present, who pass, one after the other, in front of him, to be very quickly moved out by the guards, always vigilant and all strong, once the interview is over. At my turn, I approach him, followed and surrounded by my technicians and their gear. John Paul II sees us and comes to me with open arms to greet me with a hug, then he asks me: "Well then, have you come direct from Paris?"

"Yes, Holy Father."

"And our friend Stanislas Dziwisz isn't here! Poor fellow: he broke his arm . . . He organized everything, and now that we are here, face to face, he is in hospital!"

"Yes, I did hear about it."

(And, faced with the guards, with difficulty! John Paul II couldn't know how much I had needed Stanislas Dziwisz for the last half hour—when I could really have done with him in good health, at my side, to keep the suspicious guards at bay.)

He looks at me with a half-smile and tells me to ask my questions. Under the eye of our camera, I ask him:

"Most Holy Father, before the war, is it true that nearly all your childhood friends were Jewish?"

"Yes."

"The majority of them were killed. Only three or four escaped death."

"Yes, it's terrible."

Some words, in their brevity, which does not say in those few instants what the expression on the face of John Paul II gives away: he changes ceaselessly, passing from one serious look to another, darker, more serious.

I ask him: "Your surviving friends escaped death thanks to the generosity of some Christians: were you one of them? What did you do for the Jews?"

I am waiting, I swear it, for another answer from the one he gives me. Many people have told me: he was one of the people who took risks for the Jews. We know, for example, that he made false papers for them during the war.

Now John Paul II answers me: *"I do not wish to claim attributes that I do not possess . . ."*

I must, perhaps, link this to an other question. I cannot. This answer is so direct, so frank, and so unexpected that I stay tongue-tied. So, he thinks what he did is not important! Not enough to make him a Just . . . And fixed to the spot, I look at him: his eyes are impenetrable. I do not know what more to say, what to think, what to do. I stammer out a "Thank you, Holy Father," and our audience is finished. A fraction of a second later, the guard pointed at my equipment: "Good, it's finished, move on," and we are on our way to the exit.

I have reflected for a long time on this answer, on his humility. I ask myself if I am not risking, by keeping this interview such as it is, giving the impression that I wanted to trap the Pope. To sum up, to be able to suggest that this Pope is no better than his predecessor of the time of the Second World War, Pius XII. But that is not my idea, far from it! As for the suggestion, John Paul II, during wartime, was a young man, twenty-four years old, while Pius XII was a sovereign pontiff in power, at the peak! Finally, there are many independent witnesses, which tends to establish that the young man in question, that's to say, the future John Paul II well and truly helped his Jewish friends during the war.

In fact, Karol Wojtyla, . . . in love with a young Jewish girl, wrote songs (he wrote the words, and his best friend, a Jew, the music) and plays, which he put on with his friends (more Jews), when he had to hide in the Bishop's palace in Cracow, pursued by the Occupation authorities because the anti-German pieces which he played exasperated them to the nth degree, . . . what did he do, in this Bishop's palace?

For certain, he found Faith. He became religious—without dreaming that, one day, this path would lead him to sit on the Throne in the Vatican, that is to say, to assume the highest spiritual responsibility for a huge number of believers. Far be it from me to underestimate the essential character of the young Karol Wojtyla when he took Holy Orders!

On the contrary, I want to draw attention to this point: at the same time as he was deepening his adherence to his faith, this young man participated in making, inside the Bishop's palace, false papers destined for Polish members of the Resistance and Jews.

But, this is how he sees it: John Paul II thinks very little of it, that it is nothing. Before his unsettling reply in the audience hall, I have had occasion to ask him about it, and, it is true, he always eludes such questions, although without lying about the presupposition that he had, in fact, made false papers.

If only there had been more like him, doing, like him, this *"nothing!"*

To satisfy my scruples, I am going to obtain, from the cinematic service at the Vatican, the film of the visit made by John Paul II to the Great Synagogue in Rome, so that I can integrate a bit into my film, *Tzedek: the Just.*

In fact, that visit on the 13th of April 1986 was a very symbolic day. It was the first time since Saint Peter—that is since the first Pope, who made a tour of all the synagogues around the Mediterranean to preach to the Jews to abandon their religion in favor of that of Jesus—that a Pope had crossed the Tiber to go, on the opposite bank, to speak to the Chief Rabbi, Elie Toaff, and say to him: "I come to greet my elder brother!"

And, I, for my part, cannot forget that the Chief Rabbi, Elie Toaff, was saved twice by two minor country priests.

Finally, how can we not remember the declaration, adopted in 1948, by the annual Assembly of German Catholics? I cite it here as a reminder, and not as a conclusion—but could it have in it a "conclusion" to the inquest on the Holocaust? This was the declaration:

"In face of the immensity of the sufferings which have been inflicted on people of the Jewish faith, in the course of a flood of crimes never officially recognized, the seventy-second Assembly of German Catholics, driven by the spirit of Christian repentance in regard to the past, declares that the injustices which took place must be compensated."

# 55

# Postcard from the past

*"Difficult to judge."* The President of Lithuania, Vitas Lands-bergis, had said to me, *"If you are walking alongside a river and you see someone drowning not far from the bank on which you are standing, you rush to his aid—but if you are on the opposite bank of the river, that's not so simple."*

A Just man from Turkey, Selahattin Ulkumen, used the same metaphor: *"I don't understand why so many people did nothing to save the Jews. It's like when someone is drowning. I can't understand how anyone can stay passive and not give a hand to save a life."*

Today, however, other massacres are perpetrated across the world without other countries intervening, unless it is in their direct interest.

And individuals?

Have we learnt anything from History?

Fifty years after the wholesale slaughter of the Second World War and after the massacre of the Jews, can we find, any more easily than yesterday, the equivalent of those thirty-six Just men whom the Scriptures say are indispensable to the survival of the world?

I now understand better the reason why Marc Bloch always questions the dead. *"From the ninety-seventh generation,"* qualifies Eccliesiastes, *"to the very last."* Thus, to the simple country Curé, today long gone, who, by his intervention, saved Elie Toaff, the future Chief Rabbi of Rome, and his family. This

latter remembers emotionally all that era and smiles, his face
again full of wonder and recognition when he thinks of the
support given to the persecuted Jews by the Italian people.

"When we were hungry, they fed us . . .", he says.

It is necessary here to underline the role of these people,
who, in spite of more than twenty years of fascist dictatorship,
did not hesitate to come to the aid of the Jews. Thus, out of
7,000 Roman Jews, 4,000 were saved after having found refuge
in the convents in town and in the surrounding countryside.

Elongated features, short beard, hair thinning and bleached
with age, the Chief Rabbi Elie Toaff is troubled, fifty years later,
when he thinks of those who helped him and to whom he bears
a loyalty which cannot be deflected. He has forgotten nothing
of those events.

"At the beginning of the war I was a very young Rabbi in
Ancona. I was saved twice, each time by a priest. The first time
was when the Germans had taken the town in September 1943:
I was leaving the synagogue to go home, a priest rushed up to
me to tell me to go with him to his house where he already had
my family: the Gestapo was at my house! With his help I was
able to go and join the underground in Piedmont. At Rosh
Hashanah, the Jewish New Year, I went to find my wife and
child who were hidden in a local village: I wanted to take them
for that one evening to where I was living to celebrate the
festival together. Suddenly another priest rushed up to me
saying: 'Don't go there! The Nazis have raided the place. Your
group has been decimated!' And he took us to his house."

Elie Toaff is a fit septuagenarian, who speaks in a lively
manner, and is very voluble, very "Italian." He cheerfully goes
on with his story:

"Night came, I asked 'our' priest for two candles and a little
wine. 'What are you going to do with that?,' he asked. I
explained to him what we wanted to do to celebrate the New
Year: my wife had to light the candles so that I could pro-
nounce the blessing. 'Then,' he said to me, 'we will celebrate
together!' We made an unforgettable Rosh Hashanah . . . That
was several days before the liberation. The survivors came

back to Ancona and I had to reopen the synagogue. The priest Dom Celacci and I stayed very close friends right up to his death."

Florence 1943: the great American art critic Bernard Berenson, hunted by the Gestapo, wrote from his hiding place that "even a Dominican Hebrew scholar has had to flee his monastery, for fear of being arrested, and has sought refuge with me." He also reported that another priest had been arrested for having hidden a Jew and that the Cardinal of Florence, Elia della Costa, declared himself guilty and demanded to be imprisoned in the priest's place.

It was in that atmosphere marked by violence and denunciation that the Mother Superior of the Convent of the Sisters of the Franciscan Missionaries of Mary, in Florence, decided to open the gates of her institution wide to the persecuted Jews. "Because it was our duty," they will tell me . . . "Because it was natural."

In Italy there are Just people by the hundred, but the story of the Franciscan Sisters of Florence touched me more than many others. Perhaps because of the glow on the faces of the rescuers and, also, the terrible pathos of the story of the Jewish child they snatched from death.

Mother Sandra, that's to say. Sister Ester Busnelli was at the time the Convent bursar. With her long white habit, bearing a simple cross and chain, a motherly look full of compassion, she offers a silhouette and profile typical of a good Sister of the Church. She is a lively woman, with a piercing look. At first she has to overcome her natural reserve and timidity. That period of history and her life is engraved on her mind, and she brings it back in a spirited manner. Her spontaneity of speech, her laughter, even to her raising her voice passionately, enchant me. She even expresses this cry of protest, completely sincere and totally candid:

"But me, I love the Jews! Without them we wouldn't even know who Christ was! Yes, I love the Jews! We worship the same God as they, don't we? We are one, we have our roots in Judaism . . ."

On hearing that, I recall Sister Ludovica, at the Convent in Plody, Poland, for whom *to save a Jewish child is like saving the Infant Jesus*. At my request, Sister Ester Busnelli, or rather Mother Sandra, returns to the dark years of the war: "Our Cardinal, Elia della Costa, told us we must help the Jews, even at peril of our lives. When the Germans came, when they invaded our Convent, I felt a kind of spirit come to me from Our Lord. We were all young, in those days. Those Jews needed us, we could not just stand there with our arms folded!

"I think that was it. Look at the senior nun, with whom I worked, Annie Lombardi: there you see someone full of courage! Me, I had a quite a bit, but she was much more courageous than me! She asked the Mother Superior to allow her to leave with them, with the Jews! Remember her name, go and see her: she will also tell you what happened. She is called Sister Emma Luisa under her religious name."

"Did many Jews pass through your convent?"

"Yes, lots, all the time. Especially from the nights of the 26th and 27th of November 1943, onwards. We had become a transit stop for those people who didn't know where to go."

"And fear? Weren't you frightened?"

"You can be sure we were! The Germans arrived in the middle of the night, searched all through the dormitories, even under the mattresses!"

"Mother Sandra, why did you help all these Jews?"

"It was our duty, wasn't it? And, to do your duty is easy when it is with people you love. I told you, I love them!"

I cannot but follow Mother Sandra's advice; I am leaving now to investigate Annie Lombardi. I discover an old lady of eighty-five, who, although ill, receives me in a very friendly way. White hair pulled back in a chignon, long and angular-featured, she talks easily. Her voice and her attitude seem to me to bear witness to a certain inescapable Goodness. Watching her, observing the movements of her hands when she speaks, I sense that I have a whole being in front of me, altogether, someone who *could not retreat* before injustice. A great air of compassion lights up her face when I question her on the subject of the Jews she sheltered during the war. From her wheelchair she listens to me, looking serious, then smiles before answering my question:

"Why?"

"Because I hurt for them. Because nobody wanted them. Because you have to help your neighbor, don't you?"

"When did you start to help the Jews?"

"In 1943. They came asking us for shelter. I looked after the domestic side of our life. They were mixed, Jews and non-Jews. We gave the Jewish refugees food like the others, we served them at table, and they each had their own room. The Spigliosi Palace is huge. At that time, one of the Jewish community, Mme. Vardi, lived in Florence: it was she who begged me to welcome into our accommodation these Jews who were running away, who were coming from everywhere, in a never-ending stream, because they were trying to escape from the Germans. It was terrible. I cannot allow myself to hate anyone, but I had to recognize that Hitler was an animal!"

"Were you afraid?"

"Well, truth to tell, not really. If I have to die, that's God's will, isn't it? I am a very strong character. Certainly, that war with the Germans became more and more awful, and a tragic situation. What times! We always lived tensed up. With anguish in our hearts for all those people to be protected. But, for myself, no, I was never frightened. I thought that it was indispensable to do what we did, that *we had to do it!*"

"What went on when the Germans arrested little Emanuele Pacifici and the other Jewish women who were staying with you?"

"That evening, when the Germans came to arrest them, I could have spat in their faces! I did insult them, I wanted to stop them from arresting those women. They told me if I didn't stop, they would take me away too. I said 'OK! I'll go with them! Take me too!' But they didn't do it because I was a Catholic. That evening, when they were taking them away, those lovely girls . . . they hung on to me crying! It was horrible. I don't want to think about it; it makes me sick, yes, sick . . ."

It is thanks to Mother Sandra and Annie Lombardi that I meet Emanuele Pacifici, the one they well and truly saved. He is the son of the man who was the Chief Rabbi of Genoa at the time (Ricardo Pacifici). He belongs to that Jewish community that has lived in Italy for more than 2,000 years—twenty-one centuries, in fact: since the time of the Maccabees! Rome, Milan, Trieste, Turin, Florence, Genoa, Venice, Livorno, Ancona, and also in Naples, Salerno, Tarento, Reggio di Calabria: so many names tied to the history of Jewish culture.

Emanuele Pacifici is a somewhat plump man, balding, aggressive, bubbling with vitality. Twinkling eyes behind thick glasses, voluble, nervous, full of life as he must have been in those painful days, fifty years ago, he tells me of his saga—that his rescuers may sometimes, inadvertently because of their great ages, have misled me about details:

"You cannot imagine the atmosphere in Italy when on the 25th of July 1943, Mussolini was relieved of his responsibilities. Soldiers left their barracks, everyone was shouting; everywhere people were burning the fascist emblems! We thought the war was over—it was only beginning! I was only twelve when the Germans invaded Italy on the 8th of September 1943. At the time a Catholic priest helped my father. He was called Don Francisco Repetto, and was the secretary to Cardinal Boetto of Genoa. Every evening he found a new place for my father to hide so that he could have peaceful nights. He was an exceptional person. He saved the lives of many Jews. As for me, I was taken to one of my mother's friends near Pisa. But, hardly a month later, a priest from Genoa came to advise us to move on with all haste: in spite of all the precautions he had taken, my father had been arrested and they were frightened that he would talk under torture. A fortnight later, he was sent to Auschwitz; he was gassed on arrival."

Now we will talk about the atmosphere in Italy at the time, and the monstrous ransom levied by the Germans on the 26th of September 1943: fifty kilos of gold for the lives of the Roman Jews! These latter were not wealthy. They hastily organized a collection among the Italians and also asked the Pope to help.

Pius XII consented to lend fifteen kilos if it was needed: the collection from the people would be enough.

Unfortunately, all this effort did not stop the Nazis—once more in their progression of infamy, once more going back on their word—from organizing, on the 16th of October 1943, a huge roundup in the course of which 1,259 Roman Jews were arrested, 896 being women and children.

They did the same in Genoa on the 3rd of November, in Florence on the 6th, Milan on the 8th, and Venice on the 5th of December. Primo Levi was arrested in December 1943 and deported to Auschwitz.

Around that time, the young Emanuele Pacifici and his mother, armed with a letter of recommendation from Cardinal Boetto in Genoa, arrived in Florence and knocked, without success, on the doors of several convents.

"Everywhere," remembers Emanuele Pacifici emotionally—his voice trembling—"they would say to us: 'Terribly sorry, but we're absolutely full.' And every door that was shut in our face was one less hope of life. Until that day, about six o'clock in the evening, we received the answer: 'Come in.' That was at the Convent of the Sisters of Carmel, and it was Mother Sandra who let us in. The next morning I was transferred to the College of Santa Marta. That saved my life. Mum was to come the following Saturday to bring my things . . ."

Emanuele Pacifici's voice breaks, and tears roll down his cheeks: "I was waiting for her. I was waiting for Mum. We were at the window, other children and me. She never came."

I remember what Mother Sandra had told me, she whom we thought might not have too clear a memory of the events: "I don't remember the dates anymore, but anyway, when the Germans hunted the Jews, it is a fact that we hid them in the Convent. I remember Emanuele Pacifici arriving one evening with his mother. We only took in mothers with babies. Now, Emanuele was already twelve, he was no longer a suckling. However, we allowed him to spend the night there in a chair beside his mother, because we didn't have any more beds. And the next day we sent him to a boy's college, Santa Marta at Settiniano. Alas, the next night his mother was arrested. He was saved because he was at the college. Up to the last moment we tried to save his mother. We pushed her into a side room in the hope that in the confusion . . . Then we tried to put her in the infirmary with the sick. But, with the accurate files held by the SS, there was no means of escape from them. She was caught and taken to Verona with the other Jews they had rounded up that day. We never heard of any of them again, so sad!''

The evidence of Mother Sandra is so moving that it is as if from *another world*. From beyond time . . . , in 1950, about to leave for Auschwitz, a message from his mother arrives for Emanuele Pacifici: a postcard, bearing the Verona postmark, dated 1943!

Actually, before the Gestapo had finished rounding up all the refugees in the Convent of Carmel at Florence, the senior nun, Annie Lombardi, was able to slip in among them and gave each of them a stamped postcard. Emanuele Pacifici's mother had thrown this card out of a train window after hurriedly scribbling some words on it. That train took her to her death in Auschwitz. On that letter from out of the blue, from a letter one feels must have been transported by the twists of fate, she sent wishes that all her family would see each other again. It is the last piece of evidence of his mother's existence that Emanuele Pacifici possesses. She had been dead *seven years* when he received it.

When I went over this episode with Mother Sandra, at first her face looked serious, before clearing with a big smile.

"But thanks be to God! Emanuele was saved!''

# 56
## Passive complicity

I have the feeling that before presenting the story of Professor Francesco Gabrielli, I should explain the reasons which led me to introduce him into this book.

Several of the people in Poland, Holland, and France who were saved have spoken to me about this complicity—sometimes passive—which has been necessary for the Just to carry out their actions. Now, up to this point, I have not interested myself in any of these anonymous "spectators" of events which I have described.

Professor Francesco Gabrielli, eminent specialist in Arab literature, belongs to that category of men who still fascinate me: those who have *done nothing*. In Rome, during the war, he had as neighbors the Modiglianis, a Jewish family whose son Enrico was to become a Deputy in the Italian Parliament. Professor Gabrielli, today, is an old man with a long thin bony face, thin hands, full of gestures saturated with culture and learning. He receives me in a friendly way and we are now sitting in his office. The walls are carpeted in books, rare works, polished editions of the Koran. His face watches mine. He awaits my questions with interest and curiosity. He knows, as we have spoken previously, what we are going to be speaking about.

"Professor," I say to him, "before the German invasion on the 8th of September 1943, what was the situation of the Jews in Italy?"

"It began to deteriorate in 1938. Between 1938 and 1943 there was a situation, perhaps a little less fraught, less tragic for them, than in Germany. But after 1943, after the 8th of September, their situation worsened so much that it became the same, everything taken into account, as that in the other European countries."

"Did you have any Jewish friends at the time?"

"Of course, yes. At the University. Even if, after 1938, they had to give up their jobs, abandon their posts."

"How did you react to the brutal Nazi repression?"

"Ah well, it was awful for me. I think I experienced the most bitter feelings in my whole life. I am not Jewish; moreover I don't have any Jewish relations. But in all I learned, Christian and liberal, I always felt, I have always seen, the persecution of the Jews as a manifestation of the most ignoble barbarity in Europe.

"In 1943 you lived with your family in the Monteverde area of Rome. Did you know the Modigliani family? Were they your neighbors?"

"No, No. We didn't know them! That family who called themselves 'Macchia,' and whose real name we did not know until after the war, arrived in our block in September 1943, after the German invasion."

"Did you think they were a Jewish family?"

"Ah, . . . yes. In fact I did think they must have been Jews. But we never asked them the question. There were other signs. They said they came from Pescara. We came from there ourselves. Now, they didn't have a Pescara accent—but, a Roman one; we were a bit puzzled at that . . ."

"What were your relations with them?"

"Good neighbors. And that, under this pressure which we all shared from the situation at the time, the war and its ramifications. There was also an official in the Resistance living in the same block, Fuliolari, with whom we had a good relationship. His house was a sort of refuge for his friends, rather . . . for all the people who become your friends in such times as those."

"Were you frightened for them? Did you ever doubt for a minute that the SS would not come to the apartment to arrest them?"

"Yes, we were frightened. We didn't know what risks they were running. We weren't sure . . . Then, selfishly, perhaps, we were frightened for ourselves."

"And at the liberation?"

"The 1st of June 1944, thanks to the military superiority of the Allies, brought the liberation that was welcomed with relief by nearly all the population of Rome. I remember the last day of the German Occupation, with the German trucks going back up the Via Aurelia to leave Rome. There was an explosion of joy, after all these months, all those horrible years!"

"After the war, did you ever see the Modigliani family again?"

"Yes, I went to visit them several times after the liberation, at their new address. Then we lost touch. Recently, I learnt that Mr. Enrico Modigliani, the Deputy, recognized my daughter, who works in the Civil Service for the Chamber of Deputies. But I have never had occasion to see Mr. Enrico Modigliani."

"Mr. Gabrielli, I have a surprise for you: Enrico Modigliani is going to come and see you. He has told me, that after so many years, he would like to meet you again."

"That will be a pleasure and a joy for me. He was only a child at the time. I must say that it will give me great pleasure to see someone who lived with us, with me, with our family, fifty years ago, in such a tragic and dangerous period!"

That meeting will take place soon, and will be one of cordiality, kindness, and goodwill. But before that I must visit Enrico Modigliani, to evoke this same tragic and dangerous period of history when he lived in the same apartment block as Professor Gabrielli.

Enrico Modigliani is a calm and gentle man. He has a high bald forehead, with white hair cut very short, coming down to a neat beard that frames a warm expression on his face. He has a child's view of the wartime events, as he was then: "At the time of the German invasion, I was six years old."

"Do you remember that time well?"

"I remember the days which followed much better!"

"How were your parents and you able to survive?"

"We lived in Rome, but at that time we hid in the country. After fascism collapsed, on the 25th of July, we stayed in the country and were still there when the Germans invaded Italy on the 8th of September. And my father intuitively had us stay there rather than returning to town. That's what we did until the 16th of October when they started deporting Jews. We learned that the Germans had gone to search our house in Rome. Then we fled: we were known in the country; they would have found us easily. We had to move. We therefore went back to Rome with real false papers, under false names. We called ourselves 'Macchia,' and not Modigliani any more. There were people in the Civil Service who furnished false papers for Resistance members and Jews."

"And is that how you became neighbors with Professor Gabrielli?"

"Yes. We didn't go back to our own house, but to a Jewish friend's apartment; they had left it for us as they had gone to hide in a convent. And Professor Gabrielli lived in the block. No one knew our real identity, nor where we came from. But there was a sort of sympathetic silence."

"And, what was Professor Gabrielli like then?"

"I knew his children better. Giovanino, in particular: he was nine, I was six, and we all played together with the other children in the flats. I remember his father: very austere, severe—a real professor. Later, I learned that he was one of the greatest experts in Arab literature in Italy. He used to tease me by calling me 'Macchilino'."

"Did your parents and the Professor get on well together? Did he know you were Jewish?"

"Actually, he never said whether he knew who we were. He obviously had suspicions, but he had no proof. Especially, perhaps, our accents which were not from Pescara, where we said we came from, but well and truly Roman. He knew

Pescara. He must have guessed something about it. At the beginning of June 1944, when the Germans left and the Americans entered Rome, everyone was very joyously able to talk about it at last, to confide in each other. Everyone was able to reveal who they really were and my father told Professor Gabrielli our name. I remember: they were on the terrace, and the Professor murmured 'Yes, yes . . . I knew who you were.' "

"Is that the only time your father and the Professor ever talked about your situation and your Jewish identity?"

"Yes. Absolutely. You know, from our side, from fear of denunciation, we were wary of compromising these people whom we liked very much."

"Have you ever seen the Professor since?"

"No, but I have met his daughter who works in the Parliament building."

"Do you think the Professor's attitude leaned more in the direction of Good or Evil? What do you think of someone who acted neither for nor against you?"

"Well now, I think that it was mostly good. Because he did nothing *against* us, that was already a lot. To act *against* us was obligatory. Therefore, to do nothing was to defy the law and the authorities. To do nothing was definitely to do good. There was a sort of sympathetic silence established between us—and that helped us, and gave us hope."

Enrico Modigliani is upset, but he pursues his story, albeit in a somewhat trembling voice: "You see, I am always very emotional when I think of that period, and I find it very hard to control . . ."

After this double interview, a series of hypotheses is forming in my mind. But, first, can we consider Good, with its manifestations of human solidarity, in the same way as Evil, with its cortege of culpabilities?

I have already described the four degrees of culpability established by Karl Jaspers apropos crimes committed by everybody. Taking this view, but reversing the viewpoint, I must ask what the different degrees would be, the different identifiable categories in the positive attitudes of men during the Second World War.

First of all there are the *Just:* those men and women whose absolute solidarity with regard to others appears so natural that, to take it to the limit, one could believe it to be instinctive. One can lift from this what Spinoza called the *right way of life.*

There are those that I will call *humanitarians,* committed to either political, social, cultural, or religious activities (or a combination of all or some). Their actions in saving the Jews tends towards a willingness, a conviction, a humanist tradition.

There are also the *solidaires:* The believers in solidarity. They saved Jews to help the persecuted, but also to oppose this type of Nazi power.

A fourth category applies, that of the *charitable.* This comprises individuals who inspired by pity, carry out limited acts of charity—for instance, by throwing pieces of bread to the unfortunate. We can explain this type of act towards *a piece of bad luck witnessed by us* as a reaction to a fear that one day such bad luck might come our way, or happen to one of our family.

And, finally, there is the largest group, consisting of the men and women whom I will call the *passive humanists.* This is comprised of people who, as in the instance of Professor Gabrielli, did not have the courage nor strong enough personal or political motivation to participate themselves in the rescue of the Jews. And—living in the same town, the same street, or the same apartment building as the escapees, whom they knew, as well as knowing the Jews' hiding places—they would have been able to denounce them under the laws of the period. But they did not! Their compassion did not allow them to commit such infamy. No doubt pity was not far away, but its presence in man, however slight, is preferable to a brutish insensibility.

At this stage in my observations, one fact becomes clear— and raises a new question: I have to admit that without the action, however limited and minimal, although real enough, of these different categories of individuals, the Just would not have been able to carry out their good deeds—to have been Good . . . or good. But, on the other hand, can we not ask this: without the existence of these Just people, without the example of their daily way of life, would all the others, would all the others of whom I have been speaking, have felt the need to accomplish their own deeds? And would they have been brave enough?

Evil, one knows only too well, is contagious. Is Good also?

# 57

# Eichmann thwarted

It is difficult in Italy to question people here about the Just without the name of Giorgio Perlasca being brought up. He is an Italian who fought for Franco in Spain and who saved thousands of Jews from Budapest in Hungary.

The Italians are very proud of Giorgio Perlasca. Articles and a book have been published about his story. But for a long time now nobody seems to know where he is, what he is doing, or even if he is still alive! It is thanks to the Jewish community in Milan that I discover his whereabouts: someone tells me he lives in Padua. Arriving in Padua, I learn that he is not here, but I find out that he is at the Pension Pace, near Lake Isco where, it appears, he is on holiday. I set off once more.

The car tires crunch on the gravel at the entrance to the Pension Pace, the Pension of Peace. I am near Lovere. Not far away, the day before, Lake Iseo was still sparkling in hot sunshine. Today, however, it is raining, and the old people in this restful place have to abandon the park and the floral gardens. The guests are limited to the lounge and hallways inside, on the ground floor. Among them, resting in the company of his wife, Giorgio Perlasca: the man I have come to see.

I do not know that this interview that this Just man is going to give me will be his last. [He died shortly after my visit to the Pension Pace. The recording of his discussion with me allied to the video pictures which we took on my visit, from now on, are

276

most valuable and irreplaceable documents.] In the lounge of this hotel in which everyone is gathered, our discussion is the center of attention. At the request of Giorgio Perlasca, we speak in Spanish: he is aggravated by the manner of some of the guests and does not wish to satisfy their curiosity. It is true that in Italy he has become—although a long time after his heroics—a personality. As it was for Wallenberg in Sweden, perceived as a Just among Justs, and with whom Perlasca liaised in Budapest during the war.

Graying hair cut very short and standing up like a brush, Giorgio Perlasca replies directly to my questions. His look conceals a touch of defiance or veiled irony. Sometimes he tilts his head to one side as a sign of complicity or as if looking for tacit assent, with the hint of a smile at the corner of his mouth. He screws up his eyes behind imposing dark glasses, of which the cord frames his bony, yet open, face. He seems to like giving surprises, even being paradoxical. During the whole of our interview, and in spite of the seriousness of the subjects which we are discussing, while maintaining his grave air, there is always this glimmer of perpetual amusement constantly in his eyes. In fact, this man is not used to such attention. An Italian, originating from Padua, he became half-Spanish by his way of things: he joined the International Fascist Brigade and participated in the Civil War on Franco's side. Republicanism, the Left, and antifascism were, to him, his adversaries. It was not these values which led him to save Jews—but, confirmed man of the Right that he was, he still had no sympathy with the anti-Semitic theses of the Nazis. When the Second World War breaks out, he is in charge of economic exchanges between Italy and Spain; then, still with his reputation as an influential businessman, he is sent to Budapest to develop contacts with Hungarian enterprises. Although Italian, he still operates for the benefit of the Franco regime in Spain. While deprived of all diplomatic status, he has his contacts in the Spanish Legation in Budapest. We will see how he used this situation to best advantage . . . not without risks.

I look around me. The lounge in the Pension Pace is all

steamed up with the humidity and appears ready to burst. It is overloaded with old people, crowded together because of the bad weather, in a space designed for five to ten people rather than fifty. Many of them are deaf, and everyone is talking very loudly in the echoing room. It is in the midst of this confused babble and, to cap it all in Spanish, that Giorgio Perlasca is telling me about his adventures. Smoking one cigarette after another, each one lit from the still burning stub of the previous one, he excitedly relives that "Hungarian" period of his existence. In the middle of these people playing cards, shouting to make themselves heard, or some staring vacantly into space apparently oblivious to the world, he has no difficulty in appearing infinitely younger, more alert, more alive. His voice alternates between a mischievous irony—when he talks about the obsessive shadow of Eichmann, whom he met there—and sheer emotion—when he talks about the fate of the Hungarian Jews of that time.

"On the 15th of October 1944: in the Spanish Legation in Budapest, there are 300 Jews being sheltered there. They had all been rounded up by the Hungarian fascists, who delivered them to the Nazis to send them for deportation. They had all been loaded into goods wagons in Budapest railway station, under the personal surveillance of Eichmann. It was awful! *Awful!*"

The 15th of October 1944: that was the day when the Hungarian Nazis, the "Swastika" men, supported by Eichmann, took power in Hungary: they replaced the previous fascist regime in Hungary, which they considered too "moderate" in regard to the Jews. It is worth noting the ruthless determination of these people: 1944, the final year of the war, the Germans beating retreat on all fronts, and a man like Eichmann knows very well that the Reich has been defeated. However, with dogged wickedness as much as fanaticism, he decides to deport the maximum number of Jews possible so that they can be exterminated before the Allied victory. This organized crime, this systematic genocide becomes worse as time races by: toward the horror it will be able to practice right up to the last moment.

In Hungary at that time, there were 403,000 Jews, of whom 16,000 were refugees from Austria, Slovakia, and Poland.

"One day," Giorgio Perlasca recounts," I arrived at the Spanish Legation in Budapest and saw a huge crowd pressing against the door. But, at that moment, I knew there was nobody in the Legation. The Spanish government had refused to recognize the new regime after the coup d'etat and had recalled its representatives. Then, without asking permission, I took over and started giving out refugee cards, official Spanish documents, to all these Hungarian Jews. With those the Nazis couldn't arrest them . . ."

Eichmann's race against time provoked another: that concerning the Jewish community in Hungary, and which consisted of trying to save the lives, of the greatest number possible, of these people threatened with extermination right in the final minutes of Hitlerism.

On one side, then: Eichmann, whose whole reason for living seemed to be mixed up with this obsession of annihilating the Jews, and who was striving to organize the deportation of the maximum number of unfortunates that he could send to the gas chambers, despite the imminent arrival of the Red Army.

On the other: the group called "the Five." This group of five represented in Budapest the neutral countries (Sweden, Switzerland, Spain, Portugal, and the Vatican) who tried to snatch as many as possible of the victims from the hands of the Nazi commandos and their chief, that lugubrious officer of death, Eichmann. In July 1944, to reinforce the group of Five's capacity to act, King Gustav V of Sweden hurriedly dispatched a special envoy to Budapest: Raoul Wallenberg.

"Did you know Raoul Wallenberg?"

"Yes. He worked to save the Ghetto. I met him at the goods station in Budapest where I had an appointment with a very important SS Colonel whom I didn't know. In the distance I saw the German Officer, and I asked Wallenberg who was there with me: 'Who is that officer?' Wallenberg replied: 'That's Eichmann . . .' "

"And that happened at the station?"

"Yes, at the station where they handled the cattle . . . and the Jews. Every day the representatives of the 'Five' went there to try and wrest some Jewish children from Eichmann's fanaticism. I went as well. But my main work was at the Spanish Legation. The few people still working there had only one desire: to go home as quickly as possible. In the absence of all authority, and because of my notoriety as an influential business man, they let me do what I wanted. So, every day I delivered refugee cards, and I looked for places where the maximum number of Jews could hide, in the different apartment buildings that Spain owned in Budapest. I even rented houses and hung out Spanish flags to make them 'Diplomatic Buildings,' in principle inviolable by the Germans and their Hungarian Nazi allies."

In response to the activities of the group of Five and all the others who were attempting to save the Jews, Eichmann had another 80,000 Jews rounded up. At this, Giorgio Perlasca accompanied by Raoul Wallenberg, the Swede, and de Furker, the Swiss, asked to see the Prime Minister.

"At the end of the discussion," tells Giorgio Perlasca, "I said to him that if the Spanish Government had not had reassuring news on the subject of the Jews, within twenty-four hours, they would immediately proceed to arrest the 13,000 Hungarians resident in Spain! It was a complete bluff, as I did not have the slightest idea of the Spanish Government's intentions and, besides, there could not have been more than 100 Hungarians in Spain, including all their diplomats. I was saved by the fact that this Hungarian Nazi, Prime Minister through the intervention of Eichmann, was uneducated: he did not know the real number of his compatriots who lived in Spain . . ."

"And, what happened?"

"He thought about it, then he sent an emissary to negotiate. This fellow proposed to release all the Spanish Jews—that is, those with Spanish certificates. I told him: 'No, Sir! Not the Spanish Jews, *all* the Jews!' "

Many of the Jews were going to owe their lives to this piece of bluff that, in the first instance, was apparently going to succeed. But the Nazis, furious at being deprived of part of their prey, were going to send a telegram to the Foreign Ministry in Madrid: having had doubts after their meeting, they wanted to verify the official accreditation of Giorgio Perlasca in respect of the Spanish Legation in Budapest. This telegram even asked if Perlasca was authorized, by the Spanish government, to intervene on behalf of the Jews.

Now we must remember that, at this time, Giorgio Perlasca was acting on his own initiative, "squatting" in some way in the Spanish Legation using official documents and seals to fake up those famous refugee cards which allowed Jews in Hungary to escape the Nazis. If the Spanish authorities in Madrid had sent a truthful answer—that is: Giorgio Perlasca is not one of our diplomats, he does not represent the Spanish government in any way—then that would have been the end of him and his activities! The thousands of Jews that he had hidden in the different Spanish "diplomatic properties" in Budapest would have soon been captured and deported.

"Actually," Giorgio Perlasca vows, "I didn't have one contact in the Spanish Government . . ."

For days and days, he tells me, he prayed to God that the telegram would be lost, so that no answer would ever come from Spain . . . At the end of two weeks of anguish, a reply arrived from the Foreign Ministry—it's a godsend, a stroke of luck, a miracle! In essence, the text, unsigned, which is unusual for diplomatic documents, but well and truly committing the Madrid Government, said: *"The actions of Mr. Giorgio Perlasca are in absolute conformity with our instructions. He is actively encouraged to pursue them."*

The anonymous hand that sent this extraordinary reply from Madrid is an unknown Just, an unknown warrior of the Good. This official of the Foreign Office, with his decisive gesture, contributed to the protection of, and supported, the rescue operation put in hand by Giorgio Perlasca in Hungary, in compiling this simple telegram, he had saved thousands of Jews whom Perlasca had collected. Now Perlasca, in conjunction with the group of Five and Raoul Wallenberg, were able to continue to lean on Eichmann all the time, putting Jews out of reach of his murdering hands.

"Did you meet Raoul Wallenberg later?"

"Sure I did. The last time, after our interview with the Hungarian Prime Minister, he asked me if he could hide in the Spanish Legation because he felt he was in danger. I told him yes, and I suggested that he go there right away with me. He said to me: 'No. Not now. I will come later on, this evening.' I never saw him again."

"And Adolf Eichmann?"

"I met him four or five times. We talked about the Jewish question. Whatever we spoke about with the group of Five, you know . . ."

Thus, Giorgio Perlasca was able to save 5,200 Jews from the death trains which Eichmann was hatefully filling, with icy determination, just before the Soviets arrived. (And then, at his trial in Jerusalem in 1962, the same Eichmann dared to reply, "Not guilty," fifteen times to the fifteen indictments of his crimes against humanity!)

In all the diplomatic buildings belonging to legations in Budapest gave refuge to 25,000 Hungarian Jews. Of the 403,000 people making up the Hungarian Jewish population, more than half were able to escape death, often thanks to men like Giorgio Perlasca.

"Have you ever met any of the people you saved?"

"Yes, I've met them in Budapest, in Israel, and in America. Some have been to see me. They are old now. I see people of sixty or seventy years old who are surprised I don't recognize them—when I knew them they were ten, fifteen, or twenty!"

"How old are you, now?"

"Eighty-two . . . and a half . . ."

"Why did you do all that you did? Why did you save Jews you didn't even know?"

Giorgio Perlasca looks at me with an amused smile: "You ask me that? . . . First, because I saw they were in danger. And then, because I can't stand persecution of people for their race or culture . . . No, I can't stand it! Even today!"

"Why do you think so few people tried to save the Jews? Why did so many of them do nothing?"

"You had to have the opportunity to do something. Me, at that time, there were things I could do. You know, I wasn't an hour from . . . Well, I did what I could."

"The opportunity . . . yes, I see that. But it takes courage and a certain willingness as well, doesn't it? Were you frightened?"

"Frightened, I don't know. Perhaps. The anguish waiting for that famous telegram . . . ! Yes, I suppose so. As for willingness . . . having the opportunity to act, I couldn't not take it. Nothing anyone said: I decided to take action. I wasn't going to refuse to do what I had decided to do! . . ."

Giorgio Perlasca makes me cast my mind back to that other Just man come from far away, very far away: Tempo Sugihara, the Japanese Consul who saved thousands of Lithuanian Jews caught in a pincer movement between the Germans and the Russians. To take his action, Tempo Sugihara, acting Consul, had to break his government's rules. Giorgio Perlasca is also an improvised Consul of a country that is not his own, delivering safe conducts to thousands of Hungarian Jews—and another Just, who is himself unknown, sent him support from Madrid, even though he did not know him and without advising his government. How can we not be puzzled about these Just people who, from instinct and from one country to another, invent their own ways of saving lives?

# 58

# Castles in Belguim

Henri Bergson wrote that there exist *"some things for which only intelligence is capable of searching, but which cannot be found by intelligence alone. Only instinct can find them, but instinct never looks for them."* Now those Just men, who found without looking, by instinct, contradict this reflection.

In the hope of exploring this problem in more depth, I accept an invitation from the organizers of the International Congress of Hidden Children. It is being held in Jerusalem. For the second time in half a century, the saved and their rescuers are going there to exchange their memories, their joys, and their tears. It is there that I will meet my first Just from Belgium: Andrée Guelen.

Andrée Guelen is a distinguished looking woman. With silver hair, wearing a pearl necklace and gold earrings that reflect the pearls, she speaks with her head held high and very erect. Everything about her is correct. Sometimes, briefly, she stares into space, way up, as if to enhance her memories. A hint of attention to detail emerges, and she immediately tells of her role, at the time:

"First of all, I want to make something clear: I was only one member of a network. I wasn't the organizer; it was Yvonne Jospa who started it all. I was just a little foot soldier, but a little soldier who had the best of the work as I had contact with the children! Fifty years later I still have this contact. Then, to the question you asked me—why did I do this work—I will answer with another: what could I say to my children, today if I had not done it?"

I am touched by this reply as the obvious dignity makes no claim for herself, only gives out a sense of moral necessity. Nevertheless, this projection in time, toward the future, toward her children, "her own" (at a time when she was not yet a mother), makes me ask another question: "Did you really think that at the time? What age were you then?"

"I was twenty . . . Let's say that, at the time, I was burdened by the idea that later I would not be able to admit to myself that I had done nothing. Before being contacted to join the network, I had already, on my own, started my work by hiding Jewish children with my family. Because of the requirements of the network, I accepted, when I joined, that I had to leave my teaching post."

"Were you from a Catholic family?"

"No. I belonged to a family who were freethinkers."

"How many children did your network save?"

"The CDJ (Comité de defense de Juifs) network saved around 3,000 Jews."

"Three thousand?!"

"Three thousand children, yes. Across Belgium we knew there were another 5,000, thanks to other networks like our own, and the efforts of individuals. Our network managed to hide 3,000, more or less."

There were 50,000 Jews in Belgium before the war: 25,000 were deported. Of the 25,000 others, 15,000 owe their lives to the CDJ network—and, among them, the 3,000 children Andrée Guelen is speaking about.

Her story, brief, moving, spurred me to question other Belgian witnesses. *If the concept of the route is long and involved, it is short in practice.* Now, at the moment this proverb came to mind, I did not expect to be sent to meet someone whom, although I know him well, I do not know the extra dimension in which he is a Just man.

Haroun Tazieff is a famous man. We know the intrepid scientist, the former Minister, the storyteller with the harsh warm accent. We know less about the Resistance member, and why, although we know about his research into volcanoes, on the other hand, he has never mentioned his participation in the rescue of the Jews. Discretion of the Just that I have come up against, more than once, in this research.

"During the terrible winter of 1941–1942," I say to him, "you were in the little castle of Ramée, in Belgium, on the north slope of the Meuse valley, between Liège and Namur. You had with you a group of young people, of whom the majority were Jews: What were you doing, then?"

"No," exclaims Haroun Tazieff, "not the majority: all of them! They were all Jewish! What was I doing there, with them? Things began at the beginning of the winter of '41. I had not yet become a vulcanologist then: I was an entomologist. I was the assistant to the Professor of Entomology at the Agricultural Institute, Raymond Menet, an extraordinary fellow. One day he came to me and asked if I would take responsibility for a fake School of Agriculture which he was going to open in the country, in a place he had yet to find! The idea was to place young Jews there to protect them from the roundups that were beginning to become severe in Belgium. There were to be twenty-four young people, aged from twelve, fourteen up to twenty, twenty-one, who would be accredited with being agricultural students—while I was supposed to be their mentor, their professor.

"I accepted, and that is how, with the caring Jewish community in Brussels and Antwerp, that institution came to be created in the little castle at Ramée.

"We spent a very hard winter there, as the whole of Europe was badly hit that year. In fact, as to agriculture, weeks passed without being able to dig the soil, we couldn't even hoe: it was as hard as stone. The rivers froze, we could walk across the Meuse on foot. I remember we had to break the ice on the well. That was a difficult period. we had practically nothing to eat, save carrots and occasionally potatoes and beetroots. As for meat or fish, it didn't bear dreaming about! At the castle, then, we had to tighten our belts. It was in those conditions that we passed the winter and the early spring months together."

"Did you assess the danger of this situation: you, at the head of a sham school for Jewish children, possibly facing eventual rounding up or the descent of the German army or the Gestapo?"

"I thought about it, yes. But I always loved taking risks; the professional life I entered after shows that well enough. Risk gives me pleasure, it is the spice of life to me. The fact that I was at risk didn't bother me at all. On the other hand, I had shivers up my spine for the kids I was there to protect."

"Do you know," I interrupt, "that I have met one of those young men from your colony at Ramée? He remembers you. He is now a university professor. He is called Haim Vidal Sephila. Do you remember him?"

"Haim? He is the only one I have ever met again out of all the boys . . ."

Without doubt, chance is the master of more than half the things we try to do. Chance then has made it that Haim Vidal Sephila is one of *my* old friends. He is a voluble man, full of fun, who lives in the inner suburbs of Paris in a villa in which he and his books fill a whole floor.

"At the time," he tells me, "I was a Zionist and I dreamed of becoming an agriculturist so that I could go and live in Palestine. In the autumn of 1941, I started my studies at the Jean Bloom Agricultural Institute where Haroun Tazieff was the principal. Towards the end of the first term, that was the 24 of November 1941, I received a letter telling me that, as a Jew, I could not continue my studies there. Just at that time, the Association of Belgian Jews had decided to create a School of Agriculture and Horticulture. I didn't know anything, yet, about the organization, but I was contacted to become a sort of teacher in this institution. That's how I became involved at Ramée and met Haroun Tazieff. To me he is an extraordinary man. I admire him. He represented simplicity and sanity— both physical and moral."

"You spent a very hard winter in his company."

"Yes, that was the winter of 1941–42. I remember. We had to go and look for water in a convent, nearby, and we went with a barrel that we had to manhandle along the icy roads—and, some days, we even had to break the ice on the well! But Haroun Tazieff inspired us."

"When did you meet him again?"

"I repeat, I have an indelible memory of that man. There was a sense of profound humanity about him. It was quite by chance, at a conference in the Sorbonne, where he was showing a film about water. I passed behind him at the end of the seminar and gave him a little tap on the shoulder. He turned round and exclaimed: 'Haim!' "

"Your timetable was truly amazing: you were at Ramée, in this little colony that protected you from the Germans, but you kept going to Brussels on a bicycle to keep up with the course you were forbidden to follow! How did that finish up, this mad desire for study?"

"At the time, not very well. It was after Haroun Tazieff left. Because I was Jewish, Brussels University was closed to me, by decree of the Occupation authorities. But the University authorities had got round the interdict by transforming courses into public lectures to which everyone could go, not only students. No more need, then, to exhibit my student's card or any other proof of my being a student. I only had to hide the fact that I was Jewish. To get into the building, I had to be careful to take off my yellow star, which was held on by six press-studs. When I came out, I put it on again. One day, I forgot to put it back on; I was picked up coming off a tram, very close to my parent's house, and taken away. In the end I was deported with all the other Belgian Jews who had been arrested. At Auschwitz-Birkenau, I became number 151752."

"This number . . . You know it by heart!"

"Of course! For two years that was my name! Look, it is still there, tattooed on my arm. My name disappeared. No more Haim, no more Vidal, no more Sephila—nothing! I was only *einhunderteinundfünfzigtausendsiebenhundertzweiundfünfzig!*"

# 59

## To save a number

A number, 151752, was condemned to death, and a man, Haim Vidal Sephila, was saved. What symbolism!

I will have to come to the end of my research.

But an insidious, insistent question comes, as if from the bottom of my conscious being, that has tormented me since beginning of my research, giving me no peace:

"And *you*, honestly, what would you have done in the same circumstances?"

"Me?"

"Yes, you!"

I would have liked to say, and I would like to be able to answer in all sincerity, that I would have acted like the Just. But at this *me*, this profound question that tolerates neither lies nor evasion, I can only answer truthfully: *"I do not know."*

To be sure, I have a ready-made answer: at the time I was on the other side of the barbed wire, one of the persecuted, one of those who needed saving. But the inner *me* will not be satisfied with this type of excuse: in fact, if the necessity of becoming a rescuer could not present itself to me during the period of the Holocaust, that could greatly concern me tomorrow. Perhaps even from today onwards.

Submitted to successive waves of questions without answers and more and more oppressive introspections, I think about Raymond Halter as one dreams about a safety belt in the middle of a storm.

Raymond Halter is a priest whom I met here several years ago, in Alsace, in the parish of Benfeld. Perhaps we have common ancestors as, originating in the Bruche valley, we may even be of the same family.

I am not trying to transfer my doubts and questions to another Halter—in the hope that he, a Catholic, can more easily answer. The Bible does not say: I put before you life and death . . . , but rather: *"I put life and death before thee"*—as if to underline, if we have not already understood, that all choices, and above all, a choice of this nature, is individual. Each and every one of us must take responsibility for himself before God, or man, or even his own conscience.

It appears to me that this sudden desire to question a Halter on his conduct during the war corresponds with *my wish* to once more verify that my observations apropos the Just are well founded.

After all, this man bears my name!

For weeks now I have looked for him in vain. He has given up his Alsatian diocese, and no one knows where he has gone. In Alsace I have questioned dozens of Halters about him, all astounded to learn that they have a Jewish cousin. This difficulty in finding him has had the effect of arousing my curiosity. Obstinacy helping, I at last find him outside his church. On the fascia, a very simple inscription: *Notre Dame d'Afrique.*

More than a Parish, Notre Dame d'Afrique is one of the most important educational centres in Abidjan. When I arrive, hundreds of young Africans are playing on an immense piece of ground which stretches from the Chapel right down to the banks of Lake Ebrie. Apart from his clothes, the man I knew, in days gone by, has not changed.

In Alsace Raymond Halter wore a surplice. Here in Africa he is wearing a floral shirt. Only the wooden cross hanging on his chest indicates his calling. Father Halter is a robust type, with a huge face. The sweetness and brightness of his look often filters out from behind his glasses, in glances of amused astonishment. We sit ourselves down in a hut open to all the winds and full of young people.

"My father's family, like your own," he says to me, "is originally from the Bruche valley, between Stermen and Haguenau, in Alsace. But after I was born, in 1926, my parents moved to Doubs, close to Montbeliard."

"What did you do during the war?"

"At the height of the war I was seventeen, eighteen years old."

"And your father?"

"He was a market gardener. I remember very well . . . He used to hide strangers in the barn: Jews, people from the Resistance . . . One day I even discovered an English airman!"

Thus, the father of this other Halter, originating far away from Alsace, had, perhaps, been one of these Just men of whom I am looking for traces everywhere!

"And the Germans?" I asked him.

"They often came to the house because someone in the village was always denouncing us. They always raided us at nighttime. But, luckily, they never found anyone with us. My father had built hiding places under the barn . . ."

"Why did he do it?"

"Because, to him, it seemed the natural thing to do!"

"Weren't you frightened?"

"Me? Yes, once. It was on the 14th of November 1944, in the morning. I remember it as if it was yesterday. The Germans had made a new search of the village and, once more, found nothing. At that the German Commandant decided to take a dozen young men as hostages. I was one of them! . . ."

"What happened then?"

"A piece of luck! An unexpected piece of luck! The French army supported by the Allies advanced on Montbeliard at the exact moment when the Germans took us out to be shot!"

"You were nearly shot because of your father's generosity. Have you two ever talked about this episode after the war?"

"We were in it together. I never, ever, reproached my father for having helped someone, saved people."

"Even if that could have cost you your life?"

"Even if it had cost my life . . . I am going to tell you a

secret: only twice in my life have I felt exceptionally moved. The first time, at the age of eighteen, was when I learned that some people like us had done nothing to save others. Then I felt ashamed. And the second time, a little later, when I realized the scale of the disaster—when I learnt about Auschwitz—I remember, I felt a feeling of anger like I have never felt since! And, that's when—and I'm saying this in public for the first time—I decided to become a priest . . ."

"Why a priest?"

"Because I understood that the disaster was not only physical but moral. That we would have to rebuild the world, certainly, but also man's *soul*."

# 60

# The belt is buckled

This enquiry is close to its conclusion. Perhaps, out of scrupulous attention to detail, stringency, I should have travelled to a few more countries to question some more witnesses, but would I have discovered any different elements or more convincing arguments? Would these other witnesses have modified the idea of Good that has come out in these pages or contradicted the stories of those I have already met? I do not think so. Even if doubt has never left me, my conviction is absolute: Good exists.

*"It is a strange and long war where violence tries to stifle truth,"* Pascal noted in the *Provinciales*. And he reinforced it with: *". . . all the efforts of violence cannot weaken the truth, and only serve to show it to advantage."* I think that it is also true in spite of and, perhaps, even because of the Holocaust. I also know that the war for truth is never completely won. That history continues as do the massacres. Today's killings do not yet equal—because of restraint, because of technology at their disposal, by the very size and systematic nature of the project—the extermination, yesterday's *Final Solution:* every day, however, it proves that hate and violence are not disarmed nor have any intention of quitting the battle. I will now present you with the essence of the second part of Pascal's reasoning that will counterbalance the first: *"All the lights of truth can do nothing to stop violence, and do nothing but irritate it to excess."* And the philosopher goes on to explain:

*"When force meets force, the more powerful destroys the
weaker; when one counters argument with argument, those
which are true and convincing confound those which are only
vanity and lies: but violence and truth cannot do anything, one
to the other."*

This was also Maimonides's opinion. In a different field: his
diagnosis contained more nuances. In this permanent war
between Good and Evil, between the forces of light and the
forces of darkness, he wanted to think that, thanks to the Just
in the world, the balance could, at least for a moment, lean in
favor of Good.

*At least for a moment:* their profound pessimism did not
prevent either the Jew Maimonides or the Catholic Pascal from
having hope. This is what each of them declared while secured
to a safety belt called God.

And the others, those who don't happen to have the luck to
have access to this safety belt, are they condemned to drown?
I don't think so. But, to answer this question, is it not urgent
to root out—from under the rubble of the ghettos and the
camps if we must—the old idea of universal man to try to
give the true meaning to the word *humanism?* From where
comes the idea, which I have already expressed, of a *History of
Hope.*

The belt is buckled. What more to add? I have never
believed I would be able to find a definitive solution to the
problems that have assailed man since the dawn of time. I have
attempted to answer some of these questions, the most urgent,
in the light of recent history. Some of the others, perhaps, may
be answered by the *professional thinkers.* For my part, I can
only repeat what Saint Augustine said to his friends the Rabbis
in the fourth century in his faraway Hippo: *"I remember that I
have a memory, a will. I understand that I want, that I remember.
I want to want to remember, I want to want to understand."* (*On
the Trinity,* book X)

Like him, I want to want to remember and understand. That
was the reason for this long journey across fourteen countries,
across the place of my birth and the Holocaust. I had to find the

*saved ones,* those who were able to escape from hell and who survived because they found hands to help them.

Such a journey could only be accompanied by the desire to understand their rescuers: the Just. These Just men whom Abraham, the Patriarch, searched for with such passion and despair:

*"Will Thou truly destroy the Just with the wicked? Perhaps there are fifty Just men in the center of the town: will Thou also have them perish, and not pardon the city for the fifty Just who are in their midst? Far from Thou to make such a choice! To make the Just die with the wicked, a fate which treats the Just like the wicked! Is it that He who judges all the Earth will not render justice unto it?"*

How many men, from each generation, have questioned the Eternal in this way?

Now, Just men have existed—like air, water, and all the other indispensable elements of life, to protect life. If they had not been there, would we still ask these questions? Would we even exist in this world?

I might, perhaps, never have entered into this venture, into such commentaries, if Hannah Arendt had not encouraged me, with her praise of the *"nonprofessional thinkers* [who], *different from the professional thinkers,* feel *the need of reassurance of others who share in their incertitudes."*

Perhaps my luck rests in my "naïveté," in my "nonprofessionalism," which has led me, not to question God on the subject of Good and on the existence of the Just, but to go out and look for them.

I can now affirm that not only have they existed, but that they exist today. That there are more than fifty, more than 100. That there are truly thousands of them: simple men and women, simply banal and simply good. They have names like Irena Sendler, Kaethe Schwartz, Zaneiba Hardaga, Annie Lombardi, Selahattin Ulkumen, René Raoul . . . For this book I have stopped at thirty-six.

But why *thirty-six?* Because the Talmud says this number is indispensable if the world is to be saved?

Lacking specific graphic signs for numbers, the ancient Hebrews used the twenty-two letters of their alphabet. Each one of them corresponded to a numeric value while their combination to form a larger number equally formed a word. This method, *guematrie,* was used in the Kabbala for fine analysis and metaphysical divination.

Thus favorable dates for Jewish ceremonies were, and are still today, 17 and 18: 17, Tov, means "Good," and 18, Hai, "Life."

Thirty-six is twice eighteen, that is to say, *two times life*—or *life of a life*—that of the rescuer guaranteeing the life of *the saved one.*

Was it not this that the Talmud secretly intended by signifying this number of thirty-six Just men: that thanks to the Just, life protects life?

Thus, these things become clearer: Good is Life. Life—and everything which contributes to its protection, to perpetuating and ennobling it. The opposite of that which has as its object to damage, degrade, or even deny it.

War, for example, is Evil. As is oppression. Likewise unemployment, famine, and homelessness.

There are those who, on the side of Evil, work towards the limitation of life, toward its destruction—and there are those who stay on the side of Good, on the side of life, and who do everything to preserve it.

Among these Good people, above all, are the Just.

To the extent that most men, believers and nonbelievers, tend toward the same ends: the celebration of life in support of less violence and in favor of justice, will, perhaps, make it possible, with exposure to the experience of these Just men and women, to see that love and generosity sometimes lead us to understand others better than we understand ourselves.

It is true that the believer thinks that the humanist nonbeliever is wrong, and vice versa. But both of them know that they are united by the same destiny, in the same, more and more complex fight against Evil.

This fight, from now on, without doubt, will manifest itself in actions and not only with the unfolding of ideas: this is how the Just have asked *the question about Good*, about the existence of Good, not in the form of concepts, but by deeds, in a concrete way. Also, they have given a place to solidarity, that is to say, to acts of goodness for the benefit of all.

# Index